BUCKNELL REVIEW

Untrodden Regions of the Mind: Romanticism and Psychoanalysis

STATEMENT OF POLICY

BUCKNELL REVIEW is a scholarly interdisciplinary journal. Each issue is devoted to a major theme or movement in the humanities or sciences, or to two or three closely related topics. The editors invite heterodox, orthodox, and speculative ideas and welcome manuscripts from any enterprising scholar in the humanities and sciences.

This journal is a member of the Conference of Editors of Learned Journals

BUCKNELL REVIEW
A Scholarly Journal of Letters, Arts, and Sciences

Editor
PAULINE FLETCHER

Associate Editor
DOROTHY L. BAUMWOLL

Assistant Editor
ANDREW P. CIOTOLA

Contributors should send manuscripts with a self-addressed stamped envelope to the Editor, *Bucknell Review*, Bucknell University, Lewisburg, PA, 17837.

BUCKNELL REVIEW

Untrodden Regions of the Mind: Romanticism and Psychoanalysis

Edited by
GHISLAINE McDAYTER

Lewisburg
Bucknell University Press
London and Toronto: Associated University Presses

© 2002 by Associated University Presses, Inc.

Associated University Presses
440 Forsgate Drive
Cranbury, NJ 08512

Associated University Presses
16 Barter Street
London WC1A 2AH, England

Associated University Presses
P.O. Box 338, Port Credit
Mississauga, Ontario
Canada L5G 4L8

The paper used in this publication meets the
requirements of the American National Standard for
Permanence of Paper for Printed Library Materials Z39.48-1984.

(Volume XLV, Number 2)

ISBN 0-8387-5517-8
ISSN 0007-2869

PRINTED IN THE UNITED STATES OF AMERICA

Contents

Recent Issues of BUCKNELL REVIEW

The Philosophy of John William Miller
Culture and Education in Victorian England
Classics and Cinema
Reconfiguring the Renaissance: Essays in Critical Materialism
Wordsworth in Context
Turning the Century: Feminist Theory in the 1990s
Black/White Writing: Essays on South African Literature
Worldviews and Ecology
Irishness and (Post)Modernism
Anthropology and the German Enlightenment: Perspectives on Humanity
Having Our Way: Women Rewriting Tradition in Twentieth-Century America
Self-Conscious Art: A Tribute to John W. Kronik
Sound and Light: La Monte Young/Marian Zazeela
Perspectives on Contemporary Spanish American Theatre
Reviewing Orpheus: Essays on the Cinema and Art of Jean Cocteau
Questioning History: The Postmodern Turn to the Eighteenth Century
Making History: Textuality and the Forms of Eighteenth-Century Culture
History and Memory: Suffering and Art
Rites of Passage in Ancient Greece: Literature, Religion, Society
Bakhtin and the Nation
New Essays in Ecofeminist Literary Criticism
Caribbean Cultural Identities
Lorca, Buñuel, Dalí: Art and Theory

Notes on Contributors

GUINN BATTEN is an associate professor of English at Washington University of St. Louis. Author of *The Orphaned Imagination: Melancholy and Commodity Culture in English Romanticism,* she is advisory editor for Wake Forest University Press's distinguished Irish Poetry Series. Currently she is completing a book on contemporary poetry from Ireland.

JOEL FAFLAK is an assistant professor of English literature at Wilfrid Laurier University. He is editing De Quincey's *Confessions of an English Opium-Eater* for Broadview Press and co-editing (with Julia Wright) a collection of essays entitled *Nervous Reactions: Victorian Recollections of Romantic Writers.* His other current project is *Subjects Presumed to Know: Romantic Psychoanalysis.*

GHISLAINE MCDAYTER teaches in the Department of English at Bucknell University. She has co-edited *Romantic Generations: Essays in Honor of Robert F. Gleckner* and has published several essays on nineteenth-century literature. She is presently completing her book *Convulsions in Rhyme: Byromania and the Birth of Celebrity.*

TORIL MOI is James B. Duke Professor of Literature and Romance Studies at Duke University. Her most recent book is *What Is a Woman? and Other Essays* (1999). She is also the author of *Simone de Beauvoir: The Making of an Intellectual Woman* (1994) and *Sexual/Textual Politics: Feminist Literary Theory* (1985), and the editor of *The Kristeva Reader* (1986) and *French Feminist Thought* (1987).

MARC REDFIELD teaches literature at Claremont Graduate University. He is the author of *Phantom Formations: Aesthetic Ideology and the Bildungsroman* (1996) and *The Politics of Aesthetics: Nationalism, Gender, and the Rhetoric of Romanticism,* forthcoming.

SOPHIE THOMAS is a lecturer in English at the University of Sussex. The essay included here is part of a forthcoming book on the fragment in Romanticism, parts of which have appeared in other journals and collections. She is currently co-editing a book of essays on Romanticism and visual culture.

FRANCES WILSON teaches in the English department at Reading University. She is editor of Lady Caroline Lamb's *Glenarvon* (1996), *Byromania: Portraits of the Artist in Nineteenth- and Twentieth-Century Literature* (1999) and author of *Literary Seductions: Compulsive Writers and Diverted Readers* (1999). She has also written several articles on nineteenth-century literature and is currently writing a life of the courtesan Harriette Wilson.

Introduction

The word *romantic has* come to mean so many things that, by itself, it means nothing. It has ceased to perform the function of a
verbal sign.
　　　　—Arthur O. Lovejoy, "On the Discriminations of Romanticism"

A FTER Arthur O. Lovejoy wrote this qualification of Romanticism's ideological homogeneity, a battle ensued between leading figures in the critical world. René Wellek, in particular, rushed
to the defense of Romanticism as a unified and coherent category.
He claimed that while "the terms 'romanticism' and 'romantic'
ha[d] been under attack for a long time," Romanticism nonetheless
signified "a unity of theories, philosophies, and style, and that these,
in turn, form[ed] a coherent group of ideas each of which impli-
cate[d] the other."[1] We are justified, he argued, in referring to the
Renaissance and Baroque. Why not the Romantic?

Wellek's question is well taken. What is it about Romanticism as a
field of literary study that has invited such an orgy of self-conscious
angst? In recent years this apparent trauma of critical identity has
been continued and has evolved into repeated examinations of Romanticism's state of health, whether it be in Jerome McGann's influential *Romantic Ideology* or in the countless conference discussions
given over to panicky debates about Romanticism's immanent
demise. As Marc Redfield quite rightly puts it, "the handwringing
much in evidence in recent books and anthologies written or edited
by professional Romanticists has no real equivalent in, say, Victorian
studies, where even the most politicized cultural critics seem able to
go about their business without worrying that the regal name of
their professional field might be a synonym for 'ideology.' " Most
recently, of course, the issue of Romanticism as ideology has given
way to still another debate: Romanticism as psychology. The historical frustration with Romanticism's incoherent identity—despite its
apparent preoccupation precisely with defining poetic subjectivity—
has spawned an attempt to define the "true Romantic" *mentalité* in
the so-called New Psychology, or "brain science." Psychoanalysis as
created by Freud, with all its attendant anxiety about scientificity

11

and indeterminacy, seems only to have fed what, for lack of a better term, we might call the Romantic identity crisis. Thus, as a recent web page on the subject announces, past "psychoanalytical readings of the 'infant babe' passage in *The Prelude* apply a flawed model of infant development to the poem and in so doing misread the passage."[2] The new empirical psychology and cognitive neuroscience, on the other hand, set out to uncover the true operations of infant development, offering the reassuringly measurable evidence of empiricism. Thus we are encouraged to use neuroscience in the hope that it will yield "rules for the development" of language, question whether linguistic signs are indeed "arbitrary," and test the early cognitive scientist's proposition that the mind is "best understood as a computational device."[3]

In this turn to empiricism away from "flawed" models of interpretation, we might well be reminded of a similarly exhausted Wordsworth who, "wearied out with contrarieties" in the moral dilemmas of reform, turned instead "towards mathematics, and their clear solid evidence."[4] It would seem that Romanticism as a field, no less than its most prolific poet, has become frustrated by the vagaries of interpretation in its struggle to "find itself." Now, like Keats using the "new brain dissection techniques"[5] or like Wordsworth confronted by a French body politic he no longer recognized, we too want to "probe / The living body of society / Even to the heart" in order to understand the minds we study without fear of misconstruing their meaning.[6]

What is perhaps most significant about this recent "reinvention of psychology" in Romantic studies is the manner in which it seeks, through scientificity, to resurrect Roland Barthes's "dead author." As Mary Thomas Crane puts it in her forthcoming book *Shakespeare's Brain: Reading with Cognitive Theory*, the New Psychology "provides a compelling way (in the wake of poststructuralist critiques of authorship) to bring the author back more forcefully into the equation of culture, subjectivity and language through which meaning is produced."[7] Not only are the authors given authority over their text once more, but now the critic may gratefully and gracefully step back from the interpretive spotlight. In short, it is no longer imperative, as with poststructural models of analysis, to be endlessly self-reflective and self-conscious in the production of analysis. Literary meaning comes not so much from within, but from without. We need not engage in the endless and all too indeterminate struggle of understanding Self in order to analyze Other. For, as the cognitive theorists note, there is a new (and as they themselves suggest, not altogether fortuitous) return to universality here; language halts its annoyingly poststructural slide into the arbitrary.[8] But as Toril Moi illustrates through her use of Stanley Cavell in the essay she contributes to this volume, such a linguistic fantasy partakes of what he names the "fantasy of inexpressiveness": for Moi our silence in fact expresses a wish "for a state in which words would have absolutely objective meanings. This is a yearning for a language which would not depend on the intervention of human subjectivity for its meanings" and relies on a fantasy of "an inner private subjectivity unreadable and unreachable by others." This is not to say that the critics of the New Psychology are so naive as to believe they can ever evade such interpretive subjectivity, but it is to suggest that critics such as Crane conceive of this problem as one arising out of a poststructural insistence on the slipperiness of signification. They blame poststructuralism for a slippery state of affairs that they would "correct" with the dispassionate tools of science. For Moi, however, "the question is not about reference or the floating of signifiers" but about taking responsibility for our words, and I would add, for our desire. In short, in its effort to evade the supposedly "self-obsessed" chain of signification associated both with psychoanalytic and poststructural thought, the New Psychology threatens to immerse itself in an altogether different interpretive problem. While fleeing the frustrating self-consciousness and even self-flagellation of recent Romantic criticism, it engages in a reluctance to make itself known to others and to reveal itself *as* a desiring subject.

Notably, this flight from critical self-consciousness is one that makes complete sense in the history of Romanticism, if only because the Romantic poets themselves were consistently accused of being self-obsessed and overly self-conscious. From William Hazlitt's infuriated cry that Lord Byron could only write about Byron, to John Keats's stinging nomination of William Wordsworth as the poet of the egotistical sublime, a worrying self-consciousness seems to have haunted both Romantic writers and their critics far more eerily than any "darkling" gothic vision of Anne Radcliffe's invention. All of which makes it almost predictable that, as Joel Faflak points out, the term "psycho-analysis" should first have been coined by Coleridge. Arguably, then, New Psychology is simply taking in a new direction a critical interest in understanding the Romantic mind that has marked Romanticism as a critical field since the beginning. Indeed, in a now classic collection of critical essays entitled *Romanticism and Consciousness*, Geoffrey Hartman identifies self-consciousness as a singularly gothic cultural trauma of the period since it creates a "kind of death in life, as a product of the division in the self."[9] Harold Bloom goes on to argue that "subjectivity or self-consciousness is the salient problem of Romanticism, at least for modern readers, who tend to station themselves in regard to Romantics depending on how relevant or adequate they judge the dialectic of consciousness and imagination to be."[10] For these older critics, as for the New Psychologist Romanticists, studying poetry was at least to some extent synonymous with studying the poet. While the New Psychology might "enable us to read Romantic-era representations and theories of the unconscious, of language, of mind and its embodiment in a fundamentally and productively new manner,"[11] M. H. Abrams tells us that the Romantic period saw the beginnings of a new era in which "the total poem, hitherto an image of manners and life, ha[d] become a dangerous betrayer of its author."[12] For both critical schools, no matter their methodological differences, it is the poetic mind that is the subject under scrutiny. By better understanding the poetic unconscious we might better come to understand the poetry.

Nor, again, is this new to modern criticism of Romanticism; from the nineteenth century until the twenty-first, the Romantic poet's supposed insistence on personal expression has indicated to its critics that the poem as a vehicle exposes his darkest desires. This, as John Wilson of the *Edinburgh Review* claimed, was the most dangerous and the most disgusting innovation of the new "great" works of poetry. The poet evidenced a "strange and unsated desire of depicturing himself . . . His wild temper only found ease in tracing out, in laying bare to the universal gaze, the very groundwork, the most secret paths, the darkest coverts of one of the most wayward and unimaginable minds ever framed by nature." In fact, for this critic, Byron's *Childe Harold's Pilgrimage* is nothing more than the poet's disgusting attempt to "feed the curiosity of the idle that he might array an exhibition to their greedy gaze."[13]

While the poets themselves might perceive of their titanic battle with self-consciousness as a terrifying engagement with a Shelleyan "life-in-death," it would seem that the critical gaze of Romantic readers from the nineteenth century to the present day has taken pleasure in and become irresistibly fixed before the spectacle of these "naked" subjectivities. Whereas the Bloomian model of psychoanalytic criticism focused on Freudian constructs of Oedipal narratives, ego formation, and the unconscious, the New Psychology simply attempts to "dig a little deeper" into neural paths for its poetic disclosure. "Laid bare" to our view, whether on the analyst's couch or the surgeon's table, these poets become the objects of our "greedy gaze."

My point here is that it has been all too tempting in both old and new critical schools to fall into the fantasy that somehow or other we can gain access to the "true" workings of the poetic mind uncolored by our own interpretive desire—that we can gaze upon the naked truth of the poet's mind without recognizing our own desire *in* that gaze. Such a fantasy has led to some worrying critical methodologies in the past, where the critic played the unbiased analyst to the troubled consciousness of the poetic subject. Such critical examinations of Romanticism have usually become forums in which to castigate and pathologize the poet for his or her narcissism, perversion, obsessional neurosis, or hysteria. As Guinn Batten has pointed out in her recent work *The Orphaned Imagination: Melancholy and Commodity Culture in English Romanticism,* there has been, in fact, an active anxiety in critical circles about the need to "cure" the melancholic artist of his solipsistic, unproductive, and perverse creative process:

> Haunted by the figure of the melancholic, whose very sloth—fueled by concupiscence—may nevertheless engender art, those who promote the "healthy development" of an individual or a society might well fear that beneath the demands and satisfactions of communal forms of symbolic exchange . . . lurk unmet needs that may easily find expression as private perversion, whether the site for its enjoyment is the bedroom or the study.[14]

Thus, in critical studies such as Barbara Schapiro's *The Romantic Mother: Narcissistic Patterns in Romantic Poetry,* the Romantic poet is psychoanalyzed to reveal, for example, Keats's "unresolved feelings towards the mother image" rooted in "profound infantile experiences of loss and betrayal" which threaten to transport the poet into "a narcissistic regression" and the avoidance of reality his poetry enables.[15] More alarmingly, in a 1972 biography of Caroline Lamb, Henry Blyth not only accuses Byron and Lamb of being both "mentally and physically sick, and that each was in urgent need of treatment," he goes on to claim that what both writers needed was a little less indulgence in fantasy and a little more discipline.[16] What Caroline thought she really needed was "to be hit" by her husband. Placing himself in Caroline's fantasy space, the critic imagines that:

> What she would have liked was for William to have been deeply outraged. He should have displayed an uncontrollable jealousy and forbidden her ever to look at another man again. And he certainly should have hit her. She would have screamed hysterically if he had administered a sound spanking, but she would have respected him. [17]

Needless to say, this fantasy of flagellation originates with Blyth rather than with Lamb. Here, a (thoroughly naive) psychoanalytic approach has been used as a stick with which to beat the poets in a rather embarrassing episode of critical flagellation, bringing to mind a version of Freud's own examination of sado-masochistic desire. "A Child Is Being Beaten" becomes "a poet is being beaten." But for us, just as for Freud, the most significant factor in this fantasy mise-en-scène of being beaten is what is repressed. The very affect of the fantasy of flagellation is one that enables shifting identification between passive and active role-playing since the subject may identify alternately or simultaneously with the disciplinary husband, the childlike Lamb, and the critical voyeur. Even the "originary" moment that inspires this fantasy is never "real" but a phantasmagoric construction. As Jean Laplanche insists, it was "never remembered, it has never succeeded in becoming conscious. It is the construction of analysis."[18] And what is such a phantasmagoric construction but the very operative process of criticism? The Romantic subject studied is never real, never remembered, but created in the analytical process and is "no less a necessity on that account."[19]

This, of course, is where the issue of the new cognitive and neuroscientific theories hope to act as a corrective, removing the historically ambiguous and unchartable procedures of Freudian analysis—a vagary that tormented Freud as well—with more empirically grounded evidence. But ironically the New Psychology, in its very critique of Freud, slips into the very error with which Freud himself had to struggle. I am speaking here of the danger of not recognizing the operations of countertransference in the critical process. If we as critics fail to recognize and control the desire in the critical gaze that is necessarily transferred to our object of analysis, we (no less than Freud) will be incapable of *seeing* it. To return to the above scenario, what is repressed both in the New Psychology and in the sado-masochistic fantasy of literary flagellation is not so much the actual "historical" trauma of Romanticism, or even the Romantic writer's life "laid bare" by critical analysis, but rather the fact that this construction is precisely a fantasy *which emerges through critical analysis* itself. That is, no matter how many empirical facts we can rally to our cause, no matter how "naked" our subject might be, it is in the very process of interpretation that meaning emerges. In the critical fantasy of being able to "reveal all" about its subject—in this case, the revelation of the "true" Romantic ideology or the "truth" of the poet's mind—our critical gaze reflects back upon ourselves. As Slavoj Žižek reminds us, whereas we imagine that we can "see it all," our gaze actually "falls into ourselves, the spectators, which is why the image we see . . . contains no spot, no sublime mysterious point from which it gazes at us. It is only we who gaze stupidly at the image that 'reveals all.' "[20]

The common complaint that psychoanalytic criticism fundamentally degrades its object in the analytical process, or that there is a violence done to the subject through this kind of emotional intrusion, thus needs to be inverted. Far from the Romantic subject being opened up and exposed as an object of our voyeuristic pleasure, it is the spectator himself who effectively occupies the position of the object. The real subjects are the Romantic writers, while we as their critics are reduced to a paralyzed object-gaze. Inevitably, as Freud discovered in his abortive treatment of Dora, without the recognition of our own operations of desire, *we* become the objects of analysis, paralyzed by the gaze. As Sophie Thomas points out, the powers of transference in the reading process are ones that repeat the analyst/analysand relationship in ways that demand constant critical self-awareness. For while Freud's failure to recognize this oversight led to the untimely termination of Dora's analysis, our own failure most frequently results in an interpretive paralysis in which our textual conclusions endlessly circle around our own unrecognized critical desire.

What is the force behind this critical fantasy in both old and new psychological modes of criticism and why has it emerged with such virulence within the field of Romanticism today? Freud's insistence that the psychoanalytic meaning of events does not originate in the past, per se, but rather in the way that past events are interpreted and reenacted in the present, is of vital importance here. As Freud discovered, it was not the *remembrance* of an "historical" trauma that was essential for successful analysis and cure, but rather the *construction* of this event—a distinction, which as Ned Lukacher has remarked, indicates how Freud has "radically altered the very notion of Truth" in his work by disrupting the traditional hierarchy of "memory" over "construction."[21] What this means is that it is not the originary event that signifies, but rather the manner in which this event has been interpreted and signified in the present. Thus, for Žižek, "if the trace of an old encounter all of a sudden begins to exert impact, it is because the present symbolic universe of the subject is structured in a way that is susceptible to it."[22] Paradoxically, then, Romanticism is important to us as an event because of what we are, not because of what *it* was. Searches for the "actual" Romantic past, whether it be Jerome McGann's corrective attempts to expose the "real" Romantic ideology or the empiricism of the New Psychologists, are revealing not because they might succeed in their efforts, but rather because their efforts indicate an ongoing wish to "fill in the gaps" and to rewrite the past in such a way as to produce an unbroken narrative from origin to present.[23] Indeed, as Zizek goes on to point out, what is important to recognize is:

> How *this retroactive causality, this "re-writing of the past," is inherently linked to the problematic of the "missing link":* it is precisely because this chain of linear causality is always broken, because language as synchronous order is caught in a vicious circle, that it attempts to restore the "missing link" by retroactively organizing its past, by reconstituting its origins backwards.[24]

Thus, Romanticism, perhaps more than any other literary field, has obsessively sought its identity, its origin, and its primal scene in order to understand not simply who we are, but how we have fallen from what we once were. We might remember once more McGann's effort to escape the "false ideologies" of Romanticism and retrace some allegedly pure and unsullied truth that "predates" critical constructions of Romanticism.[25] Such a task is impossible not simply because we can never escape ideology, but also because the primal fantasy of recovering such origins—of filling in the gap between history and interpretation—can only be a fantasy since to fill in the gap, as it were, would eradicate the meaningfulness of the very category "Romanticism," thereby erasing the subject we sought to explore.

This is the paradox of the impossible gaze of the primal scene— something with which the Romantic poets themselves were thoroughly familiar. Thus Byron frequently expressed the desire that his writing (significantly, often about himself) would "remove himself from himself." Beddoes, as Frances Wilson points out, obsessively attempted to silence himself in the very act of writing, while Keats considered the greatest poets to be those who could, chameleonlike, offer up their own identity on the altar of poetry. In short, for these Romantic poets, the act of "seeing themselves" could never be enacted without an erasure of self, and like Psyche gazing down upon her unknown love, it is only in the moment of loss of self or subjectivity that self-awareness can be achieved.

Evidently, these Romantic poets seemed to have recognized that the fantasy gaze that reveals "all" is inherently perverse. Thus, when we examine Keats's "Ode to Psyche," a poem that expressly deals with issues of poetic identity and critical desire, we encounter a poet who not only seeks to understand who he is as a poet, but also what a poet might have been in his unfallen originary moment. And notably, that poet gazes with the eyes of Satan. In fact, when the narrating poet wanders into a glen only to discover the sleeping Psyche and Love embracing in a bower, his astonished gaze represents nothing so much as the impossible gaze of the primal scene. Here, wrapped together in a blissful union are the poet's "parents" in the moment of his conception:

> Surely I dreamt to-day, or did I see
>   The winged Psyche with awaken'd eyes?
> I wander'd in a forest thoughtlessly,
>   And, on the sudden, fainting with surprise,
> Saw two fair creatures, couched side by side
>   In deepest grass, beneath the whisp'ring roof
> Of leaves and trembled blossoms, where there ran
>   A brooklet, scarce espied:
>
> (Ll. 5–12)

One might imagine that in such a vision, the poet would have been party to a true insight into his identity, gazing as he does upon the originary moment before what Wordsworth would call the "fall into language."[26] Certainly there seems to be hope for such a revelatory moment. Psyche is described in terms that relate her to the first mother in that other Eden, Eve. She and Love lie "couched side by side / In deepest grass. Beneath the whisp'ring roof / of leaves and trembled blossoms." Milton's Christian parents in *Paradise Lost,* much like Keats's pagan couple, sleep together, "the loveliest pair . . . Under a tuft of shade that on a green / Stood whispering soft, by a fresh Fountain side" (book 4, ll. 325–26). But what this means, of course, is that the speaker gazing upon the pair is placed in the position not simply of voyeur, but of Satan himself. The poetic persona looks upon the entangled pair with envy for their prelapsarian poetic state in a manner that clearly mirrors Satan's own recognition of his lost past. But when we analyze what is being seen here, we realize it is not actually what the poet thinks he sees. In fact, this couple does not signify paradise lost, but rather paradise *regained.*

If we recall the myth of Psyche, it is only after this mortal woman has surrendered to the temptation to "know" the mystery of her husband's identity and is cast out of paradise that she is ultimately united with Love in her immortal status. Keats' s narrating poet describes the couple in paradisiacal terms, but in fact the world of poetry has already been lost and won. The poet's gaze, so seemingly penetrative into the "truth" of his origin, is revealed to be the perverse gaze that must inevitably fall back upon itself as desire. That is, just like the Romantic critics who seek out the "true" moment of Romantic ideology's inception, what is revealed in our gaze is not the "reality" but rather the fantasy constructed in the process of analysis. Thus while Keats's poet may fantasize about "untrodden regions of [his] mind," the path he treads is far from "pure":

> A rosy sanctuary will I dress
> With the wreath'd trellis of a working brain,
>   With buds, and bells, and stars without a name,
> With all the gardener Fancy e'er could feign,
>   Who breeding flowers, will never breed the same:
>
> (Ll. 59–63)

Keats, perhaps more than his narrating poet, is well aware that behind his gaze is a "working brain" which creates a vision grounded in his own desires by his own Fancy. The naked sanctuary of poetry is ultimately "dressed" in the very moment we fantasize we have penetrated to her "rosy" core.

All of the following essays in this issue of the *Bucknell Review* acknowledge, in some manner, this Keatsian awareness of the effects of interpretive desire; they complicate and explore the premise that we can ever penetrate, uncover, or embrace the "core" of Romanticism as its "virgin choir" or even as its "pale-mouthed prophet," treading across its sacred realm without ever imprinting upon its surface. Indeed, the obvious gendering of such critical fantasies is an issue that Guinn Batten takes up in her " 'Time Feels Unclocked': Romantic History, Gender, and a Poetics of Hysteria in Recent Irish Poetry." In this essay, Batten takes on the formidable and much-needed task of rethinking literary criticism's response to issues of authenticity, universality, and the anomalous in Irish poetry. Focusing on the many recent Irish poets who have been influenced by English Romanticism, Batten challenges the frequent "scapegoating" of the male Romantic poet by recent postcolonial and feminist studies which tend to present figures such as Wordsworth as the representatives of a dominant culture that silences or buries the more "authentic" native subjects of Irish nationalist and republican traditions. Drawing on the theoretical work of Slavoj Žižek, Batten argues that such uses of "history" to expose the "true" and particular voices—and sufferings—of the Irish are contrary to the versions of history offered by Ireland's contemporary Irish poets, in which the past returns as hysteria. As Batten argues, it is in the "far more surreal . . . return of the ghosts of the past as they are embodied in the hysterical and spectral forms of a "late" capital that we encounter the strangeness that marks what is taken to be normal in Irish culture, notably as the empire of the New World Order has succeeded

England's. Through her analysis of Medbh McGuckian and Ciaran Carson, Batten shows how, paradoxically, it is the very hystericization of the Irish subject that ensures its "resistance to a noncontradictory ideological interpellation." Further, as the work of these poets reveals, the past, far from being eradicated by the universalizing claims of a dominant and colonial culture, has been preserved "through unconscious acts of bodily incorporation as well as by conscious poetic imitation" of forms of Romantic poetry. What such incorporation achieves, Batten shows, "is a preservation that restructures that consciousness and comfortably dissolves the categories of Self and Other, whether 'colonist' or 'colonizer,' 'Catholic' or 'Protestant,' or 'marginal' and 'canonical,' within the intestinal cavities of the poet's memory."

It is precisely on this issue of incorporation and fragmentation that Sophie Thomas concentrates in her "The Return of the Fragment: 'Christabel' and the Uncanny." Here Thomas explores the psychological dynamics in operation between text and reader, but in Thomas's work it is the formal structure of the work under examination that creates the transferential effect in need of analysis. Taking on the contentious subject of the fragment poem, Thomas focuses on the "restorative efforts of reading" and our repeated attempts to analyze and understand what is presented to us as fundamentally "unspeakable" and mutilated. As Thomas notes, "Christabel"'s lack of resolution creates a dynamic with its reader similar to that between a therapist and her analysand. We, like Freud in the case of Dora, are confronted with a mutilated subject, "the beauty of which can only be appreciated by those who have knowledge or imagination sufficient to complete the idea of whole composition." We seek out the meanings in the fragmentary text before us, reading and rereading in our attempt to position it within a whole and thus comprehensible narrative—a response which places this poem firmly within the realm of "uncanny" affect. After an exhaustive examination of the critical attempts to explain away, complete, or repeat "Christabel"'s meaning, Thomas goes on to suggest that the origin of the poem's power for us is precisely in this transferential quality; "the presence of the fragment, as a persistent reminder of the remainder, may be seen as the allegorical presence within a text . . . of its own 'death': its own necessarily incomplete incompletion."

Joel Faflak's " 'On Her Own Couch': Keats's Wandering Psychoanalysis" similarly examines the relationship between the Romantic text and the psychoanalytic process. Specifically, Faflak examines the ways in which "Romanticism's psychoanalytic tropes and mechanisms disclose a *process* of imaging psychoanalysis before its codification by theory." For Faflak, Romanticism replicates and anticipates Freud's later desire to "rationalize the irrational" inasmuch as it too sets the stage for the battle between the two realms that are so uneasily paired in Coleridge's term, *psycho-analytical:* the phantasmatic/literary versus the scientific/rational. For Faflak, this contestation is also evidenced in the unstable gender economies we find in Romanticism, specifically in its representation of Fancy as the feminine interiority of unreason that masculine ideology repeatedly attempts to marginalize. What Faflak's sophisticated reading of Keats shows, however, is that such marginalization precisely reveals the instability and volatility of gender economies. Following the work of Freud, Julia Kristeva, and Judith Butler, Faflak argues that while (masculine) Romanticism privileges interiority, "the privileging itself frequently manages what threatens this interiority from within, not unlike how Freud's dreamwork systematizes the unconscious so as to colonize it." Faflak argues that Romanticism as it is manifested in *Endymion, Hyperion* and the *Fall of Hyperion,* presents a sort of "primal scene" that—operating through fantasy—both discloses subjectivity in the narrative scene projected and simultaneously deconstitutes it in the impossible scene of its origin. Keats's poetry, then, sets the stage for an important drama, narrative mise-en-scènes in which psychoanalysis appears "as the articulation of gender's 'phantasmatic structure' within identity's formation."

In Marc Redfield's "Masks of Anarchy: Shelley's Political Poetics" the concept *Romantic ideology* is once more the subject under discussion. In this case, however, Redfield, through a reading of Shelley, offers a critique of Jameson's appropriation of the psychoanalytic notion of the unconscious. Redfield rewrites the political unconscious as the iterability, slippage, and ambiguity that makes politics possible—he rethinks the idea of a political "unconscious," that is, as the essential drift, the chanciness, that (in Redfield's Derridean analysis) forms the condition of possibility of political communication and action. This permits a new reading of Shelley's claim about unacknowledged legislators, since, as his subtle reading of *The Cenci* argues, there is a parallel between the sense of numbness incurred by this play's sadism and Shelley's famous description of the poet. Both, Redfield notes, are for Shelley "tools blind to the sensation they elicit or the meaning they perform." What this means is that we are confronted by a reading of poetry as a political form of violence—a theme which contradicts some of Shelley's most cherished themes. For Redfield, this contradiction reveals a "vibrant ambiguity" in Shelley's work which shows us that since "poetic words do not understand what they express, or feel what they inspire, poetry functions as the political unconscious of aesthetics precisely to the extent that poetry opens aesthetics to the contingency of history and the constitutive uncertainty of futurity."

Focusing on the personal more than the political unconscious, Frances Wilson's essay " 'Strange Sun': Melancholia in the Writing of Thomas Lovell Beddoes" examines how the Romantic disease of self-consciousness is taken to its logical conclusion in the act of self-annihilation. Far from supporting Geoffrey Hartman's assumption that the Romantics sought to overcome self-consciousness and re-turn to a sense of unification, Wilson argues that Beddoes, a poet who certainly sought to write himself free of self, attempted to do so by dismembering both his physical and figurative corpus. Dissecting limbs, disemboweling copies of his poetry, and ultimately commit-ting suicide, Beddoes provides the example of a poet who probes only further into the wound of subjectivity in his effort to "push lan-guage and the self as far as they could go—beyond signification, rep-resentation, and identity." Using the theoretical structures of Kris-teva's work on melancholia, Wilson examines a body of work that seeks its own dismemberment and annihilation through its merging with the Kantian Thing at the threshold of the sublime. Writing for Beddoes, argues Wilson, is an act of undoing, that paradoxically haunts subjectivity in the moment of its dissolution. For while it is true that Beddoes could write himself "apart" in his dissection of the "I" that is the writer and the "I" that is written, such a division signified not simply a dismemberment but also a plurality—the end-less signification of language itself which only ends in death. For Wil-son, then, it was in his carefully plotted suicide that Beddoes's ulti-mately achieved his creative goal—a creation beyond signification.

As we have already seen, such themes are closely related to Toril Moi's "A Woman's Desire to Be Known: Expressivity and Silence in *Corinne.*" Moi, in her analysis of Madame de Staël (one of Romanti-cism's most underread authors), argues for an understanding of *Co-rinne* based on an eighteenth-century aesthetic awareness of theatri-cality and expressivity. This is a novel that specifically addresses the effects outlined by Joyce McDougall as the three traumatic finitudes psychoanalysis has historically studied: the fact that there are Oth-ers, the fact that we can only be one sex, and the fact of death.[27] Corinne's struggle, as Moi explains it, is to be simultaneously ac-knowledged as a human being with access to the universal (what Moi defines as the public sphere in which values are being fought over) *and* as a woman—a sex which traditionally has been seen to suffer an erasure of proper identity within this realm. Staël struggles against the aesthetic standards established so influentially in her

time by philosophers such as Hegel who refuse to acknowledge
women as self-conscious subjects. As a result, Staël is forced to mark
her heroine with an excess of femininity precisely in order to illustrate her desire to be recognized as the Other, which is to say an
independent subjectivity apart from masculine desire. Her "expressivity" in opposition to the normative feminine dictate of silence is
thus an attempt to position Corinne simultaneously outside of the
theatrical realm of inauthenticity, while guaranteeing her position
as a self-conscious subject. Her failure to do so successfully, argues
Moi, is not evidence of her own lack, but rather that of the world's.
Writes Moi: "the ultimate realization of human finitude is doubled
by zealous protection of her own, separate and secret interiority. Corinne's dying words affirm her intense conviction that she has remained *unknown*," proving that this is indeed a world unworthy of
her. Arguably the only alternative for a woman who *cannot* be known
as Other, is death.

This collection of essays does not pretend to be the final word on
the issue of Romanticism and psychoanalysis, nor does it even present a unified theoretical school from which to approach the issue.
Rather the essays compiled here do the work of showing the range
of theoretical possibilities open to the critic when taking on the
complicated and often treacherous realm of the unconscious in the
literary corpus. No less than the individual unconscious, the unconscious of the literary body resists and denies interpretive analysis,
leaving us the difficult task of reading with responsibility and with
the recognition of our desire in the process of the construction of
meaning. But if there is a single question addressed, a central moti-
vation shared by all of the above essays, it is that which Freud articu-
lated in his essay on "Creative Writers and Day Dreaming." How,
questions Freud, does this "strange creature," this creative writer,
"manage to make such an impression on us with it and to arouse in
us emotions of which, perhaps, we had not even thought ourselves
capable."[28] At the center of all analysis, then, is this fascination *with
our own desire* which, as Byron notes in the fourth canto of *Childe Harold*, is the very source of creativity:

> The mind hath made thee, as it peopled heaven,
> Even with its own desiring phantasy,
> And to a thought such shape and image given,
> As haunts the unquench'd soul—parch'd—wearied—wrung—and riven.
>   (4. 121. 1086–89)

This collection illustrates that the "desiring phantasy" of our own
unconscious—a phantasy that literally peoples the void of interpre-

tation with desire—will continue, productively, to haunt the literary corpus.

GHISLAINE MCDAYTER

Notes

1. René Wellek, "The Concept of 'Romanticism' in Literary History," *Comparative Literature* 1 (1949): 2.

2. Nancy Easterlin, "Psychoanalysis and the 'Discipline of Love': Wordsworth's Babe in Developmental Persepective," http:/www2.bc.edu/~richarad/lcb/fc/ne.html.

3. See Alan Richardson's web site "Literature, Cognition and the Brain" at http://www2.bc.edu/~richarad/lcb/wip/ar.html. His work is part of his book in progress entitled *British Romanticism and the Science of the Mind.*

4. William Wordsworth, *The Prelude 1799, 1805, 1850,* ed. Jonathan Wordsworth, M. H. Abrams, and Stephen Gill (New York: Norton, 1979), 10. 899, 902.

5. Richardson, http://www2.bc.edu/~richarad/lcb/wip/ar.html.

6. *Prelude* 10. 874–75.

7. Mary Thomas Crane, *Shakespeare's Brain: Reading with Cognitive Theory.* Forthcoming from Princeton University Press. Web site http://www2.bc.edu/~lcb/fc/mtc/html.

8. Of course, the "universal" argument for poetry has long been pitted against psychoanalytic readings. Bernard Blackstone, for example, writes: "the attempt to interpret art in terms of psychological theory must necessarily fail because it ignores the hierarchical disposition of things; the high dream cannot be explained through the low dream and in great art we are dealing with states of experience which are, literally, God-given. If art is the freeing of the mind from the personal image, as Mr. Eliot has said, it is also the freeing of the mind from the enclosing structure and reactions and conditionings, from the habit-energies of accumulated past experiences inadequately responded to." In *The Consecrated Urn* (London: Longmans Green, 1959), 135. New Psychology is leery of precisely this kind of "hierarchy" between the "high dream" of art, and the "low dream" of psychology, and Richardson specifically addresses the issue of "universality" in his "Rethinking Romantic Incest: Human Universals, Literary Representations, and the Biology of the Mind." Forthcoming in *New Literary History.*

9. Geoffrey Hartman, "Romanticism and Anti-Self-Consciousness," in Harold Bloom, *Romanticism and Consciousness: Essays in Criticism* (New York: Norton, 1970), 50.

10. Harold Bloom, "Nature and Consciousness," in Bloom, *Romanticism and Consciousness.*

11. See Richardson's web site, n. 5, above.

12. M. H. Abrams, *The Mirror and the Lamp: Romantic Theory and the Critical Tradition* (London: Oxford University Press, 1953), 236.

13. Andrew Rutherford, *Byron: The Critical Heritage* (London: Routledge & Kegan Paul, 1970), 149.

14. Guinn Batten, *The Orphaned Imagination: Melancholy and Commodity Culture in English Romanticism* (Durham, N.C.: Duke University Press, 1998), 9.

15. Barbara Schapiro, *The Romantic Mother: Narcissistic Patterns in Romantic Poetry* (Baltimore, Md.: The Johns Hopkins Press, 1983), xiv.

16. Henry Blyth, *Caro: The Fatal Passion* (New York: Coward, McCann & Geoghegan, 1972), 3.

17. Ibid., 77.

18. Jean Laplanche, *Life and Death in Psychoanalysis*, trans. Jeffrey Mehlman (Baltimore, Md.: The Johns Hopkins Press, 1985), 99.

19. Ibid.

20. Slavoj Žižek, *Looking Awry: An Introduction to Jacques Lacan through Popular Culture* (Cambridge, Mass.: An October Book, 1993), 110.

21. Ned Lukacher, *Primal Scenes: Literature, Philosophy, Psychoanalysis* (Ithaca, N.Y.: Cornell University Press, 1986), 21.

22. Slavoj Žižek, *For They Know Not What They Do: Enjoyment as a Political Factor* (London: Verso Books, 1991), 202.

23. One of the most interesting examples of this fantasy can be found in Jerome Christensen's most recent examination of Romanticism, *Romanticism at the End of History*. Here he suggests a critical strategy in which the reader becomes a co-conspirator with the Romantic poet: "Yet a conspiratorial theory of Romantic poetry can, I urge, be justified by its ethical application. It renders the ineffable not as the unspeakable subject of the gothic or the phenomenal overload of the sublime but as the artisanal tact of the good collaborator. Conspiratorial intimacy is a breathing together—an occasion of mutual implication that, fortunately, is not capable of being rendered in language that all who run may read . . . Historically constructed, Romanticism remains under construction in the history we are making." But what is not fully clear is exactly why such secretive conspiratorial work is necessary. In short, what force are we conspiring against, and who seeks to invade our interpretive space? Who threatens Romanticism from without? See Christensen, *Romanticism at the End of History* (Baltimore, Md.: The Johns Hopkins Press, 2000), 3.

24. Žižek, *For They Know Not*, 203.

25. See Jerome McGann, *The Romantic Ideology: A Critical Investigation* (Chicago: University of Chicago Press, 1985).

26. William Wordsworth, "Essays upon Epitaphs," in *Selected Prose*, ed. John O. Hayden (London: Penguin Books, 1988), 371.

27. See Joyce McDougall, *The Many Faces of Eros* (New York: Norton, 1995), xv.

28. Sigmund Freud, "Creative Writers and Day Dreaming," in *The Standard Edition of the Complete Psychological Works of Sigmund Freud*, ed. and trans. James Strachey (London: Hogarth Press, 1953–1974), 9:141–53.

BUCKNELL REVIEW

Untrodden Regions of the Mind: Romanticism and Psychoanalysis

"Time Feels Unclocked": Romantic History, Gender, and a Poetics of Hysteria in Recent Irish Poetry

Guinn Batten

Washington University of St. Louis

Here is a stone with a stone's mouth inside,
a shell in which a lighter shell has died,

one with a honey bullet in the heart,
one that has lain full-length from the start.

The leaves are tongues whose years of blood are locked
in the wrong house, time feels unclocked

or has been dead too long by now to cast
its freshly slaughtered shadow from the past . . .
                    —Medbh McGuckian, "Script for an Unchanging Voice"

That music in my heart I bore
Long after it was heard no more.
                    —Wordsworth, "The Solitary Reaper"

I N postcolonial studies as in Romanticism, challenges to received history have focused on the excavation of whatever local and minority particulars, claimed to be more "authentic," have been banished by the imposition of the universal, and universalizing, claims of a dominant culture. Canonical, male English Romantic poetry has been a particular scapegoat in such critiques, but so have the legacies of the Romantic Age that have shaped a masculine republican tradition in Ireland. While for American feminists Eavan Boland may be the best-known such critic of Irish Romanticism, postcolonial scholars are also likely to be familiar with David Lloyd's critique of the same in *Nationalism and Minor Literature, Anomalous States*, and, most recently, *Ireland after History*.[1] Likewise, Seamus Deane in the Oxford lectures collected as *Strange Country* constructs his own in-

29

dictment of a nationalist literary history that, he claims, has ignored "real" history. It has done so, he argues, so that it may "offer itself as a body of writing that—throughout the many and disastrous changes the society that produced it has undergone—nevertheless continues to represent the unchanging and unchangeable spirit of the Gael." What Deane particularly deplores is the fact that this literary history, establishing its own version of a Romantic "canon" that is Irish, makes a universalizing claim that "depends on the exclusion from literary history of the dynamics of historical change and particularly, the actuality of historical atrocity." Note his derisive use of the word "cure" in the following:

> Literary history is the cure for other forms of historical investigation. It produces, more successfully than they, sameness out of difference, triumph out of disaster, the success of representation out of a culture that for a century had been trying to find effective ways of dealing with the conviction that it had not been represented or could not be represented.

Deane concludes *Strange Country* with a final thrust at what he perceives to be the self-deluding denial of economic history rendered by most literary responses to "history" in Ireland: "normality is an economic condition; strangeness is a cultural one."[2] Yet in recent Irish poetry we may in fact find keen readings of Ireland's economic history as it exists both within a larger and global context, and within the more intimate and sexual sites of the body, where the "normal" itself is exposed as "strange."

In the surreal poems that have appeared in Ireland since the most recent phase of the Troubles began in 1968, the canonical English Romantics appear with surprising frequency, and by no means do they make such appearances only as figures of culpability. Neither are the Romantics always English: in recent poems by Medbh McGuckian and Ciaran Carson, a shared earlier interest in Romanticism generally has been extended to Ireland and to France in the 1790s. In these poems as in those written by such other Irish poets as Paul Muldoon, Thomas Kinsella, John Montague, Michael Longley, Derek Mahon, and Seamus Heaney, the presence in various senses of "Romanticism" has been part of their innovative approach to the representation of matters that are, through the tools of the historian or the structures of everyday language, unavailable and unrepresentable. Perhaps surprisingly, what may well be in their poetry most unrepresentable in its very "strangeness" is not the local particular attributable to what has misleadingly been characterized as a "tribal" atavism or even the occluded entity that Lloyd now calls the "non-modern." Far more surreal, in "normal" Irish life as in Irish poetry, has been the return of the ghosts of the past as they are reembodied in the hysterical and spectral forms of a (literally) "late" capital.

We must all hope, as peace-loving and humane citizens of the world, that the ideological promise of prosperity will unite the island under a rule of peace as the more visible ideologies of sectarian politics have not, offering the real possibility that sectarian violence—and the state's sometimes violent and often repressive response to sectarian violence—will at last come to an end. Nevertheless, if we are also skeptical of smoking the pipe of peace with the same authorities that have made tobacco a major third-world product, then the longed-for peace under the terms of the New World Order will bring its own, less visible, costs. In this sense, economic conditions in a contemporary Ireland on the verge of becoming "normal" are, as is universally true across the globe, stranger than fiction. The representation of that strangeness requires not fiction—not even the gothic novel grounded, in Ireland, so clearly in horror—but in fact poetry, a genre that contemporary Irish poets have uniquely, and successfully, redefined by returning at once to the English Romantics (including the *Lyrical Ballads*) and to the mixed hybrid of the ballad popularized in Ireland's own Romantic Age.

I

Of course, it is no surprise to Romanticists that the "sameness" to which Deane refers, the inevitable consequence of the "transcendental" and universalizing aims of any literary historicism, remains under attack. Whether the universal is condemned in its republican, Romantic, or Enlightenment versions, it elicits scholarly suspicion, despite recent readings of Kant's legacy by Gayatri Spivak, Slavoj Žižek, and Anthony Cascardi that are by and large sympathetic. In investigations of Irish as of English literary canon formations, what Lloyd has called the "anomalous" (literally, if we consider the etymology of that term, that which is not *sem*, or "same"), may not simply be "woman" (although of course the anomalous, whatever it may be, is quite likely to be gendered as female) but, indeed, whatever subject is denied full representation in an allegedly representative government or in the aesthetic productions of its culture.

The conventional representation of violence in relation to historical change and its contemporaneous literary productions goes, over simply, as follows. The democratic state is inaugurated by a brief or extended period of "Romantic" revolution, a violent phase during

which it is commonplace that an exciting and innovative literature
emerges (England in 1798, the first and second Irish Renaissances
in this century). At last emerges a state founded on the Enlightenment ideals of individual freedom and historical progress. Yet there
is always disillusion, and nowhere more so of course than in the
foundation of the Irish Free State on narrow and sectarian principles. But more typically, while the state founded on constitutional
freedoms may claim to have freed itself from an oppressive past, one
which repressed the true spirit of its people, and may make good on
that claim not by recourse to church doctrine but to secular universals, it will nevertheless always deem certain subjects to have made
insufficient "progress" on the road to citizenship to become representative participants in the political process.

Marxist readings of the Enlightenment have for some time noted
that the literally heady revolutions it spawned were essentially
spurred by middle-class economic values rather than full democratic
participation for all classes and both genders. And we can witness in
the Celtic Tiger as elsewhere the success of that bourgeois revolution. One of the most eloquent and extreme of such critiques,
Adorno and Horkheimer's *Dialectic of Enlightenment* argues that any
totalizing universal, of which modern capital is the supreme example, does violence to what it had to exclude in order to be "representative" of the whole.[3] The purpose of the aesthetic, Adorno writes in
Negative Dialectics, is to speak on behalf of that which suffers silently
on the outskirts of modern history.[4] In the particular case of nineteenth-century Irish history, Lloyd has observed that standard portrayals of the Irish as "innately" prone to violent self-expression
downplay the regular presence of state violence in the everyday lives
of the Irish while exaggerating acts of violence committed by
"mobs" against the state. In Ireland, Lloyd writes, the " 'frequently
lamented want of a middle class' " coincides with the exaggerated
and repeated representation of the lawless, atavistic Irishman as
rural and bog-trotting. The so-called lack of a middle class, which is

> conceived as the lack of a locus of stability, has to be rethought in terms
> of the historical existence of a middle class that was the site of maximum
> instability, whether in terms of its fluctuating economic situation or in
> terms of its political or social affiliations." (*AS*, 140)

Yet the "anomaly" of Irish culture in late eighteenth- and early nineteenth-century Ireland extends beyond questions of class and the
misrepresentation of Irish identity as antinomian. In *Anomalous
States*, Lloyd concludes that in contemporary Irish historicism, the

nationalist and the revisionist converge in proposing that the "end of this history of violence" lies in the very end of history—the "emergence of the state":

> [violence] is what summons into being the emergence of a modern state apparatus in Ireland: a national police force, administration and legal system, education and even parliamentary democracy. Violence is understood as an atavistic and disruptive principle counter to the rationality of legal constitution as barbarity is to an emerging civility, anarchy to culture. In one thing, both tendencies concur: the end of violence is the legitimate state formation . . . From such a perspective, violence is radically counter-historical, even against narrative, always represented as an outburst, an "outrage," spasmodic and without legitimating teleology . . . Nationalism itself requires the absorption or transformation of justifiable but nonetheless irrational acts of resistance into the self-legitimating form of a political struggle for the state. (*AS*, 125–26)

But as Ireland begins the process of devolution, what is likely to be absorbed is the state itself, as a global economy increasingly enables the world's major economic players to intrude, in Ireland as elsewhere, into the affairs of nation states.[5]

Recent feminist scholarship has conjoined with Marxist and postcolonial critiques of Irish nationalism, decrying portrayals of "woman" in Irish culture as particularly representative of violence, from Kathleen ni Houlihan to Yeats's Helen and Leda. One of the most sophisticated examples of such scholarship as it pertains to Irish poetry is Marjorie Howes's *Yeats's Nations*, which extends the critique of representative government and literary strategies of representation to the anomalous category of "woman" in a modernizing Irish state. Howes has particularly drawn our attention to the ways in which "woman" as a category in Ireland has been feared as representative of the hysterical mindlessness of the mob, an analysis that should evoke for Romanticists Neil Hertz's pathbreaking study of the headless body and the sexualized mob in the French Revolution. What is particularly effective in Howes's analysis is her stress on the "internal contradictions that mean nationalism is never identical with itself," particularly as it is figured in "ambivalence." In contrast to Homi Bhabha's hopeful and homogenizing reading of that term, Howes rightly focuses on the gendered particulars that lead to "various ways for nationality to lack identity with itself."[6] While Howes's focus in her readings of Yeats's attunement to that lack is on the figure, and the actual examples, of "woman" in Ireland, I will suggest that we might enlarge that ambivalence, that "lack" of identity which, as Žižek suggests, paradoxically ensures the success of ideological interpellation, to consider the anomaly that is also "masculinity" in a time of violence in Ireland, or perhaps in any state, particularly as that anomaly is represented in Irish poems governed by what I am calling here a poetics of hysteria. Although it is beyond the scope of this essay, and "hysteria" as I discuss it here, I would suggest that we need to consider more broadly the importance of various strategies of the "negative" in modern Irish poetry to represent, formally and thematically, the contradictions constitutive of the anomalous states of "being" Irish. In this sense they offer a vital alternative to what have become, to a certain degree, fairly moribund readings of English Romanticism in the academy. The poets cited earlier follow Yeats in being not the "last" but perhaps the "latest" Romantics, both in their attunement to the speech of the dead and in their, in various ways, antithetical poetics.

II

To what degree can any poetry fulfill what may well be the supreme (though some recent Romanticists might argue, the supremely misguided and self-deluding) hope of the English Romantic: to speak authoritatively on behalf of the "oppressed," or even the "repressed"? Wordsworth's "The Solitary Reaper," cited in the opening of this essay, has, in recent Romanticist scholarship, perhaps become the paradigmatic pariah in this regard. I put that term "repressed" in quotation marks, of course, in part because it is a term few of us still believe has validity beyond its binary relationship with "desire." But I also draw attention to the term "repressed" because it continues to gesture toward the controversial intersection that we inevitably must approach as literary historians who are at once sympathetic to feminist and to postcolonial issues and engaged in critiques of capitalism: the intersection of public history and psychoanalysis. In Ireland, as elsewhere, the fact that public "reality" and private "fantasy" may be as difficult to consider simultaneously as they are impossible to separate might lead us to remember Freud's case history of an hysteric. In his study of Dora, Freud concluded that her symptom—aphonia—suggested that, against her will, she had something to tell that she could not tell or perhaps even that she did not consciously know. The hysteric expresses her secret as a bodily "speech" that is debilitating or even painful but irrepressible. In his failure to cure Dora, Freud arrived at two of the most controversial topics in psychoanalysis, topics that now underwrite Žižek's persuasive analysis of why the ideology of global capital succeeds in interpellating even subjects postmodern in their cynicism, in Ireland as elsewhere: the seduction theory and transference.

More broadly, as Žižek has argued, every modern subject is, by definition, an hysteric.[7] We think we are subjects, but in fact we think *from* the place of an *object.* The symptom bespeaks on the body's surface a secret object within ourselves that we unconsciously enjoy too much to surrender it consciously, an object that we think we are resisting but to which we have in fact already yielded. That symptom is the body's mute testimony to the subject's traumatic entry into the symbolic order. Yet this estranged, protesting, but also enslaving, object within ourselves, like desire itself, is neither private nor our own. Rather, even if we cannot define what "it" is, the fascinating object, and our desire *for* it, offer testimony to our identification with the desire of an allegedly "enlightened," unified, and unifying Law of the Father that pretends to be *beyond* the desire of contingent subjectivity. That Law, that universalizing ideology, has been internalized *as* our own, contingent desire, even as we have already yielded, as objects, *to* that desire of (which is to say, that lack within) the allegedly seamless ideology. Paradoxically, such yielding to (and such identification with) what proves to be itself an irrational, hysterical Law of the Father (even as we continue, consciously, to believe that the Law remains representative of universal reason) is the indispensable origin of articulate speech, of conscious subjectivity, and, one might argue, of the paradox of an ongoing belief in nationhood and national identity in the face of increasing globalization.

Yet in recent poems from Ireland, some of which are in various senses spoken in the language of hysteria, that secret object seems ambiguously to be at once a residue of interpellation and something that has refused, across the centuries, to *be* interpellated. This anomalous object, which Yeats would have confidently identified as "daimonic," carries us to the most intimate and urgent connection of the self to a public history of colonial oppression that is effacing itself as a now-devolving Ireland becomes an active agent in a global economy. Can poetry represent the very forces that struggle at once to speak and to remain secret within the final site of neocolonial contestation under the New World Order: the unconscious? That hysterical object, as Irish poets may help us to understand, may well be what Lloyd calls "an incommensurable set of cultural formations occluded from, yet never actually disengaged with modernity" (*IH*, 2). Yet their rendering of its "liberation" from "historical ideology" is far stranger than even Lloyd's sophisticated analysis of the returning revenant because they are more skeptical than he of that revenant's capacity to be itself co-opted by ideology, which is to say, to become complicit with the modernity of capitalism.

As readers of poststructuralist theory, and particularly as feminists familiar with Judith Butler's adaptation of Foucault's cautionary tales of power and "repression," we are familiar with the difficulties of defining identity as something "real" that has been repressed or buried. Yet we may nevertheless find ourselves drawn, both as Romanticists and as scholars in postcolonial studies, to academic or poetic representations of minority literatures as the "real thing" that is "repressed" by a Law of the Father whose agents we can more or less easily unmask. As the popular but also academic success of two Irish poets—Eavan Boland and Seamus Heaney—who have themselves written academically on this subject might attest, even the theoretically savvy scholar may continue to believe that a native writer may "speak" for, to represent *as* a speaker, those excluded by colonial, and English, structures of authority and by that authority's important arm of enforcement: official history.

Boland in "Outside History" writes of the importance, and impossibility, of "nation" for the Irish woman poet: "At the very least it seemed to me that I was likely to remain an outsider in my own national literature, cut off from its archive, at a distance from its energy. Unless, that is, I could repossess it" (*OL*, 128). In particular, she blames canonical literature for "the absence of an expressed [female] poetic life which would have dignified and revealed mine" (*OL*, 134). Noting that "the majority of Irish male poets depended on women as motifs in their poetry," Boland argues that such motifs rendered women "passive, decorative, raised to emblematic status." Particularly when the entity to be emblematized is the nation, Boland concludes that male poets have deprived women of "their roots in a suffered truth": "it seemed to me a species of human insult that at the end of all, in certain Irish poems, they should become elements of *style* rather than aspects of truth" (*OL*, 135). She continues: "Dark Rosaleen. Cathleen ni Houlihan. The nation as woman; the woman as national muse" (*OL*, 136). But that deprivation has not been without its compensations for the contemporary woman poet willing to repossess, as a woman, "the wrath and grief of Irish history."

Woman as she is figured as a muse of darkness either to light the way to tribal wholeness or to expose "the exact / and tribal, intimate revenge" has perhaps received its most well-known personification in Seamus Heaney's "Punishment."[8] One of many poems of excavation in his volume *North*, criticized, we might note, by (among others) Ciaran Carson for its alleged advocacy of violence, this poem echoes what Heaney has described in "Feeling into Words" as a poetics of historical and etymological excavation. Alluding to *The Prelude*'s reference to "the hiding places" of "power" where "the spirit of the past" is "enshrined," Heaney observes:

> Implicit in those lines is a view of poetry which I think is implicit in the few poems I have written that give me any right to speak: poetry as divination, poetry as revelation of the self to the self, as restoration of the culture to itself; poems as elements of continuity, with the aura and authenticity of archaeological finds, where the buried shard has the importance of the buried city; poetry as a dig, a dig for finds that end up being plants.[9]

For Heaney, the Irish poet most often cited as "Romantic," the poem is a project in self-retrieval that also authorizes the poet's special, indeed synecdochal, relationship to national identity.

As Boland concludes, in a paragraph that begins "my particular darkness as an Irish poet has been the subject of this piece," . . .

> But if these circumstances displaced my sense of relation to the Irish past in Irish poetry, they also forced me into a perception of the advantages of being able to move, with almost surreal inevitability, from being within the poem to being its maker. A hundred years ago I might have been a motif in a poem. Now I could have a complex self within my own poem. Part of that process entailed being a privileged witness to forces of reaction in Irish poetry. (*OL*, 151)

Heaney, in a more succinct summary of how the experience of a displaced "helicon" may make darkness itself a means of recovering the self, writes in "Personal Helicon," "I rhyme to see my self / To set the darkness echoing" (*OG*, 14). At the depth of the well of literary history lies, for both poets, a true history, an authentic community of Irish farm life or of independent Irish women, a true self. (We might note, in passing, how different is such certainty from Wordsworth's own reflections on reflection in *The Prelude*.)

Boland is suspicious of what she calls "the technical encounter," the "aesthetic maneuver"—"once the image is distorted, the truth is demeaned" (*OL*, 152). Yet in two of the most exciting recent collections of poetry from Ireland, both of which are poetic responses to the 1798 Rebellion (and, more generally, to the Romantic Age that emerged with such republican movements as the United Irishmen in the 1790s), a male and female Irish poet share strategies that make historical spadework seem crude, and interrogations of literary history seem beside the point.[10] In Carson's *The Twelfth of Never*

and McGuckian's *Shelmalier,* history returns as a bodily symptom that
is also poetic form, whether that body is male or female, and
whether the subject allies its politics with terrorism or with the
armed state. Both collections, which make particular demands on
American readers given the wealth of local and historical particulars
of which they are composed, require us to read across poems for
seemingly anomalous tropes that accrue, with repetition and varia-
tion, meaning and authority.

III

In these collections published in 1998, McGuckian and Carson
each, in their different ways, render the public memorials occa-
sioned by another centenary of the 1798 Rebellion into acts of memory that are visceral in their violence, but also in their sexuality. Such
acts are at once communal and private in this, the most recent, fin
de siècle. Addressing the dead heroes of '98, McGuckian in *Shelmalier* writes "You are dissolved in me / like the death of a century."
This internalizing of outer history into the inner spaces of the body
might suggest that the female poet in Ireland, in the anomie of postmodernity as in the agon of the Romantic Age, remains literally, in
her possession of such sexualized sites of burial, "anomalous."[11]
Like the hysteric, she may delude herself that she is peculiarly capable of bearing secrets and of bearing illusory lives to be reborn. But
there are enough acts of homosexual violence in Carson's *The
Twelfth of Never* to suggest that, in violent contests for ideological vic-
tory, the male body may also be the site, even if only in surreal contexts, of violent entry, interrogation, live burial, and, in its various
senses, possession.[12] In Carson's "Crack," recruitment officers
(whether for the army or for the rebels, we are not told) dress their
recruit in "raffish crinoline and ruff" before abusing him with the
eponymous, hallucinogenic illegal substance to make him "crack."[13]
"Come dawn, they asked me to fulfill my woman's role," the poem
ends. Even in a poem more wistful than openly threatening, "The
Londonderry Air," the speaker, mourning the death of a "Danny
Boy" (who of course persists in the very title of the air), writes in
language that could as easily belong in *Shelmalier.*

> I never saw him more, yet he resides within my soul
>
> Like some strange seedling of the plant of Liberty,
> That breeds eternally beneath the Northern Star,
> Returning as the blossom on the whitethorn tree.
>
> (*TN,* 60)

We might wonder why such surprisingly dark poems emerge at the very moment when a devolving Ireland seems ready to take on new life in the Land of the Forever Young of late capital. Never has Ireland been represented as (to use Carson's term) such a "dead domain," even in such commanding collections as Yeats's *The Winding Stair*, Kinsella's *Notes from the Land of the Dead*, or Montague's *The Dead Kingdom*. Throughout Carson's *The Twelfth of Never*, "the future history / Of Ireland free" seems, by turns, to be either an anomalous subject's hallucinogenic, nightmarish holiday in the Tir na nOg of a Republican or Loyalist vision, or an entire culture's armchair escape to the now commodified, commercialized Republic of Bord Failte where "You'll find you will succumb to their endearing charms / For sometimes they cohabit with the living dead" (*TN*, 78). Where McGuckian searches, as she claims in her Author's Note, within the self's interiors to at once retrieve and redress a history of Northern republicanism that had been denied to her, in Carson's poems, to the contrary, the speaker seems an unwilling captive to the competing demands of several histories and of futures that might be either Irish or Japanese in the global twenty-first century. These survive only, but effectively, as the part objects of dead hands, dancing shoes, "martyrs' groans," and emblems that, while emptied of any but sentimental significance, are nonetheless capable of raising (in various senses) recruits ("Wrap the Green Flag Round Me," *TN*, 30). To McGuckian's innovative but nevertheless deeply catholic hagiographies Carson opposes a sometimes savage parody of the rituals of a Republic whose constitution is founded on catholicism. In the literally shadow state of "Erin," vampiric, "haemo*globic*" ceremonies are, in a sense, merely the unstaunched wound of Ulster's Protestant Red Hand as it seeps across the border into a more prosperous, "globic" economy. Note Carson's perverse sexualization of Republican martyrdom and catholic sacrament in "Jarrow":

> I found him lying where they'd raked him with a harrow.
> I kissed his wounds and thrust my bloodied lips to his
> To breathe life into him, that we might see tomorrow.
> I felt him pulsing as his *was* became an *is*.

> (*TN*, 55)

Yet if "history" as it haunts the present for a future redemption is approached and even defined differently by these poetic contemporaries, both poets at once seek, and seek to escape *from*, "memory." Willingly or reluctantly, they establish an identification with, rather than objectification *of*, the dead heroes and lost objects of Irish and

literary history. To appreciate fully the ways in which they have redefined how we might think of poetry, identity, and history, let us consider how these poets depart from the models of historical "recovery" offered by Boland and Heaney.

The spade that digs, that in Heaney's hands serves as an extension
of a subject's aggression, in McGuckian's strange, Celtic twilight of
"Pass Christian" becomes itself an object of love: "Like a lip or
spade, a scooping tongue or scooped ladle . . . a twilight uncleaned
from the day before / earned the eventual coolness of my love" (*S*,
18). In that poem, "fruit trains" carry their cargo from the warm
south across a troubled border to the north for preservation—"their
extra-large windows powerfully possessing / the writing arm of
space." Here McGuckian literalizes the fruitfulness of what she has
described as a poetic apprenticeship in which she bodily *became* a
dead poet, John Keats,[14] while also enacting the process of "preservation" *as* the still-troubled border-crossing of economic exchange
in an island where the Good Friday Agreement has yet to be fully
enacted.

From a different standpoint, Carson's poetry makes pointless
both Heaney's spadework and Boland's politics of gendered, national identity, precisely because the male body carries within itself
not a "racial unconscious," and not only a genetic code, but rather
an ineluctable incorporation of, among various legacies, the very
musical and storytelling traditions, English or settler, that would
seem to have excluded him. He puts the word *salt* back into its origins as a medium of exchange and barter, but also reminds us of its
associations with loss and the dangers of the backward glance. In
Last Night's Fun—a cheerful, and even exuberant, alter ego to *The
Twelfth of Never*'s far more sinister explorations of the communal
memories revived nightly in Irish "crack"—Carson writes that the
traditional tune, whatever its origins, rather than the musician, is in
charge of its own recovery, making the body its instrument: "It
seems that the tune recalls itself, in some absentminded lull between
some other tunes, when everyone except you has put down their instruments."[15] And that alien drive may place not only the voice but
also the singer in the powers of others. Carson recalls in the same
volume that his father once found himself delightedly invited in to
sing "The Ould Orange Flute" in a Protestant household on the
Twelfth of July, only to have his identity betrayed and his person
jeopardized.[16]

Through the salt mines of memory or the saline caves of the body
(to use tropes favored by both poets), the past is preserved through
unconscious acts of bodily incorporation as well as by conscious po-

etic imitation, a preservation that restructures that consciousness and uncomfortably dissolves the categories of Self and Other, whether "colonist" and "colonizer," "Catholic" or "Protestant," or "marginal" and "canonical." (We might note, for example, the intestinal tropes in McGuckian's side-by-side poems, "Pass Christian" and "Using the Cushion.")[17] Yet bodily darkness is not simply internal; it is also on the surface and symptomatic, as in McGuckian's use, in the latter poem, of the word "melanic." As a consequence, the past in these poems of 1798, far from being brought to light so that the living can go on with their lives in a secular, nonsectarian, and progressive future, continues literally to feed on the poetic body and, perhaps, the body politic, manifesting itself, like the death drive, in symptoms that seem more alive, more urgent than the body's present, and human, needs. For the drive—whether it is a daimonic repetition of the tune or the insistent voice of the dead—has no respect for the precarious humanity of faith, hope, and charity.

Yet there is no point in identifying that drive, in these poems or in contemporary politics in Ireland, oversimply as, on the one hand, a tribal atavism that disrupts the peace of a state founded on Enlightenment principles, or, on the other, with a charged, Romantic energy or even Benjaminian utopianism that would throw off the repressiveness of that state. Neither does that drive, as these poems help us to see, manifest the inevitable truth that one community's utopia is necessarily another's dystopia, or the seeming fact that a majority and middle-class community will inevitably define violence as disruption of a law that protects private property while a minority that is more likely to be prosecuted than defended by the law will define it as such suspensions of, or exceptions to, the rule of Law as the Special Powers Act. (In a moment, we will see how Carson makes reference to that Act in his poem "Salt of the Earth.") In *Shelmalier* and *The Twelfth of Never*, the dead, themselves bearers of special powers (as in the Irish term *údar* that Dillon Johnston has connected with the "secrets" of Irish poetry), haunt the living because they are, in these revivals of a gothic Romanticism, undead in the most uncanny sense: bodily possession, unconscious repetition, a site of maternal origin that becomes a place of death.[18]

The voices that possess the speaker include those of dead English poets, as in "Salt of the Earth," which features a canonical Romantic poet known for his own plagiarism of, or possession by, other poets' voices (and other transcendental philosophers' ideas). Coleridge, of course, is also well known for his addiction to foreign substances, including a drug whose flower (the poppy worn by Protestants in

honor of World War I veterans) is an important emblem in modern
Northern Irish politics as it was of the Opium Wars in an earlier
century:

> STC gazed at the page illuminated
> By a candle as he sprinkled his thesaurus
> Over it to see the words hallucinated
> Into sentences. He felt like Saul at Tarsus.
>
> .   .   .   .
>
> Crumpled Coleridge took an age to be re-born—
> Poppy the emblem of Death and the Special Powers.
>
> (*TN*, 17)

Coleridge, who appears frequently in *The Twelfth of Never*, was of
course known for cozily squatting in the forms, as in the houses, of
others but also for making those forms strange, and estranging. Like
that Romantic forebear, the speaker in *The Twelfth of Never* seems un-
expectedly to have summoned ancestral voices prophesying war
through his adoption of the French alexandrine sonnet. It is a form
peculiarly suited to Carson's deliberately alienated, and alienating,
approach to the Year of the French. Like Coleridge, Carson's
speaker in "Digitalis" is himself possessed by flowers of evil (*TN*, 46).
Slipping his fingers into a foxglove, he is possessed not only by the
digital part object of the "Red Hand," but also by a republican Fran-
cophilia that is itself haunted by the guillotine:

> Since I got my fingers stuck in a Witch's Glove
> One night, my writing hasn't been the same, I fear;
> And something's always whispering within my ear
> About the murky underworld of goblin love.
>
> That's when Mr Stump takes over—he who writes these lines
> In automatic carabine—and I succumb
> To all his left-hand fantasies of fife and drum,
> Where soldiers sometimes use their guns as concubines.
>
> Or often he describes a land across the sea,
> Where all men are uniformed in sailor blue—
> His conversation's like the stumbling of a bee
> Within a Fairy's thimble—blushful Hippocrene—
> And then he starts this cuckoo's rumour about you:
> That's when I clamp him in my paper-guillotine.
>
> (*TN*, 46)

Another dangerous flower, the rose of Ireland in Carson's "Dark
Rosaleen," provides the occasion for a poetic forced march into

James Clarence Mangan's mind, into Carson's own past poetry (notably "Hamlet," which appeared in *Belfast Confetti*), and into the international history of the ballad form. It suggests the presence, in every case (including his own) of personal gain, propaganda, and perversion (note the repetition of the "whitethorn" blossom of "Londonderry Air"), all of which promote the conscription of troops for whatever war, and whatever side:

> The songlines were proceeding at a daily pace
> Like invisible barbed wire or whitethorn fences,
> Running through the Monday of the market-place,
> Where fellows mongered ballads under false pretences.
>
> . . . .
> I caught one by his buttonhole, and asked him plain
> And proud, if ever dear old Ireland would be free,
> Or would our forces be forever split in twain?
>
> Could we expect the promised help from Papal Spain?
> He caught my eye, and answered me quite candidly,
> *The only freedom that you'll find is in the dead domain.*

(TN, 31)

As we may recall, in Carson's 1989 "Hamlet" the barbed wire of the Falls Road was more hopefully, and magically, transformed into the "illegible thorny hedge of time itself— / Heartstopping moments" in which the threat of violence may yet redeem the future of the causes that failed with the delay or sinking of promised fleets from Spain and France. In such redemptions, forecast in the volume's opening with a citation from Walter Benjamin, storytellers would at last make sense of history, put a "shape / On what was there":

For the voice from the grave reverberates in others' mouths, as the sails
Of the whitethorn hedge swell up in a little breeze, and tremble
Like the spiral blossom of Andromeda: so suddenly are shrouds and
    branches
Hung with street-lights, celebrating all that's lost, as fields are reclaimed
By the Starry Plough. So we name the constellations, to put a shape
On what was there; so the storyteller picks his way between the isolated
    stars.[19]

When utopia arrives, in other words, the anomalous, local, and isolated particular will at last make sense within the universal design and application of the utopian hopes of the rebellions spawned by the Enlightenment.

Yet *The Twelfth of Never,* where the Armada has metamorphosed into Coleridge's "ghostly galleon," is far less hopeful, as its opening poem "Tib's Eve" (a date named for a nonexistent saint, which means "never") picks up where "Hamlet" left off. Now, the speaker suggests, we live in a time in which historical dates, while they may occasion celebrations joyful or deadly, mean nothing:

> There, ghostly galleons plough the shady Woods of True,
> And schools of fishes fly among the spars and shrouds;
> Rivers run uphill to spill into the starry clouds,
> And beds of strawberries grow in the ocean blue.
>
> This is the land of the green rose and the lion lily,
> Ruled by Zeno's eternal tortoises and hares,
> Where everything is metaphor and simile:
>
> Somnambulists, we stumble through this paradise
> From time to time, like words repeated in our prayers,
> Or storytellers who convince themselves that truths are lies.
>
>   (*TN,* 13)

Even if storytellers were to tell the truth, perhaps no one, least of all themselves, would believe them in a postmodern, deconstructive age governed by Zeno's principle that time's arrow will never find its mark and "where everything is metaphor and simile." Here we are neither the subjects nor the objects of prayers but, rather, simply further vehicles for the repetition compulsion that is "history" *as* "prayer," a repetition compulsion in which we act but do not believe. As McGuckian writes of the dead hero's appeal to her bodily "home" for "peace" in "Pulsus Paradoxus," "Keeping magic out has itself the character / of magic":

> . . . a picture held us captive
> and we could not get outside it
> for it lay in our language in the uniform
> of a force that no longer existed.
> Peace was the target he was aiming at,
> the point at which doubt becomes senseless,
> the last thing that will find a home.
>
>   (*S,* 40)

IV

With insufficient space to discuss adequately just how fully Mc-Guckian explores the difficulty of integrating an anomalous, and lost, past into the anomalous space of the body, let us turn in conclusion to Carson's poems, where the violent integration of the anomalous into "history," and more particularly into the capitalist universal, finds form. For *The Twelfth of Never* is not only about the nightmare of history from which yet another Irish artist is seeking to awaken. Rather it concerns the worldwide, uncanny doublings that are generated by the duplicity of the forms of late capital. Indeed, we might recall that the book's title is taken not from traditional Irish music but from the ghostly past of Johnny Mathis and America's Top 40. Salt, which serves elsewhere in the volume to preserve the past, is also troped as one of the world's first forms of capital, literally the basis for military "salary" in the Roman empire. As the sun rises and sets on such empires in this volume, the acid-green of postapocalyptic Japan becomes yet another parallel world to the green isle of Erin. There, as in Ireland, the operations of global markets in tobacco, intoxicants, and salt go on without the full consciousness of any market participant. (In "Adelaide Halt," "There is a drink called Hope, and cigarette called Peace," *TN*, 16). Meanwhile the global commodification of New Age spiritualism (including, as readers of "Wiccan" lore might note, the Irish *sidhe*) converts the "yen" into "Zen." Irish "crack," both the traditional phenomenon now commercialized in "authentic Irish pubs" and the contemporary drug, are both fanciful, global commodities in these poems. In reading "The Rising Sun," we might recall that the Irish poet has himself become a commodity for transport to, and purchase and consumption within, literary institutions in Japan, as in America and elsewhere. In the strong economy of the Irish pound represented in "Let Erin Remember," well-heeled women dancers "favour emerald and cyanide," while "Each dandiprat a twist of salt beneath his wig. / This night these will be strong media of barter" (*TN*, 36). But to their Irish buoyancy corresponds a sinking in Tokyo, where "the yen declined again," expressed in "The Rising Sun" as a melancholic melody played on the symbol of Erin, the harp:

> As I was driven into smoky Tokyo,
> The yen declined again. It had been going down
> All day against the buoyant Hibernian Pound.
> Black rain descended like a harp arpeggio.

The Professor took me to a bonsai garden
To imbibe some thimblefuls of Japanese poteen.
We wandered through the forest of the books of Arden.
The number of their syllables was seventeen.

I met a maiden of Hiroshima who played
The hammer dulcimer like psychedelic rain.
The rising sun was hid behind a cloud of jade.

She sang to me of Fujiyama and of Zen,
Of yin and yang, and politics, and crack cocaine
And Plato's caverns, which are measureless to men.

                                                            (*TN*, 20)

But is the yen, or the pound, "measurable" except in the uncanny doubling that is "exchange"? Žižek himself uses the motif of the dance in *The Fragile Absolute* to illustrate that the rapid, whirling changes of late capital, its "radical secularization of social life," is in fact founded on the spectral chimera, the internal contradiction, of a "Free Trade" that no national border or "atavistic," local outbreak of war can check. It is the fundamental fact of "violence" in the twenty-first century:

> When Marx describes the mad self-enhancing circulation of Capital . . . it is far too simplistic to claim that the spectre of this self-engendering monster that pursues its path regardless of any human or environmental concern is an ideological abstraction, and that one should never forget that behind this abstraction there are real people and natural objects on whose productive capacities and resources Capital's circulation is based, and on which it feeds like a giant parasite. The problem is that this "abstraction" does not exist only in our (financial speculator's) misperception of social reality; it is "real" in the precise sense of determining the very structure of material social processes: the fate of whole strata of populations, and sometimes of whole countries, can be decided by the "solipsistic" speculative dance of Capital, which pursues its goal of profitability with blessed indifference to the way its movement will affect social reality. That is the fundamental systemic violence of capitalism, which is much more uncanny than direct pre-capitalist socio-ideological violence: this violence is no longer attributable to concrete individuals and their "evil" intentions; it is purely "objective," systemic, anonymous.[20]

Paradoxically, as the muscled and particular arm of a collection of anomalous laws in a colony is replaced, in Ireland as elsewhere, by the invisible reach of global hegemony, its effects will become increasingly uncanny. Using the example of a phenomenon that is not unknown in recent Ireland—the moving statue—Žižek in *The Plague of Fantasies* describes what he calls the "two deaths," the symbolic and the "real":

> The paradox of moving statues, of dead objects coming alive and/or of petrified living objects, is possible only within the space of the death drive which, according to Lacan, is the space between the two deaths, symbolic and real. For a human being to be "dead while alive" is to be colonized by the "dead" symbolic order; to be "alive while dead" is to give body to the remainder of Life-Substance that has escaped symbolic colonization . . . What we are dealing with here is thus the split . . . between the "dead" symbolic order which mortifies the body and the non-symbolic Life-Substance of *jouissance*. . . .
>
> Life is the horrible . . . "undead" drive which persists beyond ordinary death; death is the symbolic order itself, the structure which, as a parasite, colonizes the living entity. What defines the death drive in Lacan is this double gap: not the simple opposition between life and death, but the split of life itself into "normal" life and horrifying "undead" life, and the split of the dead into "ordinary" dead and the "undead" machine.[21]

And to further exacerbate this paradox, we might follow Žižek in observing that "drive" is the dead (or rather "undead") domain not only of Irish crack and of Romantic addicts but also of contemporary science. In that dead domain, which includes literary theory, a pursuit of knowledge *as* a pursuit of an ideal may take over every concern of the living entity, including the real concern for an alternative to the ghastly wars of the Romantic period whose part objects return in Carson's poems: peace. For this reason, it is particularly necessary for scholars of Irish culture to consider not only such broad overviews of ideology and identity as are offered by Lloyd, Žižek, and Declan Kiberd (a scholar whose recent work has been particularly important for redefining Irish studies). We must also pay attention to the exceptional (in every sense) details provided in the critical studies of such readers as Edna Longley and that remarkable poetry of the elegized particular, Michael Longley. For both of the Longleys have insisted, humanely and importantly, on the cost of the anomalous in the everyday life of a state torn by competing universals.

V

In concluding, let us summarize a few observations. In contemporary Ireland as in Romantic Europe, an individual's history, memory, and even testimony are local particulars that inevitably will remain anomalous within a community that seeks the Enlightened dispassion of the universal, whether that universal is the ideal reader from anywhere, a history that embeds the local particular within its linear and progressive narrative, or the ideal state that would be Ireland. Yet, as devolving Ireland joins the ahistorical anomie of postmodernity, this island's poets suggest that the past remains as much alive as dead, a recognition that may, surprisingly, suggest the universal appeal of poems that sometimes hinge on details of Irish history or culture unfamiliar to the average American, an appeal that is not simply the "exoticism" of a "Celtic" "otherness." In the examples of McGuckian and Carson, but also of a number of other poets we might likewise consider were there space, we may witness a persistence of a belief in the utopian universals of the Enlightenment, but also a darker awareness of what the "universal" has become in our own age. What may seem to make the modern-day terrorist, of whatever ideology, the barbaric exception to the worldwide spread of "Enlightened" Law is his or her phantasmatic attachment to the ghosts of a history of oppression. Yet in fact that attachment unites the anomalous exception to the shared belief system that supports the most Enlightened law-abiding community as it does the outlaw from the global community of accepted nation states. As Žižek writes in *The Fragile Absolute*, "one becomes a full member of community not simply by identifying with its explicit symbolic tradition, but when one also assumes the spectral dimension that sustains this tradition: the undead ghosts that haunt the living, the secret history of traumatic fantasies transmitted 'between the lines,' through its lacks and distortions."[22] If, in this very moment in Ireland's public history, where hopes for peace seem on the verge of fulfillment, there is in fact in the poems of Carson and McGuckian neither hope nor peace beyond their commodification, these poets might lead American readers to find in them the shared, and very contemporary, trauma of everyday life within the New World Order. They might even encourage American Romanticists to reconsider the possibility that Wordsworth himself, despite the fact that he was male and English, may well have spoken honestly of, and effectively on behalf of, a Celtic woman. Living on the margins of empire, her voice otherwise would have remained not only inarticulable but unavailable had that poet not borne it in the "heart," long after his own death, somatically, symptomatically, and sympathetically.

Notes

1. See Eavan Boland, *Object Lessons: The Life of the Woman and the Poet in Our Time* (New York: Norton, 1995). Hereafter *OL*, cited in the text. See also David Lloyd,

Anomalous States: Irish Writing and the Post-Colonial Moment (Durham, N.C.: Duke University Press, 1993); hereafter *AS,* cited in the text; *Nationalism and Minor Literature: James Clarence Mangan and the Emergence of Irish Cultural Nationalism* (Berkeley: University of California Press, 1987); *Ireland after History* (South Bend, Ind.: Notre Dame University Press, 2000). Hereafter *IH,* cited in the text. While Lloyd's title closely approaches that of Jerome Christiansen's own millennial publication *Romanticism and the End of History,* and while both scholars challenge the presumptions of New Historicism, Lloyd's Marxist critique of neocolonial practices of global capital is closer to my own arguments in this essay. As will become clear, however, I am unable to share Lloyd's hope that the repressed will return redemptively or his castigation of liberals who are unable to support armed resistance to the state. Nevertheless, Lloyd remains today the major theorist (Marxist, poststructuralist, and psychoanalytic) of contemporary Irish studies.

2. Seamus Deane, *Strange Country: Modernity and Nationhood in Irish Writing since 1790* (New York: Oxford University Press, 1997), 115, 197.

3. Theodor Adorno and Max Horkheimer, *Dialectic of Enlightenment,* trans. John Cumming (New York: Verso Books, 1997).

4. Theodor Adorno, *Negative Dialectics,* trans. E. B. Ashton (London: Routledge & Kegan Paul, 1973).

5. For these and other reasons, studies of globalization have become increasingly important as the next phase of postcolonial scholarship.

6. Marjorie Howes, *Yeats's Nations: Gender, Class, and Irishness* (New York: Cambridge University Press, 1996), 4.

7. See especially Slavoj Žižek's discussion of these and related matters in "Che Vuoi?" in *The Sublime Object of Ideology* (New York: Verso Books, 1989), 87–129 and, more specifically, his discussion of hysteria and subjectivation in *The Plague of Fantasies* (New York: Verso Books, 1997): "What characterizes the fundamental subjective position of a *hysteric* (and one should bear in mind that for Lacan, the status of the subject as such is hysterical) is precisely the ceaseless questioning of his or her existence *qua* enjoyment—that is, the refusal fully to identify with the object he or she 'is', the eternal wondering at this object: 'Am I really *that?*' " (49).

8. Seamus Heaney, *Opened Ground: Selected Poems 1966–1996* (New York: Farrar, Straus, Giroux, 1998), 112–13. Hereafter poems in this volume will be cited in the text as *OG.*

9. Seamus Heaney, "Feeling into Words," in *Preoccupations: Selected Prose 1968–1978* (New York: Farrar, Straus, Giroux, 1980), 41.

10. For a sophisticated reading of gender, the canon, and "hysteria" in relation to the literature and politics of the 1790s in Ireland, see Ghislaine McDayter's "Hysterically Speaking," in Ghislaine McDayter, Guinn Batten, and Barry Milligan, eds. *Romantic Generations: Essays in Honor of R. F. Gleckner* (Lewisburg, Penna.: Bucknell University Press, 2001).

11. As I have suggested elsewhere, in readings of Paul Muldoon's *Quoof,* that volume's representations of the protests in H-Block in the Eighties remind us that republican prisoners recognized that the male body has its own sexualized, inner sites of burial through which messages can be secretly conveyed.

12. See Medbh McGuckian, "From the Weather-Woman," in *Shelmalier* (Winston-Salem, N.C.: Wake Forest University Press, 1998), 33. Further citations of McGuckian's poetry are from this volume and will be cited in the text as *S.*

13. Ciaran Carson, *The Twelfth of Never* (Winston-Salem, N.C.: Wake Forest University Press, 1998), 54. All citations of lines of poetry written by Carson are from this volume and will be cited in the text as *TN.*

14. See Medbh McGuckian, "Comhrá, with a Foreword and Afterword by Laura O'Connor," *Southern Review* 31 (Summer 1995): 581–614.

15. Ciaran Carson, *Last Night's Fun: A Book about Irish Traditional Music* (London: Jonathan Cape, 1996), 28–29.

16. Ibid., 187–88.

17. In "Pass Christian," the "blue laws" of the waves "cut through the indigo roofline of my back / to the intestines, singling out the one thread / of my life where dry fronds rasp against each other." In "Using the Cushion," the orchid's "leaf edges formed a series / of rock steps into a saline cave, / where the air is not still, and a melanic / sky anastomoses" (*Shelmalier*, 18–19).

18. Dillon Johnston, "Afterword," *Irish Poetry after Joyce* (Syracuse, N.Y.: Syracuse University Press, 1997), 303–4.

19. Ciaran Carson, "Hamlet," in *Belfast Confetti* (Winston-Salem, N.C.: Wake Forest University Press, 1989), 105–8.

20. Slavoj Žižek, *The Fragile Absolute, or, Why Is the Christian Legacy Worth Fighting For?* (London: Verso Books, 2000), 15.

21. Žižek, *Plague of Fantasies*, 89.

22. Žižek, *Fragile Absolute*, 64.

The Return of the Fragment: "Christabel" and the Uncanny

Sophie Thomas

University of Sussex

COLERIDGE'S unfinished poem, "Christabel," has long held its readership in thrall, and with the force of the mariner's glittering eye, kept it in an uneasy state of attraction and repulsion. Modern readers are as enticed by its unrestrained gothicism as by the ambiguous sexuality of its central character, the predatory Geraldine. Coleridge's contemporaries, on the other hand, were almost universally appalled, and some of its early reviewers denounced its content as shockingly immoral, if not obscene. Hazlitt, for one, asserted that there was "something disgusting at the bottom of the subject . . . like moonbeams playing on a charnel-house, or flowers strewed on a dead body."[1] But the critical furor was, and still is, as much a function of the poem's irresolution as its content: much of what the poem suggests can neither be named nor carried through, and perhaps from the perspective of a Hazlitt, this was just as well. Insofar as the poem draws on gothic romance conventions, irresolution may come with the territory; gothic plots were frequently so complicated as to thoroughly ensnare their own authors.[2] And yet (to adopt the rhetoric of equivocation that so saturates Coleridge's poem) its disturbing features are implicit, if not in Hazlitt's metaphors (what exactly *is* it, one might ask, about the play of moonbeams on charnel houses, or flowers and dead bodies?), then surely in his apprehension of something not only concealed, but lurking *at the bottom* of its subject.

In the case of "Christabel," reading, it seems, enacts an excessively transferential process. First of all, the impossibility of saying or naming that "concealed bottom," the elusive ground and center of the poem, becomes not only the investigative focus but also the defining feature of critical readings: the essential state or condition of the poem is repeated in, nay transferred upon, the act of critical analysis. This is a state of affairs that the poem's incompletion, in

51

the second instance, thoroughly complicates. Because the essential dynamic of the poem presents a pressing case for resolution, the critic finds herself in the situation of the analyst in a therapeutic sense as well: gestures of completion and gestures of analysis, though not implicitly the same, become difficult to tell apart. If we are, with contemporary reviewers, invited to compare the poem "with a mutilated statue, the beauty of which can only be appreciated by those who have knowledge or imagination sufficient to complete the idea of the whole composition," we may feel some sympathy with Freud's struggles with incompletion in the case history of Dora, where he claims to have felt constrained "to follow the example of those discoverers whose good fortune it is to bring to the light of day after their long burial the priceless though mutilated relics of antiquity."[3] He "restores what is missing," using the best models known to him from other analyses.

This paper seeks to explore the relation of "Christabel" to the restorative efforts of reading, both in its time and in ours, and to investigate the transferential effects (loosely understood) implicit in the poem's incompletion: in short, to think about the bearing of the poem's puzzling central drama upon its fragmentary form *and* upon its readers. The movement of doubling or repetition this suggests recalls at least one aspect of the uncanny, but the condition of the poem as a mutilated relic of antiquity, suggests another, namely Schelling's suggestion that " '*Unheimlich*' is the name for everything that ought to have remained . . . secret and hidden but has come to light"—which informs Freud's observation that the uncanny "is that class of the frightening that leads back to what is known of old and long familiar."[4] This implies a relationship between fragmentation and uncanniness that has not been systematically taken up, but which is clearly central to "Christabel" and its readers, who are so often perplexed by that perceived void or gap at the "bottom" of the poem—a gap that figures (paradoxically) something unrepresentable, something that ought, at least, to have remained hidden: an unnameable, an uncanny, manifestation.

I

The first fragment of "Christabel" was composed, as Coleridge noted, in 1797—the second followed a few years later in 1800. The poem was first written, then, during the productive period of the *Lyrical Ballads* project, a period that included "The Rime of the Ancient Mariner" and Coleridge's best-known fragment poem, "Kubla

Khan." The similarities between "Christabel" and "Kubla Khan" are many. Both were first published along with "The Pains of Sleep" in a slim volume of 1816—itself a fragment, perhaps, of a proper book.[5] More significantly, both poems share a distinctive (and disjunctive) two-part structure, prefaced by a lengthy prose note describing the history of the poems' composition, engaging the thematics of fragmentation, and alerting the reader to the author's intention eventually to complete the work. In the early published version of the preface to "Christabel," Coleridge stated that "as, in my very first conception of the tale, I had the whole present to my mind, with the wholeness, no less than the liveliness of a vision; I trust I shall be able to embody in verse the three parts yet to come."[6] But while "Kubla Khan" explicitly projects, in the very terms of the poem, the existence of a potentially comprehendable whole (the possibility of a unifying poetic vision was at least one of its major themes), "Christabel" does not. It is, as many of its readers have observed, more radically detached from a completing context. In a sense, the similarities only make the differences all the more plain: the more decisive absence of a "whole" context for the fragment, the clear *inorganicity* of the part, make the poem a more radically fragmentary fragment.

The attempt to come to terms with the poem's insistent fragmentation was, as I have suggested, as much a feature of the poem's contemporary as of its current reception. While some of its early reviewers responded somewhat hysterically to the poem's impropriety, many readily gave themselves over to the broken promise of its form. Josiah Condor, for example, writing in the *Eclectic Review*, suggested that while the general effect upon readers will be one of disappointment ("the reader is obliged to guess at the half-developed meaning of the mysterious incidents, and is at last, at the end of the second canto, left in the dark, in the most abrupt and unceremonious manner imaginable"), the fragment will nevertheless "be found to take faster hold of the mind than many a poem six cantos long."[7] Coleridge's earliest readers frequently described the poem's effects with the language of the sublime: "For ourselves we confess, that when we read the story in M.S. two or three years ago, it appeared to be one of those dream-like productions whose charm partly consisted in the undefined obscurity of the conclusion—what that conclusion may be, no person who reads the commencement will be at all able to anticipate."[8] Hazlitt, writing in the *Examiner*, conceded that while the poem contained parts of great beauty, "the effect of the general story is dim, obscure, and visionary."[9] While the writer for the *Critical Review* thus responded to the pure partiality or particularity of

the poem, Hazlitt, with the terms "dim, obscure and visionary,"
identified the allegorical aspect of the generalized whole. And as
with "Kubla Khan," "Christabel" 's reviewers resorted to the language of disappointment, of broken promises—implicit even in the
brokenness of the poem itself: "but we fear it is from some lurking
distrust of his best resolutions, that he has been tempted to mar the
strong interest which his wild romantic tale would otherwise have
excited, by thus communicating it in piecemeal."[10]

The general problems are exacerbated, in the case of "Christabel," precisely by this piecemeal communication: by the fragment-
ing of the fragment. Since the poem is itself composed of fragments,
truncation and discontinuity are as much internal features as exter-
nal ones. E. H. Coleridge commented in his 1907 edition of *Christabel* that the poem was not just a fragment, but a "sequence of fragments"; Harold Bloom argued that "Christabel" is really a series of
poems, rather than a single fragment.[11] Even in the presence of actual material suggesting an ending (a point I shall return to below),
no one has ever tried to argue that "Christabel" is, like "Kubla
Khan," really a whole in disguise. Humphry House, for example,
after arguing vociferously for the wholeness of "Kubla Khan," comments that "Christabel" is "an entirely different matter: for not only
is it inescapably a fragment, but the two parts differ so much from
each other, that they scarcely seem to belong to the same poem."
For House, the poem is "all fragmentary and finally unsatisfying because it leads up to a mystery that is both incomplete and clueless."[12]
While this assemblage of fragments appears infinitely expandable,
then, its central mysteries, by contrast, do not lend themselves to re-
duction: as a reviewer in the *Literary Panorama* suggested, "to extract
parts from such a *morceau* is to reduce what remains to a mere
nothing."[13]

The threatening "nothingness" of the poem, the ambiguity of
what *is* present in its parts, raises the specter of what is absent in the
whole. Its fragmentation makes the question of a boundary between
the absent/present, the inside/outside of the poem, indeed of all
boundaries, thoroughly problematic. Because the poem is so radically fragmentary, the "outside" could be, as it were, anywhere. Attempts to explain or justify the poem's fragmentary form are often,
paradoxically, accompanied by an obsessive preoccupation with the
poem's inconclusion that continues to supply it with imaginative
and fully worked-out endings. The pressing question in the case of
"Christabel" seems not to be *whether* Coleridge could have continued, but rather *how*. Even though Wordsworth denied that Coleridge had a worked-out ending in mind, the source of these pro-

jected endings is Coleridge himself, who persistently claimed to have the poem entire in his head.[14] Two of these possible endings come to us from James Gillman. In the first, Christabel's story is partly predicated on the idea that the virtuous shall save the wicked. Christabel overcomes Geraldine and the evil she represents on behalf of her lover who is "exposed to various temptations in a foreign land"—for whom she must, thus, suffer and pray.[15] A similar proposition is made by Derwent Coleridge (a third possible ending), who suggests that Christabel's sufferings are vicarious and that the "holy and innocent" are made into instruments to bring their loved ones back to peaceful ways. In this version, Geraldine is "no witch or goblin, or malignant being of any kind," but an agent or spirit of goodwill.[16]

These two projections make Christabel and her sufferings the main narrative focus. Gillman's second ending, however, offers a more detailed account—one which, while plausible, has been dismissed as excessively vulgar and trivially gothic.[17] In this one, all manner of supernatural events occur. Bard Bracy hastes, as instructed, to Lord Roland's castle, only to find that it has been washed away by a flood. Geraldine, meanwhile, who appears to preside, witchlike, over the course of events, rouses anger and jealousy in the baron's breast; but once the Bard returns, and she can no longer impersonate the daughter of Lord Roland de Vaux, she transforms herself into Christabel's absent lover. Christabel responds to this dreadful double of her once-favored knight with a sense of disgust that is as distressing and mysterious to her as it is to her father. Luckily, of course, the real lover appears in the nick of time, and Geraldine is obliged to vanish as supernaturally as she appeared.[18] Christabel's passive sufferings and her timely rescue in this account are, on the surface, inconsistent with the implication in the other two versions that she must actively combat evil. Nor, many claim, do these narrative twists and turns follow necessarily from the two existing cantos. Perhaps, as Paul Magnuson suggests, this last version is a fiction produced for Gillman's benefit years after Coleridge completed the second part.[19] It is noteworthy, though, that all three endings attempt to make sense of the function of Geraldine (perhaps the most enigmatic aspect of the entire poem) and that the third continues the movement of Christabel's increased enslavement which is already the main feature of the two existing parts.

Although there is a general tendency to dismiss these phantom endings, the attempt to defend them clarifies an important issue: how much do they matter? B. R. McElderry Jr. makes a strong case for Gillman's extended ending, showing precisely how it could logically and effectively follow from the two existing cantos. Indeed, if these latter were reduced to a prose summary (an experiment he undertakes to great effect), they would sound as untenable and sensational as the proposed ending. He suggests, then, that Coleridge could have persevered without any considerable obstruction and completed the poem. McElderry uses this conclusion to make his case for the Gillman ending, but the evidence also points the other way: since Coleridge did *not* complete "Christabel," one might more accurately conclude that a paralyzing force must be coming from within the poem. Like the passing steps of the two women, "that tried to be, and were not, fast," the poem, so to speak, tried to be but was not finished. As Coleridge reiterated in *Table Talk*, "the reason of my not finishing Christabel is not that I don't know how to do it; for I have, as I always had, the whole plan entire from beginning to end in my mind; but I fear I could not carry on with equal success the execution of the Idea—the most difficult, I think, that can be attempted to Romantic Poetry—I mean witchery by daylight."[20] The precise nature of the difficulty involved, and the disruptive mechanics of this uncanny, paralyzing force, are of primary importance to the poem's fragmentary status. Coleridge finds himself, in effect, thwarted or blocked by the poem's central "Idea," which he sums up in a phrase—"witchery by daylight"—a phrase that appears to resonate with Hazlitt's flowers strewn over the dead.[21] Hazlitt's metaphor is conspicuously decadent, while Coleridge's statement in fact *defines* the uncanny, but both metaphors convey the troubling sense of something out of place, or, in the language of Coleridge's concluding fragment to part 2, the forcing together of "thoughts so all unlike each other" (l. 667). But there too, in the father's expression of "love's excess / With words of unmeant bitterness," the poet is transfixed by the distressing likeness of extreme emotions, which in a "world of sin" lack new, or even adequate, modes of expression.

II

Readers often remark on the oddly anomalous (unexpected *and* unnameable) qualities of "Christabel." Under the weight of an unspecifiable distortion, the events and descriptions often suggest a liminal state: neither one thing, nor, quite, another. The poem begins, for example, in the middle of the night, between the realm of owls and that of crowing cocks—on the verge, thus, of dawn. It takes place "a month before the month of May"—a curiously dislocated

way of saying, in effect, between winter and spring (but during neither). A thin grey cloud "covers but not hides the sky" (l. 17). Indeed the narrator's mode of questioning ("Is the night chilly and
dark? / The night is chilly, but not dark," ll. 14–15)—of asking, stating and then retracting or qualifying—aptly represents the slightly
abnormal or anomalous status of the narration. Often, unworldly or
irrational—preternatural[22]—factors intrude: Geraldine's swoon on
the threshold of the castle gate, the flaring up of the dying brands
as the two women pass, with steps "That strove to be, and were not,
fast" (l. 113), the impotence of the characters, as in a dream, to
carry out their desires, or, in Christabel's case even to speak—as
though natural agency has been usurped along with straightforward
articulation. Coleridge's equivocations, his manner of simultaneously suggesting and negating, have in themselves the effect of evok-
ing a representation of the unpresentable that is a key quality of the
fragmentary.

Such apparently anomalous features as the poem's occupation of
a liminal space, or its preoccupation with liminal states, may be thus
related to its fragmentary status. The implication, however, that frag-
menting forces arise from within the poem needs some immediate
qualification. It seems to suggest that the poem has an immanent, if
fragmentary, center, where in fact there may be, as the reviewer for
the *Literary Panorama* feared, a mere nothing. The dilemma, that is,
of not *if* but rather *where* to locate the poem's truncation, finds expression in the prevailing sense that its fragmentary state serves both
to conceal and to configure an essential void or absence at its center.
Because even an "absent" center may still be construed as a center,
it is important to stress the resistance of fragments in general to cen-
tralizing, or totalizing, forces. With this in mind, the issue of fragmentation in "Christabel" can be approached by examining the
perceived void or gap at the "heart" of the poem—the elusive bottom that summons and resists analysis in the same way a fragment
suggests and denies the (w)hole.

Whether we think of the poem as mutilated in formal terms or
paralyzed by its conceptual contradictions, its liminal and undefin-
able spaces are encountered, repeated, perhaps fulfilled, in the act
of reading. Succumbing to the paralysis outlined above, readers
must and do remain—perhaps obsessively—fascinated by the same
subtle problem that prevented Coleridge from moving on. But if
there is widespread agreement about the fragmentary status of
"Christabel," it is nevertheless noteworthy that the location of its
points of fragmentation has changed a great deal. As Marjorie Levinson has pointed out, early readers tended to view the poem as a "co-

herent fragment truncated at either end"—hence the intense interest in its unwritten cantos.[23] Modern readers, on the other hand, are
more interested in the poem's "internal fissures," and are more
likely to locate the poem's important ruptures both between the two
main parts, and between those parts and their respective conclusions. Indeed, fragmentary incoherence is present on many more
levels, impeding the poem's progress on several fronts.

The divided structure of the poem has, primarily, invited comparison of the two main parts. In addition to the obvious differences in
the time and place of composition, and the considerable effects of
those intervening years, other—often related—differences are frequently noted. Commentators often remark that the first part is particularly static and atmospheric, while the second is more concerned
with narrative action.[24] Richard Holmes, on the other hand, suggests
that the two parts are more of a piece, as they present "night and
day versions of the same inexplicable trance"; the power of *both*
parts derives from "a haunting suggestiveness of atmosphere."[25] In
any case, there is very little dramatic development: action in the second part is threatened but thwarted (Bracy's dream, for example,
delays and then finally moves the action off-stage). But while many
critics emphasize the disunity of the poem (and important differences within it), most offer at least a strategy for a unified reading.
Such readings have configured the poem's partial contents in a vari-
ety of ways: through the poem's numerous projected endings,
through its internal disjunctions—through attempts either to fulfill
it, or to show how it works *as it is*, to make, in effect, a unity of fragmentation.

While the poem's disunity poses certain problems, A. J. Harding
argues that it may effectively be read as an example of Romantic
"mythopoesis," since it addresses a strangeness in human experience in which the human soul is strikingly portrayed in a state of
temporal division and speechlessness, a state without apparent resolution. Harding argues that the poem's lapses and disjunctions are
roughly analogous with the polysemous procedures of myth, which
work through opposition and division toward resolution—
resolution achieved by "the introduction of a third, anomalous category: the *revenant*, the incarnate god, the virgin mother."[26] In the
case of "Christabel," then, division and opposition are manifested
in speechlessness, in an inability to speak because of inward disunity.
Geraldine provides at least one aspect of the anomalous third term,
but she is clearly a thwarting, rather than a resolving, figure. This
account addresses other blocking forces in the poem, but they tend,

interestingly, to be psychologized rather than mythologized, thus revealing the implicit limitations of the model.[27]

One aspect of the poem's division is related to the experience of the "praying self," an experience that corresponds to Wordsworth's sense, in book 10 of *The Prelude*, "of treachery and desertion in the place / 'The holiest that I knew of' " ("M," 211–12). The discovery of "treachery and desertion within the self"—not so much a moral truth as a truth about the disconnectedness of speech "from willed thought and meaning"—is redescribed in "The Conclusion to Part II" where the contradictions again bespeak an essential thwarting of the self. Harding suggests that Coleridge may recognize here a reflection of his own state of paralysis; embodied in the Christabel-Geraldine exchange are consequences "fatal to poetry itself: to be forced into silence, robbed of the power of utterance, is equivalent to the complete loss of 'poetic space,' the power of projecting from the self an answering and reciprocally self-confirming otherness, the power to affirm Being as the ground of the self" ("M," 216–17). Harding comments on the problems posed by Coleridge's own capacity to "freeze" the action through narrative interjection (largely in the form of speculation on past causes and future consequences). The paradoxical importance of these interventions is that they emphasize how "the hold which the poem exerts on a reader derives in large part not from the sense of narrative expectation . . . but from the intrinsic power of a central, heart-stopping image" ("M," 209). In many cases, narrative resolution fails completely to "neutralize" the effect of such images.

The drama of the divided self that Harding finds "mythic" comes across powerfully in the idea that the poem is arrested in states or images, and we might like to think of these as akin to the allegorical emblems Benjamin writes of in his work on *trauerspiel*. What seems especially interesting, though, is not the relevance of myth as such, but the bringing to bear of an explanatory paradigm that has division and paralysis as its central terms and that uses them as the basis for a unifying structural account. A similar approach is taken by Jane A. Nelson in "Entelechy and Structure in 'Christabel.' " Nelson explicitly adopts structuralist paradigms as a way of accounting for the poem's anomalies, turning in particular to Lévi-Strauss, whose observations about mythical thought were made use of by Harding: mythical thinking "always progresses from the awareness of oppositions toward their resolution."[28] Such "thought" is a process by which a mediating term is sought for irreconcilable extremes in human experience. Mediation comes once again in the form of a third category, that of the anomalous or the irrational. In "Christabel" this category is, arguably, more apparent than the extremes it attempts to reconcile, and Nelson notes that "Christabel" is "a poem of anomalous terms . . . a poem of 'middle,' often disturbingly liminal terms."[29] In a way, the poem presents both the fundamental self-division Harding discusses, and the tertiary category of the anomalous, but neither of these familiar conceptual paradigms can be properly thought to "ground" a poem that is insistently bottomless. They remain, rather, juxtaposed in a static encounter, caught at a moment of mutual stand-off, and this is more significant for the poem's incompletion than either writer stresses. Lévi-Strauss points out (as Nelson acknowledges in a footnote) that "mythical thinking" produces multiple and recurrent themes, and never develops any one of these to completion: "there is always something left unfinished"—like rites, myths are fundamentally interminable.[30]

Although critics regularly supply a bridge over the void, or posit a crossing through "Christabel" (attempting thereby to break free of what Hazlitt called the poem's "petrific" qualities),[31] others have made effective use of the poem's disintegration without making it, *faute de mieux*, an explicit strategy for a negatively achieved unity. Many of these readings depend upon an exploration of the psychodynamics of the interaction between Christabel and Geraldine, regarding it as the key to the poem's narrative of division and reconciliation. The poem is thus read in a coherent way by turning it into an implicitly unified narrative of psychological "incoherence." Jean-Pierre Mileur, for example, uses the curious relation of "The Conclusion to Part II" to the body of the poem (like the preface of "Kubla Khan" to the poem) as an instance of the "alienation of the poet from his poetry," but this alienation is now seen to proceed from Christabel, who fails to recognize the aspects of herself (bodied forth in Geraldine) which would contradict an innocent or virtuous self-image. Just as Christabel "vacillates between treating Geraldine as another person and as an extension of herself," the poem "vacillates between a moralistic and a psychological treatment of the relationship between the two women."[32] From a psychological perspective, there is a correspondence between the extent of Christabel's repression and the daimonic aspect of Geraldine and between the strength of that repression and her subsequent powerlessness. Christabel's resistance to self-recognition is, in this view, precisely what allows Geraldine to preempt her powers of speech—indeed her power to represent herself at all. And yet this is not just a battle for supremacy between two aspects of the same self; Geraldine's predation (the exact motives for which—as with the actions of all the characters—seem "hopelessly obscure or simply irrelevant") invites, perhaps demands, differentiation from Christabel on moral grounds (*VR*, 62).[33] Mileur remarks, though, that it is difficult to distinguish this moralism from just another repressive tactic, and this difficulty is called to account for the poem's incompletion: "It is precisely the difficulty of containing the psychological questions raised by the poem within the bounds of moral judgement or of identifying any point of view not implicated in the problem of psychological contingency that gives the poem its dark vision and dooms it to incompletion" (*VR*, 63). The disruptive effects of "psychological contingency" preempt the attempt to normalize the poem, to assert the priority of a given order (whether narrative, natural, or personal), and thus to complete it.

The nature of this disruption is expressed, in Mileur's account, by the abrupt departure from the tone and focus of the poem in "The Conclusion to Part II," which is seen to represent Coleridge's own comment on his poem. The passage signals a "giving up" on the irresolvable problems staged in the poem, and this signaling takes a form akin to a "word-surprise" during psychoanalytic treatment, where the patient says something not only unexpected but often in apparent contradiction to his intention. Coleridge refers indirectly to this phenomenon in his reflections on the perversity of intense feeling—a "genuine eruption of psychological contingency into everyday life" (*VR*, 64). In the analytic situation, the analysand immediately disclaims this intrusion (hence the surprise), but the disclaimer is seen by the analyst as a revealing evasion to be explored on its own terms in the patient's life history. Taken together, the phenomenon of the word-surprise and the problem of psychological contingency suggest that not only is the self fragmented, but that these fragments of self can only communicate indirectly. Thus it is neither through nature nor through any other order (the symbolic, for example) that what we say has meaning, but rather, or only, through interpretation. The analyst's attempt, against the grain, to discern or "to posit a unified intention or identity behind the diverse, even contradictory, manifestations of behaviour" (*VR*, 65) is thus as vexed as the attempt to interpret a fragmentary text, as these readings of "Christabel" show.

Mileur brings a psychoanalytic narrative to bear upon the poem, or rather, upon the poet, since Coleridge is the primary source and cause of the poem's incompletion. Others have also figured— minded and mended—the gap, not by situating it in, or as emanating from, the revisionary context of the oeuvre, but rather as fixed on Geraldine—if not on her explicitly enigmatic function in the poem then on the mystery implicit in the description (or lack of description) of "her bosom and half her side— / A sight to dream of, not to tell!" (ll. 252–53). Hazlitt makes much of the lines Coleridge omitted here, citing an early manuscript: "Behold her bosom and half her side— / *Hideous, deformed, and pale of hue.*" This self-thwarting act, Hazlitt remarks in the *Examiner,* is "a greater psychological curiosity than even the fragment of *Kubla Khan.*"[34] He finds these suppressed lines to be essential for making "common sense" of the poem's two parts, and suggests that it is precisely *because* this is so that Coleridge left them out.[35] Hazlitt was, perhaps, prescient in seizing upon this absence as significant. Richard Rand has taken up Geraldine's mysterious mark as a deconstructive *entrée*—not so much into the text of "Christabel" as into the complex relation of textuality and signification of which the poem is an example. The reader's (or critic's) attempt to interpret Geraldine's disfigurement is rebuffed, as the signifier itself—the mark—vanishes behind inferred significations. The mark, thus, signifies something which it cannot communicate (its effect on Christabel is, of course, speechlessness)—producing, in the de Manian sense, an effect, or allegory, of reading.[36]

Robert Schwartz, in a similar vein, figures the gap as that which is beyond articulation. He points out that aspects of the poem, especially Coleridge's early descriptions of the scene ("Is the night chilly and dark? / The night is chilly, but not dark."), imply the existence of "a supernatural level of perception" that ordinary language cannot capture. The ambiguous negation of the above question, like the cloud that covers but does not hide the sky, is perhaps the only way to depict a fundamentally unapprehendable state. The particular quality of the darkness suggested by Coleridge's curious questioning, for example, implies a state "expressible only as the difference between two empirically definable ones" (i.e., dark and not dark). The momentary effect of proceeding by simultaneous suggestion and negation is to evoke a representation of the unpresentable. The vague suggestion of otherworldliness becomes increasingly explicit as the poem continues so that further descriptions in turn continue to conceptualize a significant gap. As Schwartz says, "in conceptualizing the gap between these polar states the reader defines the boundaries of a world of things that is not an amalgam or reconciliation of opposites, but rather a state which is defined by what we know to be the difference between the opposites."[37] This paradoxical knowledge, an essential dynamic of the fragment itself, persists so that the suggestion of opposites results in peculiar and unexpected inversions.

As this survey clearly shows, the problem of "Christabel" 's fragmentation is implicated in a broad range of approaches to the poem. The poem's central indeterminacy, its inherent paralysis, its arrest in the sublimation of the sublime—all derive from the abyss opened up by the poem's incompletion, and critical readings alive to that central dynamic are left to maneuver in that open space. Some of the more subtle readings mentioned above cast their analytical net from a position within the poem's faultlines, but attempts to "complete" it explicitly are far from obsolete. In spite of a general consensus on the poem's fragmentation, we still encounter the critical commonplace that its meanings are to be sought extratextually—"in relation to an unrealized textual whole," and that this is something we agree to, tacitly, as readers.[38] Indeed, this is one aspect of the paradox I began with, in which the poem's unambiguously truncated state evokes an insistent degree of critical completion. Marjorie Levinson's reading of the poem is apposite here, for the paradox I am elucidating is reproduced by Levinson herself, who pronounces that the poem is a "true" fragment while supplying it with a very inventive completing context: indeed in her taxonomy of Romantic fragments, a "true" fragment is defined as one that suggests its before-and-after, its prior and future contexts or descriptive states. In her sense, then, a true fragment is *un*ambivalent about its proximity to an intelligible whole. And yet, this relationship between a pure or quintessential fragment and its concludability must be rather more complicated, for the fragment is, by definition, a highly ambivalent figure that both suggests and negates the whole.

Levinson's account of a complete "Christabel," while examining the epochal specificity or historical determinations of the poem's production and reception, *performs* its observations by beating Coleridge's readers at their own game—hands down. Levinson overturns the prevailing assumptions that "Christabel" is to be understood (and indeed berated) as the fragment of a gothic romance, and situates it instead as a romantic interval within a tragic action, the precise details of which she deduces from the existing two cantos. As she points out, Coleridge's readers and reviewers responded to "the tragic or classical dimension of 'Christabel': its visual immediacy, its dramatic procedures, its choral commentary, its stylized and abstract emotional candor, its metrical allusiveness" (*RFP*, 82). The comparison of the poem to a mutilated statue, noted above, invoked a classical sense of the fragment which could not *but* be fundamentally tragic. Moreover, tragedy has special links with the fragment: "more than any other literary form, tragedy is a passing that directs the observer's attention to what has passed and what is to come . . . tragedy seems to empty itself into the events that precede the first scene and those that succeed the last in the spectator's imagination" (*RFP*, 85). This is certainly so, but the fragment is, by definition, inscrutable on those very points: its suggestiveness, that is, coexists with a certain internal resistance. Insofar as "Christabel" is a poem about apparently *transitional* spaces, with no clear reference *either* to what has passed, or to what is to come, it is an exemplary fragment in precisely this other sense.

In Levinson's very determined account of a completed "Christabel," however, provision *is* made for the poem's suggestive indeterminacy. The classical fragment suggested by tragedy turns out to be quite radical: once a tragic structure is intimated for the "romance fragment," it follows that "Coleridge supplies an economy of action which he elucidates without diminishing the poem's apparent infinity, a function of its radical indeterminacy" (*RFP*, 96). This claim, however, sits curiously alongside the way in which "Christabel" has been configured as both a perfect example of the fragment, and as inherently completable. For if, in Levinson's terms, "Christabel" 's status as a true fragment derives from its being, unambiguously, "two parts from a tragic unity," how true (one might ask) *is* a fragment that admits of such completion? Levinson's continued interest in the extratextual coherence of "Christabel" is exceptional in recent criticism and runs against the "true-ness," or truth, of the fragment, which arguably manifests itself in the condition of the poem *as it is,* as well as in the highly problematic relation of outside to inside, of without to within.

III

Perhaps the most sustained attempts to explore and articulate "Christabel" 's fragmented state have come from the productive convergence of feminist and psychoanalytic readings. Some of these readings bring psychoanalytic observations to bear on the problem of form and thus implicitly raise the question of the feminine and the fragmentary. The feminine, in this context, may be seen as another way of figuring or understanding an anomalous manifestation such as the fragment insofar as feminine forms, as Karen Swann points out, "represent the enigma of form itself."[39] As the site of both erotic and generic "licence," the feminine is the source of the contagious ambivalence that thwarts even the narrator, who can do no more than re-present the central riddle. As Swann argues, "the narrator circles round but cannot tell the enigma of form, of the body or sign that is at once meaningless and too full of significance"

("C," 546). The "enigma of form" is, moreover, suggestively close to the interpretive riddle presented by the fragment, as that which signifies both too much and not enough.

The "contagious ambivalence" that thwarts the poem's progress has a distinctly hysterical resonance. Swann reads "Christabel" against Burton's (ironically truncated) material on hysterics in *The Anatomy of Melancholy*. Significantly, the main symptom of hysteria is speechlessness; hysterics feel themselves to be bewitched, but "cannot tell" what ails them.[40] Geraldine, in Swann's analysis, is compared to an hysterical symptom, "which figures both desire and its repression"—"She appears in response to what Burton implies and psychoanalysis declares are the wishes of hysterics—to get around patriarchal law, which legislates desire" ("C," 538–39). Answering both Christabel's desires and the indeterminacy of the narrative, Geraldine is a fantasy, "produced by the psychic operations of condensation and displacement" ("C," 540). In "Christabel," as in dreams, "there is no version of the negative: questions raise possibilities that are neither confirmed nor wholly dismissed" ("C," 540); yet, through condensation and displacement, the repressed comes to light.

Recent readings of "Christabel" that focus on gender in relation to psychoanalytic concepts such as hysteria do not attempt to make the poem whole again but rather explore with exactitude the lines of its brokenness or fragmentation. Certainly hysteria, with its own fascinating resistance to definition, makes ready use of the formulations of the fragment.[41] It is, however, the uncanny qualities of the poem that I wish to reflect on in this final section, as these cut across the categories of gender and genre, form and content, and indeed converge with some of the poem's apparently hysterical symptoms. The uncanny has several characteristic manifestations, and some of these are peculiarly, perhaps uncannily, relevant to "Christabel." First are the related phenomena of doubling and repetition— repetition of a central event, or the recurrence of names or traits. Doubling refers, on the one hand, to the appearance of two identical characters, but it also refers to the identification of the subject with someone else. Freud identifies its source as the primary narcissism ("the unbounded self-love") which dominates childhood, but adds that once this stage of life has been surmounted, "the 'double' reverses its aspect": "From having been an assurance of immortality, it becomes the uncanny harbinger of death."[42] In addition to the doubling of characters (Christabel with Geraldine, most obviously, but also Sir Leoline with his erstwhile friend Lord Tryermaine), we can include among the poem's uncanny qualities Christabel's feelings of repulsion and distress, the return in Geraldine of the dead, or of the repressed, and the seemingly compulsive repetition of conditions and poetic effects. In narrative terms, as we will see, the presence of the uncanny effectively defers resolution and conclusion.

One does not need to stray too far from current critical discourse to suggest that Geraldine is an uncanny apparition in several respects. Not only may she be seen as Christabel's double in the Freudian sense, that is, as a representative of Christabel's repression, but she has been interpreted as a return, of a sort, of Christabel's mother—thus doubled twice over. Charles Rzepka argues convincingly that much in the poem suggests that Christabel's denial of her adult sexual desire is caused by the death of her own mother in childbirth. Geraldine, in her own sinister way, represents "a surrogate mother, sexually mature and attractive," through whom Christabel can explore the question of her own (potentially fateful) womanhood ("CWM," 21). But this exploration is an encounter marked by dread and distress, for, according to this logic, the basis for Christabel's sexual repression would be her fear of meeting the same death, the same end, as her mother ("CWM," 38). The encounter with Geraldine must represent, for Christabel, the death of her mother: a moment when sex and death come to light. This representation occurs in a narration that is clearly uncanny, insofar as it repeats Christabel's apparently naive voice—and with it represents repressed content. The narration is similarly compelled (similarly paralyzed by an unspeakable dread) to present-by-hiding the poem's central riddle. That which must remain concealed (namely, the sight of Geraldine's bosom and half her side, in the touch of which "there worketh a spell, / Which is lord of thy utterance, Christabel!" ll. 267–68) has come to light, but only for Christabel. This significant revelation is unpresentable; the elliptical, repetitive, and question-begging style of the narrator repeats or doubles Christabel's speechlessness. Recalling Swann's analysis, it is because the hysteric is speechless and cannot tell her tale that she is doomed to a repetition that we may now identify as uncanny—an infectious repetition that knows no end.[43]

The poem's uncanniness, then, has been especially remarked upon in connection with its narrative presentation. Swann, for example, argues that the poem's *narrative* voices are fundamentally hysterical—as spell-bound and speechless as Christabel herself.[44] Rzepka, in his reading of the poem's repressed narrative effects, argues that the narrative contains all that *can* be told, and it does so with a certain Christabel-like naiveté that "reads like a species of ventriloquism or metempsychosis." The effect of this is uncanny, as though the narrator is a displaced or repetitive self of Christabel—but representing her from the outside ("CWM," 21–22). The narrator is thus unavoidably implicated in the uncanny representation of that which must be denied in the poem.[45] Traces of obsession and denial are accessible to the reader by their figuration in the language of the verse, but the manner of this figuration has the effect of inhibiting reflection in the reader, who is in turn paralyzed by the effects of the narration, as though by the paralyzing logic and conditions of a dream. As a result, the reader is incapable of resolving the poem's ambiguities from a position outside the poem's fictions, but Swann remarks, tellingly, that "the poem's 'fictions' seem to be about little else than these formal slippages" ("C," 542). The prevailing sense of paralysis, the poem's apparent inexpressibility, arises not from plenitude or sublime excess; rather, the uncanny elements and effects of "Christabel," the repetition through displacement of repressed desires and/as ghostly presences, in fact double (perhaps even allegorize) the unstoppable (and therefore "uncenterable") gap that marks, or demarcates, the poem.

Because of this central dynamic of doubling and repetition, the uncanny may be seen as a figure for—as well as a cause of—inconclusiveness: for how can its effects be suspended?[46] Coleridge's fragmentary poem may indeed be seen as a canny, or shrewd, presentation of the central problem. But, to read "Christabel" in terms of the *interminable* compulsion to repeat involves a certain repetition on the level of reading that fragmentary works especially invite, since completion is so often displaced, or transferred upon, the act of reading. Reading "Christabel" as an uncanny poem is itself, admittedly, just such a critical repetition, for "doubling" is ever-present in the displacement from one type of discourse to another (Christabel may not speak but we, after all, read . . . and read again). The attention to reading here has been precisely to show fragmentary transference in operation, in a way that is "doubled" by the poem's uncanniness and its fragmentary status. As a result, however, the problem of conclusiveness remains peculiarly difficult to solve.

In a sense, the impossibility of concluding (because nothing absolutely new or final can be said) says it all. The central problematic of Coleridge's poem may be given a summarizing re-presentation, if I may put it that way, by considering the double of Freud's text, its return in the form of new texts which analyze, in turn, its *own* uncanniness. Hélène Cixous, for example, reads "The 'Uncanny' " as itself uncanny, like "a strange theoretical novel," beset by a contradictory unfolding—by the presence of the author's double in the form of his hesitation.[47] Over the course of Freud's essay, many subjects, themes and difficulties are brought up and then abandoned so that the explication of the uncanny is "thwarted by Freud himself": "the complexity of the analysis and its suffocation go hand-in-hand with the uncertainty of the analyst" ("FP, " 526).[48] The *Unheimlich* is thus shown to be an indefinite domain, on the fringe, or threshold perhaps, of something else. With the repetition of key terms central to the discussion here of Coleridge's (or at least his narrator's) relation to the text of "Christabel" (self-thwarting, thresholds, suffocation) we see something of the larger operation of the uncanny, "outside" as well as "inside" the poem—something, perhaps, of what perplexes Coleridge and/or his narrator. In Freud's case, his occupation of the envied space of the writer—envied for his power to create uncanny effects at will—admits of a certain strangeness with respect to creation so that he is, "in his relationship to the writer, as the *Unheimliche* is in its relation to the *Heimliche*" ("FP, " 532).

Cixous subjects Freud's text to a thorough scrutinizing. Her comments on Freud's discussion of the uncanny in manifestations of death, on ghosts, on the return (of the repressed, of the dead, etc.), are particularly apposite for they not only address but link two matters of concern here: the representation of liminality (the "third" category of anomalous manifestations that pervade "Christabel" and come to reveal something essential about the fragmentary), and the question of the "return" in the form of Geraldine. These converge on the question of death. As Cixous points out, death is an impossible representation: it is that which "mimes," through that impossibility, the reality of death. What is more, "what is an absolute secret, something absolutely new and which should remain hidden, because it has shown itself to me, is the fact that I am dead; only the dead know the secret of death" ("FP, " 543). Is Geraldine more than an uncanny apparition? Is she more than the return of the dead mother: that is, death *itself*—at least to Christabel? The dead are powerful provokers of dread and terror because, as Freud says, if the dead return it is to carry us off with them. "In order to *carry* you *off*," Cixous points out, "it is always a question of displacement, the insidious movement, through which opposites communicate. It is the *between* that is tainted with strangeness." Everything remains, claims Cixous, to be said about the ghost, and about why its ambiguous return is so intolerable, for the return does not prove that death exists and neither does it announce death, per se. It is *only* the return itself that is confirmed. The ghost is really intolerable because it effaces the boundary or limit between two states. It is neither dead nor alive: "passing through, the dead man returns in the manner of the repressed." Death itself, Cixous suggests, amounts in the end to no more than this "disturbance of the limits" (*"FP,"*543). The ghost is constituted by this return, as much as a repression is inscribed by *its* return.

The fragment, as I have suggested above, is also that which disturbs, rather than implicates or confirms, a relation between parts and wholes—that which confirms only *itself,* and not a completing, nor even disintegrating, context. The consequent *ghostliness* of the fragment, then, which constitutes it as a kind of return, indicates a crisis of phenomenality and perception akin to the Kantian crisis of presentation implicit in the sublime (which has its own special links with death). The opposition drawn by Freud between the uncanny in literature and life, his envy of the artist's capacity to create and manipulate uncanny effects, relates, of course, to the presence of death. The *creation* of doubles is to conceal the fact that death is "always already present in life." Neither living nor dead, the double must supplement or perfect the living—and yet the double is "the harbinger of death." It is uncanny because "it cannot but invoke what man tries in vain to forget."[49] By extension, the presence of the fragment, as a persistent reminder of the *remainder,* may be seen as the allegorical presence within a text, within every text (no matter how *lively*) of its own "death": its own necessarily incomplete incompletion.

The threat posed by the uncanny is bound up by the same crisis of presentation remarked on above insofar as that which is revealed (what should have remained hidden) nevertheless eludes perception: by being repeated, doubled, and fragmented, its meaning is (allegorically speaking) endlessly displaced. The uncanny is thus, as Weber suggests, "a certain undecidability which affects and infects representations, motifs, themes and situations, which, like the allegories described by Walter Benjamin, always mean something other than what they are and in a manner which draws their own being and substance into the vortex of signification."[50] "Christabel" is uncanny in precisely this way: the poem's several degrees of fragmentation and discontinuity illuminate a complex of representational and hermeneutic factors that trouble the question of reading—the author's self-reading, as well as ours—of how, in effect, we construe the problems that fragments present us with: time and time again.

Notes

1. *The Collected Works of William Hazlitt,* ed. A. R. Waller and A. Glover (London: Dent, 1904), 2:581.

2. Donald R. Tuttle, in " 'Christabel's' Sources in Percy's *Reliques* and Gothic Romance," *PMLA* 53, no. 1 (June 1938), comments that Coleridge's difficulties completing the poem were also endemic to the gothic romances from which he partly drew.

3. Josiah Condor, in the *Eclectic Review,* 2d ser. 5 (June 1816). Sigmund Freud, *Case Histories 1: "Dora" and "Little Hans,"* in vol. 8 of The Pelican Freud Library (Penguin Books, 1977); first published in *The Standard Edition of the Complete Psychological Works of Sigmund Freud,* ed. and trans. James Strachey (London: Hogarth Press, 1953), 7:41.

4. Sigmund Freud, "The 'Uncanny,' " in vol. 14 of The Pelican Freud Library (1985); first published in *Standard Edition* (1955), 17:340.

5. The generic implications of this juxtaposition are discussed by Anne Janowitz in "Coleridge's 1816 Volume: Fragment as Rubric," *Studies in Romanticism* 24 (Spring 1985).

6. Coleridge, *Poetical Works,* ed. E. H. Coleridge (1912; London: Oxford University Press, 1969), 213. All line references in the text are to this edition of the poem.

7. Condor, *Eclectic Review,* see n. 3, above.

8. *Critical Review,* 5th ser. 3 (May 1816), reviewer unknown.

9. *The Examiner,* 2 June 1816.

10. *Literary Panorama,* 2d ser. 4 (July 1816), reviewer unknown.

11. Coleridge, *Christabel,* ed. E. H. Coleridge (London: Frowde, 1907), 17; Harold Bloom, *The Visionary Company: A Reading of English Romantic Poetry* (London: Faber & Faber, 1961), 206.

12. Humphry House, *Coleridge: The Clark Lectures, 1951–52* (London: Rupert Hart-Davis, 1953), 122, 125. House comments that this disjunction would be self-evident even if Coleridge had not, as usual, pointed it out in a preface, and that it primarily reflects the chronological break in the composition (with Coleridge's trip to Europe intervening) and the move from Somerset to the Lake District.

13. *Literary Panorama,* see n. 10, above.

14. Some skepticism has been voiced about Wordsworth's authority on this point, most significantly by B. R. McElderry Jr., in "Coleridge's Plan for Completing *Christabel,*" *Studies in Philology* 33 (July 1936). His skepticism derives most convincingly from the circumstances surrounding Wordsworth's statement, which was made to Coleridge's nephew in 1836, two years after Coleridge's death.

15. James Gillman, *The Life of Samuel Taylor Coleridge* (London: Pickering, 1838), 283.

16. As quoted by E. H. Coleridge in his edition of *Christabel,* 52.

17. See, for example, House, *Coleridge,* 128.

18. Gillman, *Life of Coleridge,* 301–2.

19. Paul Magnuson, *Coleridge's Nightmare Poetry* (Charlottesville: University Press of Virginia, 1974), 96.

20. Coleridge, *Table Talk,* ed. Carl Woodring (Princeton, N.J.: Princeton University Press, 1990), 1: 409–10 (1 July 1833).

21. It resonates as well, perhaps, with Goya's nightmares produced by the "sleep of reason" in what was still the broad daylight of the Enlightenment.

22. Coleridge had intended to affix to "Christabel" (as a kind of postface, perhaps) an essay on the preternatural which, not surprisingly, we do not have. The preternatural in fiction was, however, the subject of a brief 1818 essay in which the writer discusses, under the category of the preternatural, "the re-appearance of the dead, and the struggle of evil beings for an ascendency over human nature"—both of which are relevant to the poem at hand. In *Blackwoods Edinburgh Magazine,* no. 3, September 1818, 648–50.

23. Marjorie Levinson, *The Romantic Fragment Poem: A Critique of a Form* (Chapel Hill: University of North Carolina Press, 1986), 77. Hereafter *RFP*, cited in the text. The imitations, parodies, mock continuations—and much else—are amply documented by Arthur Nethercot in *The Road to Tryermaine* (1939; reprint, Westport, Conn.: Greenwood, 1978).

24. H. W. Piper, for example, observes that "the first part is a comparatively static confrontation of two figures that invite symbolic interpretation: the second has a good deal of varied action." In "The Disunity of *Christabel* and the Fall of Nature," *Essays in Criticism* 28 (July 1978): 216.

25. Richard Holmes, *Coleridge: Early Visions* (London: Hodder & Stoughton, 1989), 287.

26. A. J. Harding, "Mythopoesis: The Unity of *Christabel*," in R. Gravil, L. Newlyn, and N. Roe, eds., *Coleridge's Imagination: Essays in Memory of Pete Laver* (Cambridge: Cambridge University Press, 1985), 210. Hereafter "M," cited in the text.

27. It was Freud's contention, moreover, that the psychological necessitates, or leads directly to, the mythological: "The theory of the instincts is so to say our mythology. Instincts are mythical entities, magnificent in their indefiniteness." In *New Introductory Lectures on Psychoanalysis, Standard Edition*, 22:95.

28. Claude Lévi-Strauss, "The Structural Study of Myth," in *Structural Anthropology*, trans. Claire Jacobsen and Brook Grundfest Schoepf (Garden City, N.Y.: Anchor Books, 1967), 221.

29. Jane A. Nelson, "Entelechy and Structure in 'Christabel,'" *Studies in Romanticism* 19 (Fall 1980): 386.

30. Claude Lévi-Strauss, *The Raw and the Cooked*, trans. John and Doreen Weightman (New York: Harper & Row, 1969), 6; Nelson, "Entelechy," 385 n. 16.

31. As Hazlitt remarked in the *Examiner*, Coleridge's "superficial, pretty, ornamental" style is forced "into the service of a story which is petrific." Petrific (with its suggestion of what one might call the paralytic sublime—frozen, as it were, by fear) because unfigurable: a presentation of unpresentability. On the other hand, this petrific power recalls Freud's "Medusa's Head," where the male spectator is turned to stone by the terrifying threat of castration—a response related, more precisely, to the sight of the female genitals. In "Christabel," this is perhaps implicit in the sight of Geraldine's "hideous" bosom.

32. Jean-Pierre Mileur, *Vision and Revision: Coleridge's Art of Immanence* (Berkeley: University of California Press, 1982), 61–62. Hereafter *VR*, cited in the text.

33. Mileur comments, as others have, that this "inaccessibility of a causal center or source of motive" is what thwarts any attempt to turn the poem into a romance narrative.

34. From his review in the *Examiner*, see n. 9, above.

35. Hazlitt, some suppose, wanted Geraldine to bear unambiguously the traditional marking of a witch, perhaps only to safeguard his reading of the poem as fundamentally "disgusting." As Andrew Cooper points out, this comment—as motivated as that of which he charges Coleridge—shows that Coleridge's instincts in dropping the line, and thus retaining an essential ambiguity, were probably right. See "Whose Afraid of the Mastiff Bitch? Gothic Parody and Original Sin in *Christabel*," in his *Doubt and Identity in Romantic Poetry* (New Haven, Conn.: Yale University Press, 1988), 211 n. 7.

36. Richard A. Rand, "Geraldine," in Robert Young, ed., *Untying the Text: A Post-Structuralist Reader* (Boston: Routledge, 1981).

37. Robert Schwartz, "Speaking the Unspeakable: The Meaning of Form in *Christabel*," *The University of South Florida Language Quarterly* 19/1–2 (Fall-Winter 1980): 31, 32.

38. Lee Rust Brown, "Coleridge and the Prospect of the Whole," *Studies in Romanticism* 30 (Summer 1991): 238.

39. Karen Swann, " 'Christabel': The Wandering Mother and the Enigma of Form," *Studies in Romanticism* 23 (Winter 1984): 544. Hereafter "C," cited in the text.

40. Swann cites from *The Anatomy of Melancholy*, ed. Holbrook Jackson (New York: Random House-Vintage Books, 1977), 416. For a more detailed discussion of the links between Burton and "Christabel," see Swann, " 'Christabel,' " 537. In addition, as Charles Rzepka notes, one of Freud's early disciples, Sandor Ferenczi, observed that the refusal of the hysteric consciously to accept unconscious desire results in various degrees of antipathy and, at the extreme, loathing. Christabel is, clearly, so affected. See Rzepka, "Christabel's 'Wandering Mother' and the Discourse of the Self: A Lacanian Reading of Repressed Narration," *Romanticism Past and Present* 10, no. 1 (Winter 1986): 18. Hereafter "CWM," cited in the text.

41. Freud's procedures in the case history of Dora are a case in point. The case history is itself a "fragment" of an analysis, since the treatment was "broken off" by Dora; but even more remarkable are Freud's notes about his procedures, which depend on the piecemeal reconstruction of symptoms as they emerge. In Dora's case, this reconstruction extends to Freud's narrative: he compares himself, as noted above, to those whose task it is to unearth the mutilated relics of antiquity. "I have," he continues, "restored what is missing . . . but, like a conscientious archaeologist, I have not omitted to mention in each case where the authentic parts end and my constructions begin." See Freud, "Dora," *Standard Edition*, 7:41.

42. Freud, "The 'Uncanny,' " in *Standard Edition*, 17:357.

43. E. E. Bostetter in *The Romantic Ventriloquists*, rev. ed. (Seattle: University of Washington Press, 1975), 127, linked "Christabel" to Freud's "repetition compulsion," and wondered if a similar psychic operation were not motivating both the writing of the poem and Coleridge's well-documented dreams at that time, where the central situation was Coleridge's own helplessness before various, sadistic female figures.

44. Swann suggests that "Christabel" 's "narrators" are themselves hysterics (plural because, although the poem's "interlocutor and respondent mime the entanglement of Geraldine and Christabel," it is "not clear if we hear two voices or one")—hysterical because "they" are "overmastered by visions" and often stymied in their tale-telling. See " 'Christabel,' " 541.

45. This obtrusive denial on the level of narrative, Rzepka suggests in "Christabel's 'Wandering Mother,' " makes an important level of meaning—the story of Christabel's sexual repression—accessible. The point of his analysis is to reveal the "appositeness" of Coleridge's "ingenuous" narrative style (38–39), and, ultimately, to link his inability to finish or tell the tale of "Christabel," and his abandonment of poetry, to his own poetic desires and expectations.

46. Certainly Hoffmann's "The Sand-Man," a tale of the uncanny which Freud discusses at length in his essay, ends badly. Coleridge himself noted in 1823, in a less often cited reflection on the poem's ending, that "Were I free to do so, I feel as if I could compose the third part of Christabel, or the song of her desolation." *The Notebooks of Samuel Taylor Coleridge*, ed. Kathleen Coburn, 4 vols. (Princeton, N.J.: Princeton University Press, 1957–1990), 4: 5032.

47. Hélène Cixous, "Fiction and Its Phantoms: A Reading of Freud's *Das Unheimliche*," *New Literary History* 7 (Spring 1976): 525. Hereafter *"FP,"* cited in the text.

48. The problems are more precisely stated by Samuel Weber in "The Sideshow, Or: Remarks on a Canny Moment," *Modern Language Notes* 88 (1973): 1109, and

they pertain as much to "the nature of the uncanny, to its position *abseits* [off-side, off-beat], than to any peculiarities of Freud, or weaknesses in his argument." The problems, of which Freud is aware, include the following: "the central thesis, involving repression (and then surmounting) is too abstract and too formal, and the particular relation between repression, anxiety and the Unheimliche is left open: however interrelated these three are, they are not simply identical. Secondly, the status of Freud's 'evidence' remains open to question: how exemplary are the examples, if the elements they comprise are not necessarily uncanny?"

49. Sarah Kofman, "The Double is/and the Devil: The Uncanniness of *The Sandman*," in *Freud and Fiction*, trans. Sarah Wykes (Cambridge: Polity Press, 1991), 148.

50. Weber, "The Sideshow," 1132.

"On Her Own Couch":
Keats's Wandering Psychoanalysis

Joel Faflak

Wilfrid Laurier University

So she was gently glad to see him laid
Under her favourite bower's quiet shade
On her own couch.

—Endymion

I

FREUD'S admission that his case histories "lack the serious stamp of science" and read more like "short stories" than confirmed diagnoses marks psychoanalysis as a seismic confrontation between Reason and phantasy.[1] This encounter is hardly novel, given that Coleridge coined the term *psycho-analytical* in 1805. Kathleen Coburn first pointed out the neologism, but Romantic studies has yet fully to internalize its astonishing resonance within a cultural imaginary of psychoanalysis that includes, among other elements, philosophical idealism and Romanticism, as well as Freud.[2] In Coleridge's writing the term indicates a shift from metaphysics, especially from Kant's transcendental idealism, to a metapsychology arising from Coleridge's fascination with phenomena such as mesmerism, hysteria, or madness, to name only a few. For Coleridge, however, metaphysics and metapsychology, by attempting to reason *beyond* the given, also coincide in Kant's attempt to abstract the mind's categories from its empirical functioning. *That* they coincide suggests in Coleridge the attempt to fathom in (Kantian) Reason its frequently *un*rational functioning. The specter of this attempt still haunts Freud's writings insofar as their theoretical rationalism betrays Freud's desire for acceptance by the scientific community from which he emerged.[3] *The Interpretation of Dreams,* for instance, systematizes the dreamwork in the way that Kant's first Critique maps the architectonic of the conscious mind. Of course, Freud intends to educate Kant, so that where in Kant the dream disturbs philosophic and moral reflection, Freud will once and for all rationalize the irrational:[4] "dream interpretation is capable of giving us hints about the structure of our psychic apparatus which we have thus far expected in vain from philosophy."[5] Battling his own penis envy with philosophy, Freud conceives of psychoanalysis in a type of onanistic splendor. It is no mere coincidence, however, that Kant sees his critical method as "secur[ing] for human reason complete satisfaction in regard to that with which it has all along so eagerly occupied itself, though hitherto in vain."[6] In both cases, the vanity of a masculinist confidence in Reason has a great deal to do with things.

In their struggle to theorize a psyche frequently resistant to Reason, both writers set aside the psyche's "other" articulation as literature. "Literature," as Ned Lukacher argues, "is always what philosophy/psychoanalysis forgets in its progress toward the Spirit of Absolute Knowledge."[7] This struggle in lieu of literature, as it were, takes us back to a Romantic coinage of the psycho-analytical as it posits the struggle of psychoanalysis with Reason in advance of Freud. Indeed, one can argue that Romanticism, as witnessed by Coleridge's coinage, and as profoundly as Freud's own discoveries, *invents* psychoanalysis as the struggle for an identity radically divided between its scientific—by which I also mean theoretical and philosophical—and literary or aesthetic impulses.[8] Romanticism leaves psychoanalysis relatively *un*defined. That it does so, however, is precisely the point, Romanticism's way of nodding to the phantasy of Reason behind the theoretical structure or metapsychology of psychoanalysis. Romanticism's psychoanalytic tropes and mechanisms disclose a process of *imagining* psychoanalysis before its codification by theory. Psychoanalysis had to be imagined, that is, before it could be debated in theory, a debate always undone by the psychic process which made it possible. Applying literature to a psychoanalysis that literature generates and always exceeds, then, one can return to the future of psychoanalysis in Romanticism, but not as the disciplined child of a later theoretical parent.

Positing the transcendence of the *cogito* by the SUM, Coleridge's metaphysics of imagination would overcome the mind's associationism, what is for Coleridge the mere materialism of its grey matter operating like a machine. What Coleridge seems most concerned to overcome, however, is the ghost within this machine. He refers to associationism's "delirium,"[9] which amounts to a type of psychic determinism or free-associationism of the mind firing away at will beyond the subject's rational or conscious control. That Coleridge names Fancy as a third and seemingly nonessential category after his primary and secondary imaginations, then, becomes instead the symptom of a psychic autonomy Coleridge would set aside. Fancy repeats the primary imagination as the unconscious of the SUM and thus turns metaphysics into economy, mobilized by a delirium Coleridge's idealism would repress. Coleridge's metaphysics of imagination announces the *cogito*'s privilege of Reason. Addressing its interior life, however, encounters the power of phantasy as a threat to Reason's authority, a psychology Coleridge would turn into metapsychology. That Coleridge gave up poetry suggests in the first generation of Romantic writers an uneasy confrontation with this threat.

In Romanticism a telling factor in this unstable economy is gender. As Fancy comes to be associated with romance and sensibility, it signifies a wandering or interiorized discourse of the imagination feminized as the Other to masculine writing, which is often concerned with strategies for containing this threat or eradicating it altogether. This emergence of the separate spheres of masculine and feminine posits gender as a force of signification mobilizing its own system of cultural prescription, one that comes to evoke a psychical as much as biological determinism or essentialism. But the gendered "feminine" in Romanticism, as that which the gendered "masculine" would marginalize, cannot be defined only by virtue of this marginalization. The very positing of gender in any of its manifestations points to its implicit volatility and instability. Here I invoke Judith Butler's interrogation of gender's role in the social construction of subjectivities. A "feminist appropriation of sexual difference," argues Butler, reads the feminine as the "unrepresentable absence effected by (masculine) denial that grounds the signifying economy through exclusion" so that an excluded feminine "constitutes the possibility of a critique and disruption of that hegemonic conceptual scheme."[10] However, Butler reads the feminine as part of a broader economy that gender both generates and is sustained by:

> That the power regimes of heterosexism and phallogocentrism seek to augment themselves through a constant repetition of their logic, their metaphysics, and their naturalized ontologies does not imply that repetition itself ought to be stopped—as if it could be. If repetition is bound to persist as the mechanism of the cultural reproduction of identities, then the crucial question emerges: What kind of subversive repetition might call into question the regulatory practice of identity itself? . . . If the regulatory fictions of sex and gender are themselves multiply contested sites of meaning, then the very multiplicity of their construction holds out the possibility of a disruption of their univocal posturing.[11]

Marking its own essentialized and essentializing terms, gender also becomes a force of speculation by unsettling and redistributing the terms of its own signifying economy. Gender does not express an essential identity, for "gender attributes . . . effectively constitute the identity they are said to express or reveal." If identity is thus "phantasmatic, then it must be possible to enact an identification that displays its phantasmatic structure."[12] According to Butler, one can only disrupt, resist, or transform gender's positing power of subjectivity by always thinking in terms of this power's locus in phantasy. This thinking offers a constitutive articulation of the subject as the Other of gender's own constitution of identity

Romanticism "thinks" gender's "phantasmatic structure," yet not without some ambivalence. Geraldine in "Christabel" or Margaret in "The Ruined Cottage" signify a feminized excess of Reason haunting the masculinist *cogito* of Romantic imagination, just as the scientism of Freud's metapsychology is haunted by the "alien" psychology of woman. Thus, when Romanticism privileges interiority, the privileging itself frequently manages what threatens this interiority *from within*,[13] not unlike how Freud's dreamwork systematizes the unconscious so as to colonize it. Wordsworth uses the "discerning intellect of Man" to look "Into our Minds." But he also subsumes the multiple personalities of individual "Minds" within the universal "Mind of Man"[14] so as to contain within the "body" of his "gothic church" its own "sepulchral recesses."[15] In both Freud and Wordsworth, Reason tells the story of how Mind triumphs over its matter. However, Ms. B of "The Ruined Cottage," which contains "Incipient Madness" and "The Baker's Cart," the earliest writings for *The Recluse*, tells another version of Reason. These texts suggest an *inability* to understand the psyche—specifically Margaret's psyche—as the social order's trauma, just as Geraldine, a "sight to dream of, not to tell,"[16] evokes the symptom of patriarchal trauma in "Christabel." Margaret, the Female Vagrant, the Pedlar, the Discharged Soldier, Christabel's "wandering mother," the Ancient Mariner—all suggest within Romanticism an organicism disrupted by its own errant or peripatetic interiority, a site where phantasy resists Reason.

Wordsworth's texts flirt with psychoanalysis to talk through this disruption. "The Ruined Cottage" and *The Prelude* begin their deep introspection by placing their narrators on "couches" and are encounters between an analyst and analysand: the Narrator and the Pedlar, Wordsworth and the "silent screen" of Coleridge. Yet Wordsworth aborts psychoanalysis by feminizing within it what threatens Reason's masculinity. How could Margaret *possibly* understand her own mind? In "The Ruined Cottage" the Pedlar and the Narrator,

like Freud and Fleiss analyzing Emma Eckstein, reason away Margaret's madness *as* madness.[17] Significantly, then, Coleridge becomes
the repetition of the woman's dis-ease by emerging in *The Prelude* as
an effete analysand in need of the phantasy of Wordsworth's heroic
ability to overcome his own mental crisis. In both texts Margaret's
absent psychosomatic body reproduces itself in the unstable negotiation of unreason "between men," the telling symptom of a flaw in
Reason's narcissistic, masculine façade. Eventually, this symptom reproduced itself as a gendered periodic version of the "separate
spheres." Thus Romanticism itself became feminized and pathologized as what Julia Wright calls an "ineffective cultural mutation"[18]
in the larger nineteenth-century narrative of building a healthy Victorian (national) body, Wordsworthian egotism came to represent
"an unproductive attention to feeling that must be supplanted for
the patient to mature and find health." This Victorianism cured the
nervous or telling Romantic body by putting aside its excessive "self-
feeling" for the greater corporate good of the empire's body politic,
which "coheres through feeling"[19] for one's social or moral duty.

Keats is perhaps himself anxious about Wordsworthian excess
when he critiques the "wordsworthian [*sic*] or egotistical sublime,"
ostensibly for its too determinate selfhood. He offers instead the indeterminate "camelion" nature of the poet who "has no Identity."[20]
He seems to displace a patriarchal visionary tradition inherited from
Milton via Wordsworth, and thus to remain ambivalent about Romantic poetry's powerfully masculine signification.[21] Favoring feminine Fancy, "opening on the foam / Of perilous seas, in faery lands
forlorn."[22] Here ("Ode to a Nightingale) Keats seems to redress a
Wordsworthian marginalization of the feminine. Yet Keatsian identity is also perpetually "tolled back" from its feminine "vision" (l.
79) or "music" to the "sole self" (l. 72) of the poet's "egotistical"
consciousness. The poet is caught in a no-man's land of gender's
ambivalent "waking dream" (l. 79). On one hand, gender allows the
poet to distinguish Reason from unreason, or the real from phantasy, as the masculine from the feminine. On the other, however, he
then succumbs to this distinction as a type of psychic determinism
he is subsequently, out of his compulsion to repeat its prescription,
compelled to resist and transform. The drama of gender in Keats
thus takes the form of an unfolding psychoanalysis which can be
traced through *Endymion, Hyperion,* and *The Fall of Hyperion.* This psychoanalysis reads its masculine science or model of the mind as a
feminine phantasy of Reason in order to confront the masculine
and feminine as both constitutive *and* destabilizing categories within
this process.

Keats's preface to *Endymion* distinguishes between the "healthy" imaginations of manhood and boyhood, a "space of life between in which the soul is in a ferment, the character undecided, the way of life uncertain, the ambition thick-sighted" (*CP*, 505). Keats seems to put aside this mutation in consciousness within an organic movement from Romantic adolescence to Victorian adulthood. However, read against the preface's canonization, which too vehemently rejects the poem's "flaws," this marginal middle ground is also immanently transgressive. Alan Bewell argues that reviews of Keats's 1817 *Poems* and 1818 *Endymion* (particularly Lockhart's) are early responses to the poetry's "gender conflict":[23] an attention to sensuous and luxuriant imagery, associated with an effete literature of sensibility, that points to a Romantic excess not "fitting" (of) a heterosexist paradigm of Victorian social duty and self-control. As a male poet, that is, Keats is either too libidinous or not potent enough. However, Keats "enact[s this conflict] within the later poems . . . as a matter for revision. In these poems, Keats consistently rewrites the conflict between women's literature and the male visionary tradition as a conflict between his earlier and later self."[24] *The Fall of Hyperion* thus distinguishes between the poet as the picture of masculine health and as the carrier of a femininized and pathologized fanaticism. Keats's "stylistic cross-dressing"[25] borrows from a "women's" poetry of romance and sensibility at a time of Regency culture's rising anxiety about its own masculinity. Yet Keats also exploits the labor of the feminine within the larger project of constructing his own later persona as a more potently masculine writer.

However, Keats's transformation at the expense of the feminine does not accrue wholly to the masculine. The economy of Romantic psychoanalysis mobilized between *Endymion, Hyperion,* and *The Fall of Hyperion* unfolds within its identity its own "phantasmatic structure," dramatized by an internalized "subversive repetition" of gender that this identity comes to confront within itself. To differing ends *Endymion* and *Hyperion* express an essential—and essentially gendered—interiority; yet they also treat this interiority with some ambivalence. By feminizing unreason, *Endymion* would colonize romance in the service of building Keats's masculine identity as Poet. But the text unravels into a wandering scene of psychoanalysis constituting the unstable hegemony of Romance. A similar thing happens in *Hyperion* with epic, which is unsettled by a subtext of psychoanalysis in which gender also figures prominently. By staging the mise-en-scène of the gendering of these genres as if returning to the first *Hyperion* as the second text's primal scene, *The Fall of Hyperion* is equally ambivalent about its own gendered nature. However, this

ambivalence emerges as part of the text's transgressively (de)struct-
ured unfolding. This process repeats or stages the "mechanism of
cultural reproduction" in order to contest the "regulatory practice
of identity itself." Gender and psychoanalysis thus emerge as mutu-
ally contested and contesting forces in all three texts. The prototype
of this struggle occurs in *Endymion*, where Peona, to help Endymion
read the "troubled sea of the mind" (1.454), places him "On her
own couch" (1.438). Here the woman is the feminine unreason of
Romanticism as well as its female analyst, both compromised by and
resisting a masculine analytical authority the text would presume to
know. Yet Peona also facilitates in the poet, as Romantic analysand,
his confrontation with the pathology of his visionary imagination—a
confrontation with (Margaret's) madness as the projection of his
own masculinist *cogito*. The feminine, that is, resists the philosophical confidence of gender's prerogatives, dragging them to the phantasmatic scene of their own authority, a place of "no Identity" that
is both absence *and* potentiality. The feminine discloses the phantasy of Reason, opening Reason to its own internal psychic determinism but also displaying/mobilizing its performative or self-making
potentiality as a constitutive resistance to this determinism.

II

When Keats argues that Wordsworth had thought further "into
the human heart" (*LK*, 96) than Milton, he uses the discourse of
sensibility to psychoanalyze the patriarchy of epic and thus of the
visionary tradition itself.[26] But Keats reads further within the gendered economy of Wordsworth's "Reason in her most exalted
mood."[27] Wordsworth signifies Reason as a feminine subject presumed to know, yet then registers beneath her intellectual façade a
psychosomatic complex or "mood" of thought that suggests radical
doubt. As if implicitly to contain this threat, he also transcendental-
izes the embodied feminine as allegorical abstraction so as to abject
her as Other. Accordingly, the femininity of Reason is placed
beyond Wordsworth's control to more than one end. Keats directly
opposes "consequitive reasoning" (*LK*, 37), the rational gaze of
Apollonius that would eradicate Lamia's "gordian shape" as
the unreason of his "cold philosophy" ("Lamia," 1.47, 2.230).
Instead, Keats favors "speculation" (*LK*, 157) or "*Negative Capability,*
that is when man is capable of being in uncertainties, Mysteries,
doubts, without any irritable reaching after fact & reason" (*LK*,
43). Thus, when Keats names his paradigmatic theme in "Ode

to Psyche"—"I will . . . build a fane / In some untrodden region of my mind"—it is a "wreathed trellis of a working brain," of "branchèd thoughts, new grown with pleasant pain," but "without a name" (ll.50–51, 52, 61). To "name" the feminine as resistant to signification is to leave her *un*named; but it is also to signify resistance itself as a transgression *of* (masculine) signification.

This resistance discloses the psychoanalytical ambivalence of Keats's poetry. In "Ode on a Grecian Urn," speculation names the urn's beautiful "end" of being human, but according to a sublime ambivalence between "men or gods" (l.8). Immortality accrues to patriarchy, but only through a repetitive questioning of its autonomy, which "dost tease us out of thought" (l.44). As the unconscious of the *anthropos* disrupts the text's contemplation, "eternity" (l.45) becomes interminability, signaled by the urn's metaphysical coitus interruptus, which perpetually suspends the ideology of a heterosexual union between "men" and "maidens." In "Ode to a Nightingale" sensibility mesmerizes the speaker's masculine reason: "My heart aches, and a drowsy numbness pains / My *sense*" (ll.1–2; my italics). He would thus pit the empirical autonomy of his "sole self" (l.72) against unreason: "the fancy cannot cheat so well / As she is famed to do" (ll.73–74). But Fancy both constitutes and transgresses the boundaries of masculine vision. Hence, when Keats feminizes melancholy in "Ode on Melancholy," as "dwell[ing] with . . . Beauty that must die" (l.21), he suggests the eradication of the feminine but also uses it to overturn the static aesthetic hegemony of Beauty associated with a masculinist visionary tradition.

Despite their internal psychological complexities, however, the shorter and elaborately "overwrought" form of the odes still suggests within the tortu(r)ousness of Reason an immanent teleology that is less possible to maintain within romance, which frames a much broader canvas for the psyche and the economy of gender within which it emerges. In a letter of May 1818, four months before starting *Hyperion*, Keats "compare[s] human life to a large Mansion of many Apartments, two of which [he] can only describe" (*LK*, 95): the "infant or thoughtless Chamber" and the "Chamber of Maiden-Thought." This latter room "becomes gradually darken'd and at the same time on all sides of it many doors are set open—but all dark— all leading to dark passages." Beyond this indeterminate "maiden" stage, one suspects a later shift into masculine experience. A year later, however, having abandoned *Hyperion* and not yet having started *The Fall of Hyperion*, Keats describes life as a "vale of Soul-making" (*LK*, 249). A locus of both negativity and potentiality, soul-making is "where the heart must feel and suffer in a thousand di-

verse ways" in "a world of Circumstances" (*LK*, 251) which perpetually delays how the soul "possess[es] the *sense* of Identity" (*LK*, 250;
my italics). Wordsworth's gothic church organizes the psyche meta-
physically within a syncretic vision of the stable *anthropos*. Keats's
"Mansion," however, is a psychological structure inhabited develop-
mentally. Within its logic of Reason unfolds instead the heterogeneous psychosomatic field or "vale" of its functioning indetermi-
nately staged between the feminine and masculine.

Endymion develops as if to map the topography of this vale as the
emergent psychology of the imagination's unreason. This unreason
comes to suggest within the conscious form of romance the unconscious tendency of its poetic psyche to wander interminably.[28] As if
making a stock plea for aesthetic guidance and inspiration, Keats
calls this romance's "uncertain path" (1.61), just as Endymion is
"wandering in uncertain ways" (2.48). The stating of the poem's
theme—"A thing of beauty is a joy forever" (1.1)—is meant to signify the goal at the heart of romance's labyrinth in the "heart" of
the poet's soul, where beauty will register the journey's lasting effects. However, these effects are more incessant than transcendental
as Endymion becomes intoxicated by a vision of the autonomy of his
mortal self as his "sweet dream" (1.677) of Diana. "Forever" comes
to represent a painfully uncertain time. *Endymion* explores the anatomy of eternity as the interpretation of this dream as it perpetually
"[falls] into nothing" (1.678). Thus, in "lowliness of heart" the narrator "move[s] to the end" (4.29) of the text by confessing the text's
melancholy as the failure of poetry to transform "our dull, unin-
spired, snail-pacèd lives" (4.25). The intoxication of Endymion's desire for omniscience, and so for the telos of romance, becomes addiction, a melancholic dis-ease of "secret grief" (1.539) which the
text's therapy cannot overcome. This dis-ease is contingently figured
in Diana, who haunts the text as mythology's Protean mutation into
the multiple tellings of the Greek pantheon. She suggests a free-associationism, both in Endymion's mind and in the form of the text's
narrative, and thus in the psyche of romance itself, which the text
would resist. Her indeterminate presence comes to betray a temporal psychosomatic interiority "full of ache" and "gone in woe"
(3.80). As myth's pathology, she signifies the psychic dis-ease of Endymion's own contemplation, "Reason in her most exalted mood"
as a radical psychoanalysis of Wordsworthian vision: "where / Are
those swift moments? Whither are they fled?" (1.970–71). That Endymion never possesses Diana, then, suggests a masculine anxiety
toward feminine vision. But this rupture within the text's *cogito* is
also its own resistance to a masculine mastering of the feminine and

thus to colonization by romance (and Romantic) prescriptions. If uncomfortable with feminine unreason, the text appears equally uneasy about a masculine Reason that would gender away what seems integral to its own identity.[29]

Although everyone in book one's Festival of Pan is "ripe for high contemplating" (1.355), talk turns out to be cheap.[30] They "wandered, by divine converse, / Into Elysium, vying to rehearse / Each one his own anticipated bliss" (1.371–72), and "all out-told / Their fond imaginations" (1.393). This wandering rehearsal for immortality, however, suggests both anticipation and an excessive lack of fulfillment, while "out-told" suggests both apotheosis and excess. While this group mesmeric crisis is circuited through Endymion and the "agèd priest" (1.357), their "sober ring" (1.356) is also a "fragile bar / That keeps us from our homes ethereal" (1.360–61), as though philosophy is the curse preventing the *cogito*'s transcendence. Everyone "feelingly could scan" (1.178) Endymion's "lurking trouble" (1.179), but remains susceptible to its psychic dis-ease. Endymion's "senses . . . [swoon] off" (1.398) as though Reason itself becomes the feminine suspending his "sense." Peona removes him from the opening scene of masculine philosophy to one of feminine interrogation (1.407ff.) and lays him "On her own couch." Where he and the priest "discourse" as if of "one mind," Peona addresses Endymion as part of a dialogue. He begins to "ease [his] breast / Of secret grief" (1.538–39) by retelling his dream of Diana as a "second self" (1.659) that resists assimilation within his "sovereign vision" (3.183). A singing analyst, Peona plays on her lute a "lively prelude, fashioning the way / In which her voice should wander" (1.492–93), as if to recall Endymion from this self-division. Yet she "[traces] / Something more high-perplexing in [his] face" (1.514–15) which she cannot read. Moreover, her music's "deep intoxication" (1.502) is both curative and infectious. That it carries the "wandering" of her voice suggests the threatening influence of gender which she embodies/bodies forth, a contagion unsettling her "self-possession" (1.504). This countertransference uncannily repeats Endymion's trauma so that he must himself turn therapist: " 'Tell me thine ailment . . . / Ah! thou hast been unhappy at the change / Wrought suddenly in me' " (1.519–21).

As if responding to the gender ambivalence of psychoanalysis as a threat to romance, Peona then shifts to speak as romance's superego. Here the text exemplifies "woman" as having internalized cultural restraint by loathing her own dreams as the province of feminine sensibility: "*Shame / On this poor weakness!*" (1.717–18). Dismissing psychoanalysis in favor of behavioral therapy, she would cure Endymion's feminized melancholy by appealing to his sense of duty: " 'wherefore sully the entrusted gem / Of high and noble life with thoughts so sick?' " (1.757–58). Tellingly, it is Endymion who would persist in romance—"No merely slumbering phantasm, could unlace / The stubborn canvas for my voyage prepared" (1.771–72)—as equal to social action: "My restless spirit never could endure / To brood so long upon one luxury / Unless it did, though fearfully, espy / A hope beyond the shadow of a dream" (1.854–57). Yet this "Life of Sensations rather than of Thoughts" (*LK*, 37) remains unsettled by the mind's "entanglements, enthralments far / More self-destroying" (1.798–99). Thus, as the potentially transformed *anthropos* "Full alchemized, and free of space" (1.780), he remains "knit" (1.701) by an "under darkness" (1.702) that becomes the symptom of the abstract *cogito* as if divided from its inner life. Endymion settles upon "demurest meditation" (1.975), which suggests a feminine empowering of masculine contemplation that would resist normative gender prescriptions. But the "demure" discourse of sensibility also suggests capitulation so that both the feminine and masculine are compromised. He "Bear[s] up against [Sorrow]" (1.974) and would show a "more healthy countenance" (1.986). Yet he rises from his couch only "faint-smiling" (1.990). In book two, "Brain-sick" (2.43), his "old grief" (2.47) returns immediately and the text continues to unfold as an avoidance of "coming madness" (2.218). Accordingly, the text unfolds as a series of episodes wherein Endymion repeatedly "fling[s] / Himself" (2.95–96) on the ground, on couches or on beds (1.436–38; 2.95–96; 2.440ff.; 2.711ff.; 3.107–9) in order to "ponder / On all his life" (2.886–87) and to tell his dreams.[31] In each case, however, self-revelation turns to "entrancements" (2.704), a repeated catharsis without therapeutic results.

Books two, three, and four retell the text's own mythopoeia as its repeated attempt to fashion a scene of psychoanalysis that would account for Endymion's wanderings. Two specific episodes seem to bring this psychoanalysis to fulfillment. Book two's union of Venus with Adonis in his bower (2.387ff.) figures the cure of Endymion's transference with Peona, and thus the end to self-division as the consummation of his desire for Diana. Book three similarly recuperates Endymion's truncated "discourse" with the priest as the fulfilled psychoanalysis of Endymion's "discoursing" (3.723) with Glaucus, who "know[s Endymion's] inmost bosom" (3.293), so that they become "twin brothers in this destiny" (3.713). Endymion revises Glaucus' "lifeless" (3.220) identity and hears the "secret [of his own destiny] all displayed" (3.308) in Glaucus' story (3.314–711), the uncanny repetition of Endymion's unfulfilled desire for Diana. At the end of this narrative, Glaucus tears the "scroll" (3.670) that prophesies the consummation of his own fate in Endymion's. In a moment of homosocial bonding, as if to buttress the masculinist ideology of Reason, he asks Endymion to scatter its fragments on both of them as on the "files of dead" (3.770) whose Reason has, like Glaucus', been slain by Circe, "arbitrary queen of sense" (3.459). Thus reanimated, these dead turn Glaucus' "mumblings funereal" (3.748) into a "noise of harmony" (3.791) so that the melancholic dis-ease of the feminine within Reason is overcome. Here the gender ambivalence of previous attempts at psychoanalysis is reclarified in terms of the visionary trope of apocalypse negotiated between men, just as the union between Venus and Adonis confirms the text's heterosexual matrix.

Yet the parallel between Circe and Diana in book three unsettles these negotiations by suggesting that the release from unreason is instead a missed encounter with its radically transgressive feminine power. By destroying the scroll, as if to transcend language, Glaucus also eliminates any record of the feminine's murderous designs on Reason. The elimination itself, however, confirms the feminine's constitutive power within the symbolic as the occulted repetition of this order's instability, the flaw within its masculine narcissism. The most potent symptom of this trauma is book four's Cave of Quietude, "Made for the soul [itself] to wander in and trace / Its own existence" (4.514–15). As the analytical office of the text's pantheon, the cave anatomizes as if from the text's unconscious its wandering scene of psychoanalysis. As a "native hell" (4.523), "Happy gloom" (4.537) or "Dark Paradise" (4.538), where the soul is made by both "buried griefs" (4.517) and "new-born woe" (4.519), the cave seems adapted to internalize the text's ambivalence toward psychoanalysis as what Julia Kristeva would call an "indefinite catharsis."[32] Oddly, this anatomy is never fully embodied as a productive clinical response to the text's ambivalence so that the cognition of psychoanalysis remains suspended. Partly this suspension implicitly rejects what Butler calls the "disembodiment of the abstract masculine epistemological subject."[33] This abstraction is a type of Kantian *epoché* that privileges self-awareness only by bracketing it off from the volatile economy of gender by which subjectivity is constituted. Endymion refuses to take on Glaucus' identity and thus to reject entirely the embodiment of this identity's "other" gender. As the poem ends, Peona blesses Endymion and the Indian maiden as they "vanished" (4.1002) into the text's now defunct romance topography. Awkwardly expedient, this resolution repeats book two's union between Venus and Adonis, but as if now to stage a "compulsory heterosexuality" which the text would no longer defend.

Realizing his "kingdom's at its death" (4.940), Endymion discards the masculinist illusion of immortality and autonomy. Instead, he "inwardly began / On things for which no wording can be found" (4.961–62). This music, echoing Peona's "intoxication" and Glaucus' "harmony," yet left darkly unprescribed by the ideology of masculine vision—"Deeper and deeper sinking until drowned / Beyond the reach of music" (4.963–64)—suggests Kristeva's idea of the semiotic. The semiotic registers the subject's "drives" and "pulsions" as "psychical marks" and "energy charges" so that biological determinism is rethought as "always already involved in a semiotic process."[34] As a "stage" or "region . . . hidden by the arrival of [symbolic] signification" and preceding "the realm of positions,"[35] the semiotic takes the form of the *chora*, a "mobile and extremely provisional articulation constituted by movements and their ephemeral stases."[36] Kristeva associates the *chora* with the mother's body as a primal matrix of biological, cultural, and patriarchal regulation from which the (de)constituted subject emerges, a form of theoretical essentialism against which Butler herself famously reacts.[37] Refusing to identity the semiotic with the feminine, however, Kristeva uses the semiotic to posit within any symbolic economy its constitutive instability or repetitive marginality as (to return to Butler, albeit in a way she might not welcome) the very mechanism of its cultural reproduction. The semiotic thus suggests within the text's prescribed economy of gender alternate identities facilitated by the feminine as it signifies, although does not essentialize, a productive ambivalence within this economy. However, that these identities are left unexplored suggests finally that the text cannot overcome what it perceives to be flaws within its own gendered schema. Waking from his "great dream" (4.638), Endymion realizes he has "clung / To nothing" (4.636–37), while in sleep "Imagination [gives] a dizzier pain" (3.1009). He remains "full of grief" (4.107), "lost" (4.51) between masculine and feminine, Reason and unreason: "What is this soul then? Whence / Came it? It does not seem my own, and I / Have no self-passion or identity" (4.475–77). The text is prone to psychoanalysis, yet only as a specter haunting the stubborn structure of romance which, despite its tendency to wander, resists psychoanalysis's alien feminine presence.

III

Keats abandoned *Endymion* for the "new romance" (*LK*, 25) of *Hyperion*.[38] As the serial pathology of the psyche's inability to tell its "romance" uniformly, *Endymion* unfolds more palimpsestically than teleologically. *Hyperion* recasts this pathology as epic as if to monumentalize the psyche by tracing its archetypal psychic parentage. But, picking up where *Endymion* leaves off, the text manifests the previous text's rather more latent psychoanalysis of the Greek pantheon. *Hyperion* dramatizes the autonomy of masculine vision as if moving through the mirror stage of its own identity into its symbolic ambivalence. Saturn's opening speech to Thea, his female interlocutor, thus refigures *Endymion*'s mortal doubt as if from its other side in the trauma of Titanic selfhood: "I have left / My strong identity, my real self, / Somewhere between the throne and where I sit / Here on this spot of earth" (1.112–15). In Saturn's struggle to accept a lost autonomy, he is thus also ambivalently positioned between mourning and melancholia. Laplanche and Pontalis, quoting Daniel Lagache, write that the "work of mourning consists in 'killing death.' "[39] Melancholy, however, results from an inability to "sever [one's] attachment to the object that has been abolished." Saturn's melancholy results from his inability to "kill" the *imago* of his archaic patriarchal divinity, for the past, while utterly alien, is also an integral part of who he was/is. Saturn's struggle thus stages as a more overt scene of trauma the homosocial narcissism of patriarchy in *Endymion*.[40] Where in *Endymion* romance seems regressively melancholic, as if unable to accept the "phantasmatic structure" of its own gendered economy, *Hyperion* struggles to account for melancholy as this structure's constitutive and constituting nature. Without "a bent for melancholia," Kristeva writes, "there is no psyche": "melancholia . . . is not the philosopher's disease but his very nature, his *ethos*."[41] Kristeva suggests within Reason its "*impossible mourning*" for an inaccessible—and inaccessibly lost—object, what she calls the " 'Thing' as the real that does not lend itself to signification."[42] As a version of this "impossible mourning," Saturn's patriarchal vision is internalized within the text as the feminine sensibility of melancholy, as if in an attempt to transpose these categories beyond their own essential terms.

As in *Endymion*, dialogue in *Hyperion* is both the cure for and the symptom of this epic instability. At first *Hyperion* seems ready for psychoanalysis and for a concerted working through of its gender conflicts. The text unfolds as a series of encounters through which Saturn, Hyperion, and Apollo emerge as mirror images of a composite analysand who transfers his psychic dis-ease onto various analytical figures: Thea (1.23–71; 2.89–100), Coelus (1.306–48), Oceanus (2.163–246), Clymene (2.247–303), Enceladus (2.107–10; 2.303–55), and Mnemosyne (3.46–79). These scenes posit a complex communication in that dialogue frequently occurs by reading the semi-otic register of the other's face or affect, and thus by reading beyond symbolic prescription. In book one, for instance, Saturn "feels" Thea's presence before he sees her "face," which he then asks her to lift so that he might "see [their collective] doom in it" (1.97). Thea responds in book two by observing "direst strife" (2.92) in "Saturn's face" (2.91), and thus confirming his melancholy. This process constitutes reading as what Tilottama Rajan calls a "psycho-logical and not just a semiological process."[43] But even as the psy-chology of trauma is both remembered and repeated in these scenes, communication remains more projected than fulfilled. Thus more part of the text's subconscious, they comprise a psychoanalyti-cal allegory in which the subject confronts, but cannot seem to move beyond, the narcissistic construct of its own epic autonomy. Like En-dymion, Saturn can "see his kingdom gone" (1.90), but still yearns to repossess it.[44]

As a desperate subject presumed to know, then, Saturn has a "ner-vous grasp" (1.105) on reality. In the literature of sensibility, Peter Melville Logan notes, "the female body, though victimized by con-finement, is also the contagious source of the nervous epidemic; the nervous mother, in her debility, infects her offspring with a constitu-tional nervous temperament."[45] Here, however, the father's body is infected by a nervous contagion that is passed on to the text's two suns/sons, Hyperion and Apollo. Although a mirror image of Sa-turn's melancholy (in the pantheon, he would be Saturn's brother, and in the text, he signals the Titans' own internal hope for redemp-tion), Hyperion suggests an ambivalent identity between a "shape majestic" (2.372) and a "vast shade / In midst of his own bright-ness" (2.373). His "Horrors, portioned to a giant nerve, / Oft made [him] ache" (1.175–76) so that he signifies the anatomy of the text's *anthropos* dying into the life of his own psychosomatic interiority: "through all his bulk an agony / Crept gradual, from the feet unto the crown" (1.259–60). In this respect he assumes the text's arche-typal psychoanalytical pose between Saturn's downward gaze "couchant on the earth" (1.87) and Apollo's upright stance "Full ankle-deep in lilies of the vale" (3.35) and gazing at Mnemosyne.

As the *imago* of Apollo, the rising sun/son who Saturn would be-come, Hyperion emerges as key to the family romance of the text's patriarchy. The transition to Apollo is partly negotiated through Hyperion's transference with Coelus. As god of the heavens, he is both Hyperion's and the text's Father. Hyperion "[stretches] him-self in grief and radiance faint" (1.304) on the earth and talks up-ward to Coelus, the melancholic son having placed himself on the couch. Hyperion seems able to confront the unreason of an interiority that Saturn cannot: "O dreams of day and night! / O monstrous forms! O effigies of pain! / ... / Why do I know ye? Why have I seen ye? / ... / Saturn is fallen, am I too to fall?" (1.227–34). Just as Thea recognizes in Saturn a "supreme God / At war with all the frailty of grief" (2.92–93), Coelus also sees in Hyperion an "evident God" (1.338) struck with "mortal" "grief" (1.334–35). He would place Hyperion "in the van / Of circumstance" (1.343–44) so that the Titans' ascension can be realized. By the end of book two, however, Hyperion remains "dejected" (2.380) so that the father's therapy is ineffectual. As an abstract or "Ethereal presence" that is "but a voice" (1.340), Coelus demands that the patriarchy's "sons" must embody the melancholic dis-ease it has denied and thus confront the text's "sad feud" (1.321) of "son against his sire" (1.322). By turning Hyperion toward his outward duty, however, Coelus would avoid Saturn's melancholy, just as Saturn only addresses his adversarial son, Jupiter, through Thea, Oceanus, and Enceladus. Although speaking "from the universal space" (1.307) that also bodies forth Apollo, Coelus remains the disembodied signifier of Reason's masculinist, yet "nervous," desire for release from its internal dis-ease, a patriarchal psychoanalysis that does not work.

By "leav[ing]" (3.3, 7) the Titans behind, book three appears to fulfill this truncated therapy. Here Apollo encounters Mnemosyne who, as Memory, asks him to "Show [his] heart's secret" (3.76) and thus to overcome the Titans' self-forgetting. Reading a "wondrous lesson" (3.112) in her face, he feels both a godlike "Knowledge enormous" (3.113) and "wild commotions" (3.124) as he "Die[s] into life" (3.130). He seems to work through the trauma of lost divinity and thus fully to embody the psychosomatic complexity of an earlier Titanic anthropology. "During [this pain] Mnemosyne," a kind of Delphic psychoanalyst, "upheld / Her arms as one who prophesied" (3.133–34). The gesture is complex, for it suggests a visionary suspension, as well as a transforming contamination, of Apollo's Olympian body. On one hand, Apollo's "commotions" suggest confusion, covered over by the trope of apocalypse, which pretends to remove any need for mediation and thus dismisses Mnemosyne's female presence, whose feminine "confusion" stems from the fact that, as a Titan goddess, she has shifted her allegiance to the Olympians. On the other hand, however, gender productively displaces a detached Olympian "Knowledge enormous" by bodying forth in Apollo a confrontation of Reason with its own signifying economy of gender.

It is thus significant that Apollo says to Mnemosyne, "Thy name is on my tongue I know not how" (3.83). This inability to name Titanic madness is also its resistance to symbolic prescription and thus to the containment of madness by gender. *This* ambivalence suggests within the text's melancholic anatomy a subversive immanence. In Thea's "listening fear," which repeats Saturn's opening stance of "bowed head . . . listening to the earth, / His ancient mother, for some comfort yet" (1.20–21), resides a semiotic potentiality related to the mother's body, although not grounded in it (significantly, "Terra" remains *un*named in the text). Replayed more consciously in Thea's anxious readiness, this potentiality signifies a pre-Titanic "infant world" (1.26), elsewhere referred to as the "murmurs" of "[Oceanus'] first-endeavouring tongue" (2.171). These "mourning words" (1.49) translate the text's "feeble tongue / . . . like accents . . . frail / To that large utterance of the early Gods" (1.49–51) and thus signal both the negativity and potentiality of the text's melancholy. An apotheosis of this melancholy is played out in Clymene's transmutation of Saturn's grief. She "took a mouthed shell / And murmured into it, and made" (2.270–71) a "new blissful golden melody" (2.280) that eventually anatomizes the "morning-bright Apollo" (2.294). The trope of apocalypse again suppresses differences within an economy of vision. Yet this new "new" vision is productively melancholic without suppressing melancholy's ambivalence—"each gush of sounds" was a "living death" (2.281). Melancholy registers the text's flawed interiority, the constitution of the text's identity only through its endless iteration. This ghost in the machine of the text's cultural reproduction, however, also offers the possibility of alternatively authentic, albeit suffering, voices.

Another factor signifies here, however. While Mnemosyne is a therapeutic witness to the patriarchy's confrontation with its own gendered Other, she also merely reflects back to the patriarchy its own inner dis-ease. That is, Apollo's "commotions" also demonstrate how Saturn's contagion might be passed on to his son, for the male Titans, like Mnemosyne herself, are equally capable of shifting identities and allegiances. That one cannot tell from whom the contagion comes in the encounter between Apollo and Mnemosyne, then, also suggests the symptom of a patriarchal nervous disorder that Apollo, by recontaminating the feminine, would expel. Thus, Apollo, like Saturn, remains outside the transpositional economy of melancholy so that the text's desire for psychoanalysis, like that of *Endymion*, seems again oddly suspended. Judith Little argues that *Hyperion* is a "poem of contemplation, not of action," a text "working itself into a statement of evolutionary development"[46] between the Titans and the Olympians, but never getting there. The success

of Olympic contemplation, signified in the arrival of Apollo as a successful mourning of (and "morning after") Titanic melancholy, is
perpetually delayed by Titanic self-observation. The "listening fear"
(1.37) of Thea's "regard" is the analytical register of the poem's
"aching time" (1.64) (like that of Diana, "full of ache," yet more
fully anthropomorphized). This register suggests within the text's
monumental form the "unsecure" (1.168) anatomy of Saturn's,
Hyperion's, and Apollo's melancholy: Hyperion compares his own
fallen state to Saturn's, his "eternal essence thus distraught"
(1.232), and "melancholy numbs [Apollo's] limbs" (3.89). Hence,
the text begins as the monologic exegesis of Saturn's fall. Like Diana
as the pathology of myth, however, the text repeats this fall serially
within the Greek pantheon, raising the specter of patriarchal immortality, and thus of the *cogito* of epic, as a multiple personality
without cure unfolding interminably against the grain of the text's
epic desire.

IV

As shifting metaphorical selves, Saturn, Hyperion, and Apollo
form a paradigmatic narrative axis that arranges them according to
a teleology of desire rather than history. Within this teleology Saturn
is the discarded rem(a)inder of Apollo already disrupting his emergent identity. Similarly, those who precede Mnemosyne are re-
m(a)inders of a prior analytical identity infected by Saturn/Hyperi-
on's melancholy as "King" (1.52; 2.184), "god" (2.110), and
"father" (2.252). Apollo's dying into life thus seems to manifest definitively the text's latent psychoanalytic subjectivity.[47] As if not
knowing what to do with psychoanalysis, however, the text fragments
itself in a moment of trauma: "Apollo shrieked—and lo! from all his
limbs / Celestial" (3.135–36). Confronting this trauma as an inability to re-member the original text as its own identity, *The Fall of Hyperion* turns to psychoanalyze *Hyperion*'s abandoned identity. *The Fall*
thus interrogates the first text's ambivalent attempt to discipline unreason within the "egotistical sublime" of poetry's properly masculine self and thus to make poetry submit to the essentialism of gender. Moreover, cast as a dream vision, *The Fall of Hyperion* enacts the
phantasmatic structure of gender and thus performs the earlier
texts' wandering psychoanalysis as the constitutive instability of the
cultural reproduction of identity. *Endymion* and *Hyperion*, that is, attempt to prescribe a metaphysics of psychoanalysis. As metaphysics,
this process depends on the reproduction of an array of gendered

figures who also reproduce the nervous contagion of melancholy as the inability of this metaphysics to accept its own psychoanalysis. *The Fall*, however, focuses on the singular confrontation between the narrator (presumed to be masculine) and Moneta and so stages definitively within the text of Romantic gender, albeit in a radically ambivalent form, its scene of psychoanalysis.

The text's opening separates poets, those who can "tell" their dreams, from fanatics, who succumb to the dream's "dumb enchantment" (1.11). Where poetry speaks the dream's unreason, fanaticism is the symptom of its suppression by "weav[ing] / A paradise for a sect" (1.1–2) and thus perpetuating the visionary tradition's false consciousness. Whether the "dream now purposed to rehearse" (1.16) be that of poet or fanatic, the narrator says, can only be decided at the text's margins—"When this warm scribe, my hand, is in the grave" (1.18). As rehearsal rather than performance, then, this dream signifies the most indeterminate staging of identity through which the poet subverts the cultural prescription of his own identity as a model for his future readers: "Who alive can say, / 'Thou art no Poet—may'st not tell thy dreams?' " (1.11–12). By dreaming *Hyperion* as its primal scene, *The Fall* refigures the earlier text's anatomy of melancholy as part of a repetition of the past which both confirms and resists the trauma of the cultural reproduction of identity. The Titans are repeatedly drawn back to the future of an indeterminate identity to which they remain blind; as if to comprehend this indeterminacy, *The Fall* moves forward through the telling of its dream by moving archaeologically back to its own textual past, where it encounters the original *Hyperion* at 1.294 as the rem(a)inder of its unconscious.

Like *Endymion*, *The Fall* unfolds as a palimpsest of dreams and trances, as if to stage each movement through history according to its phantasmatic structure, yet so to challenge the narrator to read this structure. Within the text's larger dream, the narrator recounts his first trance as an encounter with *Paradise Lost*, the "refuse of a meal / By angel tasted, or our Mother Eve" (1.30–31). Here the text revisits a kind of primal forgetting of the feminine which then becomes the "domineering potion" (1.54) as "parent of [his present] theme" (1.46) so that the feminine's influence is both traumatically debilitating and genealogically productive. The narrator then awakens into a further dream that signifies this original trauma as the depths of an "old sanctuary" (1.61–62). That he "could not know" (1.34) what any of these "remnants" (1.33) now signify, marks in the text's present semiosis an irreparable epistemological rupture beyond which the narrator must surrender himself to the phantasy of Reason. This struggle beyond the "habitual self," as Moneta says, means "What 'tis to die and live again before / Thy fated hour" (1.141–42). Toril Moi argues that Kristeva's semiotic, because it "can never take over the symbolic," works by "*expulsion* and *rejection*," a "*negativity* masking the death-drive" yet "analysable as a series of ruptures, absences and breaks in the symbolic language."[48] The "parenting" of the poet's identity from "refuse," then, is constituted by the text's expression of its own negativity rather than as the expression of an essential identity which, as the text suggests, can only exist by a specular identification with the past. In this respect *The Fall* reads the earlier texts' encounter with the pathology of the Greek pantheon as the trauma of identity figured in yet also radically facilitated by a forgetting of the feminine.

As Cathy Caruth argues, what is traumatic about trauma, and thus about any historical experience, is not the trauma itself, the fact that it cannot be known, or the fact that it induces a traumatic forgetting, but that it cannot be taken in at one go: "pathology consists . . . solely in the *structure of its experience* or reception: the event is not assimilated or experienced fully at the time, but only belatedly, in its repeated *possession* of the one who experiences it."[49] By staging the cultural reproduction of its past traumatically, *The Fall* suggests in the masculine remembering of poetry its overwhelming confrontation with the feminine, although the poem does not presume to read its gender essentially, that is to say outside of the prescriptive terms of its own culture. The devastated landscape of *The Fall* as a "mingled heap" of "confused" (1.76) "imageries" (1.75) is a partial recovery of *Hyperion* and of a larger poetic tradition centered in Milton, both of which have been jettisoned into a cultural past whose traces the present text would read potentially as "hieroglyphics old" (1.277). However, the luxury of this primal scene of poetry, despite its "confusion," suggests a profusive Victorian commodification or staging of poetry's domestic space. Bewell suggests that Keats's poetry "arises from an urban middle-class context" that "very much belongs to an incipient Victorian culture."[50] And so the scene of *The Fall* is the "Chamber of Maiden-Thought" in Keats's Victorian "Mansion" of the mind gendered by the ideology of the "separate spheres"—yet in traumatic disarray. This is Wordsworth's gothic church turned Victorian living room in Wordsworth's "home at Grasmere," yet *anti*-domesticated by the "sepulchral recesses" of Margaret/Dorothy's madness it would hide in the profusive details of its interior.

As the narrator approaches the altar of "An Image, huge of feature as a cloud" (1.88), a voice challenges him with the "Prodigious" (1.121) burden of finding his identity in the midst of this trauma: " 'If thou canst not ascend / These steps, die on that marble where thou art" (1.107–8). The narrator undergoes a deathlike catharsis or "a palsied chill" (1.122) that "[puts] cold grasp" (1.124) on his ability to speak, as if to signify the killing effect of Reason. Like Apollo dying into life, he "shrieked" (1.125) and, "[striving] hard to escape / The numbness" (1.127–28), regains his sense(s), as if at least to read beyond *Hyperion*'s fragmentation in the textual unconscious and thus into its suspended economy of melancholy. In a type of *Matrix*-like gesture, the poet now finds himself on the far side of poetic tradition, as if within the "other" consciousness buttressing its phantasmatic façade. Here, the voice takes up the text's opening interrogation of identity: " 'Art thou not of the dreamer tribe?' " (1.198). The "dreamer" (1.200) "vexes" (1.202) the world, whereas the poet "pours out a balm upon" (1.201) it. Left to choose between them, the narrator in turn asks Moneta to interpret the landscape around him: " 'What Image this whose face I cannot see / . . . and who thou art?' " (1.214–15). The poet's encounter with Moneta models dialogue, not between two full-fledged subjects, but as the circulation of subjectivities which manifests the *possibility* of a (dis)embodied subject. Just as Saturn, Hyperion, and Apollo are versions of *Hyperion*'s emerging analysand, so Thea, Mnemosyne, and Moneta comprise an intertextual composite of the Keatsian analyst. Infected by the Titans' melancholy in *Hyperion*, Thea and Mnemosyne are now figured within Moneta's retelling of Saturn's fate, as if superseded by her ability to know the narrator's psychic history.

As it registers this history's radical temporality, however, Moneta's face is "Not pined by human sorrows, but bright-blanched / By an immortal sickness which kills not; / It works a constant change" (1.257–59) that is "deathwards progressing / To no death" (1.260–61). Tied to the previous text's melancholy, but now conscious of its effects, Moneta carries the pathology of gender as it infects the masculine visionary apparatus of poetry itself. She is the dis-ease of the text's psyche as the sickness of its immortality, figured in her fatal attachment to the mythology of Saturn's world. Hence her "power" (1.243), although "Holy" (1.136), is a "curse" (1.243). She is "Sole Priestess of [his] desolation" (1.227), the "pale Omega of a withered race" (1.288) of Titans who also signify the end of Miltonic authority. Moneta signifies the curse of Reason, not by its own unreason but by its attempt to reproduce a prescription that would gender unreason as feminine. She is the pathology of gender itself installed at the core of Romantic psychoanalysis as the attempt to occult Margaret's madness.

Moneta would also help the narrator enter into this cultural re-production as a force of transgressive articulation against its hege-monic effects. She notes that her "curse" "Shall be to [him] a won-der" (1.244). In the affect of her eyes (1.270–76) he can read his own emerging subjectivity. These eyes are both "visionless" (1.272) and "benignant" (1.270); they hold a "blank splendour" (1.274) that mirrors/reflects both her own and the narrator's own blank identities as both absence *and* potentiality (a "blank slate"). Through her interpretation of his dream, which he reads as "high tragedy" (1.275) being acted in "the dark secret chambers of her skull" (1.278), he is able to "see as a God sees" (1.304). Different from Apollo's "knowledge enormous," the narrator's ability empha-sizes a suffering imaginative vision rather than an abstract epistemo-logical autonomy. He thus is able to see within the interminable mel-ancholy of her immortality the "electral charging misery" (1.246) of the "scenes / Still swooning vivid through [her] globèd brain" (1.244–45). This semiotic negativity offers a perpetual resistance to the symbolic language poetry—and the poem itself—would use to regulate the poet's identity. Moneta appears mesmerized by these scenes and thus is figured as part of a paralyzed and specular statu-ary (1.382–88) that the previous text has now become in the textual unconscious. The narrator struggles both to resist and to read this unconscious in order to subvert its power. This subversion is provi-sional, for his "lofty theme" (1.306) is a "half-unravelled web" (1.308). He both stages and is staged by the psychic determinism of his "high tragedy," its "eternal quietude" (1.390) and "unchanging gloom" (1.391). He thus pauses at the end of canto 1, to "perhaps no further dare" (1.468) to resist an economy from which he can find no release. Canto 2 proceeds beyond the dream's "antecham-ber" (1.465) to Hyperion's "clear light" (2.49), but fragments "in-between" Saturn and Apollo as if to abandon altogether the false consciousness of Olympian ascendancy. Here the text rehearses its most radical contingency by progressing "deathwards" toward Keats himself and beyond, where gender is reproduced in the ambiva-lence of a time long after his "warm scribe is in the grave."

Where Apollo reads Mnemosyne's "lesson" as if in the "hollow" of his own brain, the poet of *The Fall* reads his identity "enwombèd" (1.277) within Moneta's "hollow brain" (1.278). By finding his inte-riority in the discourse of the Other, he marks gender distinctions as mobile and unstable. He (re)possesses himself through this au-tonomous production of gender as it discloses his selfhood to him, a radical staging of identity that subsumes the poet within its "min-gled heap confused." Alexander Gelley argues that the scene of narrative, like the analytic or primal scene, works by phantasy so that the subject is both witness to her internal drama and projected as a (de-)constituted subject within this scene's dramatic effects.[51] This imaginary theater exists within the outward drama of the subject's symbolic identity as a stage both facilitating and unsettling identity's constitution. In Keats's writings, this "stage" is psychoanalysis as the articulation of gender's "phantasmatic structure" within identity's formation. In *Endymion* the narrator attempts to read this process like "Adam's dream": the subject awakens to the realization of the dream's "essential Beauty" (*LK*, 37) as the truth of the male visionary tradition. Disillusioned of this truth, Endymion says "no more" (4.669) to this type of dreaming.[52] *Hyperion* repeats *Endymion*'s traumatic realization through the finer tone of epic, yet remains disrupted by the "Creations and destroyings" (3.116) of a gendered psychoanalysis so that neither epic nor psychoanalysis offer viable options. Casting this process as dream vision, *The Fall of Hyperion* stages the "abstract masculine epistemological subject" as the trauma of gender. Moneta's dark education of the narrator about his own unreason unsettles the patriarchal authority of the egotistical sublime, figured in the ruins of an epic identity over which she presides. In Moneta's ruined sanctuary, the madness of Margaret in Wordsworth's ruined gothic church, as the ruined cottage or domestic space of gender Wordsworth would avoid, comes home to roost in the body of the male Romantic poet.

Notes

1. Joseph Breuer and Sigmund Freud, *Studies in Hysteria*, ed. and trans. James and Alix Strachey (1974; reprint, London: Pelican Books, 1991), 231.

2. Kathleen Coburn, *Experience into Thought* (Toronto: University of Toronto Press, 1979), 4. Coleridge first used the term in a September 1805 notebook entry. See *The Notebooks of Samuel Taylor Coleridge*, ed. Kathleen Coburn and Merton Christensen, 4 Vols. (New York: Pantheon Books, 1957–1990), 2:2670.

3. Freud's desire for scientific credibility can be discerned in his early grounding in the physiological analyses of neurological disorders; in his early translation of Charcot's *Lectures on the Diseases of the Nervous System*; in his relationship with the physiologist Wilhelm Fleiss, which he protected at all costs for the scientific/medical legitimation it afforded; and in the fact that Freud calls his earliest sustained theoretical account of his research *Project for a Scientific Psychology*.

4. Freud writes of Kant's *Anthropology from a Pragmatic Point of View* (1789): "the dream exists in order to lay bare for us our hidden dispositions and to reveal to us not what we are, but what we might have been if we had a different education." In *The Interpretation of Dreams* (1913), trans. A. A. Brill, 3d ed. (New York: Quality Paperbacks, 1995), 58–59.

5. Freud, *Interpretation of Dreams*, 122.

6. Immanuel Kant, *The Critique of Pure Reason*, trans. Norman Kemp Smith (London: MacMillan, 1992), 669.

7. Ned Lukacher, *Primal Scenes: Literature, Philosophy, Psychoanalysis* (Ithaca, N.Y.: Cornell University Press, 1986), 14.

8. This is the essential point I make elsewhere, and at greater length, in a manuscript entitled Subjects Presumed to Know: The Scene of Romantic Psychoanalysis.

9. Samuel Taylor Coleridge, *Biographia Literaria; or Biographical Sketches of My Literary Life and Opinions*, ed. James Engell and W. Jackson Bate (Princeton, N.J.: Princeton University Press, 1983), 1:111.

10. Judith Butler, *Gender Trouble: Feminism and the Subversion of Identity* (New York: Routledge, 1990), 28.

11. Ibid., 31.

12. Ibid., 141, 30–31.

13. For a reading of the relationship between Romanticism and madness in relation to Derrida's rereading of Foucault's *Madness and Civilization* in "Cogito and the History of Madness," see Ross Woodman, "Shelley's Dizzy Ravine: Poetry and Madness," *Studies in Romanticism* 36 (1997): 307–26.

14. William Wordsworth, "Prospectus to *The Recluse*," in *Poetical Works*, ed. Thomas Hutchinson; rev. ed., Ernest de Selincourt (1936; reprint, Oxford: Oxford University Press, 1988), l. 41.

15. Wordsworth, *Poetical Works*, 589.

16. Samuel Taylor Coleridge, *Christabel*, in *Poetical Works*, ed. Ernest Hartley Coleridge (Oxford: Oxford University Press, 1980), l. 247. A superb psychoanalytical reading of this trauma is Karen Swann, " 'Christabel': The Wandering Mother and the Enigma of Form," *Studies in Romanticism* 23 (1984):533–53.

17. For an account of this negotiation, see my "Analysis Interminable in the Other Wordsworth," *Romanticism on the Net* 15 (November 1999).

18. Julia M. Wright, "Growing Pains": Representing the Romantic in Gaskell's *Wives and Daughters*, in Recollecting Romanticism: Transforming Romantic Writers for a Victorian Audience, ed. Julia M. Wright and Joel Faflak (manuscript under consideration), 115.

19. Ibid., 116. On the relationship between sensibility and canonical Romantic poetry and culture, see Jerome J. McGann, *The Poetics of Sensibility: A Revolution in Poetic Style* (Oxford: Clarendon Press, 1996). On the nervous body of narrative in Romanticism, see Peter Melville Logan, *Nerves and Narrative: A Cultural History of Hysteria in 19th-Century Prose* (Los Angeles: University of California Press, 1997).

20. John Keats, *The Letters of John Keats*, ed. Robert Gittings (Oxford: Oxford University Press, 1977), 157. Hereafter *LK*, cited in the text.

21. On "masculine" Romanticism and the masculine *in* Romanticism, see Anne K. Mellor, *Gender and Romanticism* (London: Routledge, 1993) and Marlon B. Ross, *The Contours of Masculine Desire: Romanticism and the Rise of Women's Poetry* (New York: Oxford University Press, 1989).

22. John Keats, "Ode to a Nightingale," in *The Complete Poems*, ed. John Barnard, 2d ed. (New York: Penguin Books, 1977), ll. 69–70. Hereafter *CP*, cited in the text. All quotations of Keats's poems are cited by book and/or line number; citations from prefaces and appendices refer to page numbers.

23. Alan Bewell, "Keats's 'Realm of Flora,' " in *New Romanticisms: Theory and Critical Practice*, ed. David L. Clark and Donald C. Goellnicht (Toronto: University of Toronto Press, 1994), 92.

24. Ibid., 92. Susan Wolfson writes: "More than any other male Romantic, Keats writes from an intense intersection of creative genius and adolescent uncertainty.

The result is to disrupt any unified syntax of 'masculine.' " In Wolfson, "Keats and the Manhood of the Poet," *European Romantic Review* 6 (Summer 1995):2.

25. Bewell, "Keats's 'Realm of Flora,'"

26. Keats wrote *Endymion* between April and November 1817. He wrote *Hyperion* between September and December 1818 and had abandoned the poem altogether by April 1819. *The Fall of Hyperion* was written between July and September 1819 and, of course, subsequently abandoned. Keats moves quickly beyond Wordsworth. In February 1818 he writes: "are we to be bullied into a certain Philosophy engendered in the whims of an Egotist . . . We hate poetry that has palpable design upon us . . . I will have no more of Wordsworth" (*Letters*, 60–61). Keats does not appear to have shed Milton's influence until September 1819, when he gave up writing *The Fall of Hyperion*: "I have given up Hyperion [for *The Fall*]—there were too many Miltonic inversions in it" (ibid., 292). In another letter he writes: "I have but lately stood on my guard against Milton. Life to him would be death to me" (ibid., 325–26).

27. Wordsworth, *The Prelude* (1805), 13.170.

28. The text's wandering is built into its composition, as if romance becomes lost in the narrative of its own telling. Keats said of the poem, "I must make 4000 Lines of one bare circumstance and fill them with Poetry" (*Letters*, 27), an aesthetic calculus that suggests in each book of almost exactly 1,000 lines a *duration* of talking, like a psychoanalytic session, through which the poet, treating his subject matter almost incidentally, explores his own psyche as the mind of romance.

29. Stuart Sperry, *Keats the Poet* (Princeton, N.J.: Princeton University Press, 1973), argues that the text shifts its allegiance from Pan, "the symbol of a form of *thinking*" (98) that is "inscrutable" and "unimaginable," to Apollo, who symbolizes "prescience and control" (116) so that the unreason of the *anthropos* is overcome by masculine Reason.

30. "What the imagination seizes as Beauty must be truth," Keats writes early in his *Letters* (37), although he was to develop a more ascetic and severe attitude toward the contemplation of beauty.

31. Responding to readings of the text's incoherencies as erotic fantasy, Sperry asks: "is it rather a chain of daydreams and reveries, best interpreted as a psychiatrist interprets the free associations of a patient and useful primarily for what it reveals concerning the quality of Keats's unconscious life?" (*Keats*, 93).

32. Julia Kristeva, *Powers of Horror: An Essay on Abjection*, trans. Leon S. Roudiez (New York: Columbia University Press, 1982), 208. She asserts: "One must keep open the wound where he or she who enters into the analytic adventure is located . . . [It is] a heterogeneous, corporeal, and verbal ordeal of fundamental incompleteness" (27).

33. Butler, *Gender Trouble*, 11.

34. Julia Kristeva, *Revolution in Poetic Language*, trans. Margaret Waller (New York: Columbia University Press, 1984), 25.

35. Ibid., 40, 43.

36. Ibid., 25.

37. See Butler's critique of Kristeva's "body politics" in *Gender Trouble*, 79–93.

38. Keats is looking past *Endymion*, written April–November 1817 and published in May 1818, the idea of which he abandoned even before completing the poem. In September 1817 he writes, "I am tired of it and think the time would be better spent in writing a new Romance" (*Letters*, 25).

39. J. Laplanche and J. B. Pontalis, *The Language of Psycho-Analysis*, trans. Donald Nicholson-Smith (London: Karnac Books, 1988), 486.

40. See Freud's "Mourning and Melancholia," in *The Standard Edition of the Complete Psychological Works of Sigmund Freud*, ed. and trans. James Strachey (London: Hogarth Press, 1953–1974), 14:237–58. Freud suggests that mourning is necessary to the production of a healthy ego, for melancholia, in its most extreme form, can lead to psychosis, the retention of the lost object as if it were alive. In "Keats, Poetry, and the Absence of the Work," *Modern Philology* 95 (1998), Tilottama Rajan argues that the work of melancholy in *The Fall* is part of its "cultural responsiveness" (349), its attempt to signify that which escapes the use-value of history.

41. Julia Kristeva, *Black Sun: Depression and Melancholia*, trans. Leon S. Roudiez (New York: Columbia University Press, 1989), 6, 7.

42. Ibid., 9, 13.

43. Tilottama Rajan, *The Supplement of Reading: Figures of Understanding in Romantic Theory and Practice* (Ithaca, N.Y.: Cornell University Press, 1990), 308. I treat these scenes at greater length in my "Romantic Psychoanalysis: Keats, Identity, and '(The Fall of) Hyperion,' " in *The Lessons of Romanticism: A Critical Companion*, ed. Thomas Pfau and Robert F. Gleckner (Durham, N.C.: Duke University Press, 1998), 304–27.

44. Saturn's inability to confront the Real of his identity, especially as he misses it projected in others, seems almost pathological. Addressing the Titans as a "fallen tribe" (2.100), for instance, he says: "Not in my own sad breast, / Which is its own great judge and searcher-out, / Can I find reason why *ye* should be thus" (2.129–31).

45. Logan, *Nerves and Narrative*, 24.

46. Judith Little, *Keats as a Narrative Poet: A Test of Invention* (Lincoln: University of Nebraska Press, 1975), 140.

47. Many readers, both explicitly and implicitly, adopt the rubric of psychoanalysis and read the poems through the narrative of a loss of (textual) omnipotence, moving from the illusion of narcissism toward a later shattering of this illusion. See Marjorie Levinson, *The Romantic Fragment Poem: A Critique of a Form* (Chapel Hill: University of North Carolina Press, 1986), 107–87; Paul de Man, "Keats: The Negative Road," in *English Romantic Poets*, ed. Harold Bloom (New York: Chelsea, 1986), 343–61; Patricia Parker, "Keats," in *Critical Essays on John Keats*, ed. Hermione de Almeida (Boston: Hall, 1990), 103–28; Barbara Schapiro, *The Romantic Mother: Narcissistic Patterns in Romantic Poetry* (Baltimore, Md.: The Johns Hopkins University Press, 1983), 54–60; and Harold Bloom, *Poetry and Repression: Revisionism from Blake to Stevens* (New York: Yale University Press, 1976), 112–42.

48. Toril Moi, *Sexual/Textual Politics* (New York: Methuen, 1985), 170.

49. Cathy Caruth, "Introduction," *Trauma: Explorations in Memory*, ed. Cathy Caruth (Baltimore, Md.: The Johns Hopkins University Press, 1995), 4.

50. Bewell, "Keats's 'Realm of Flora,' " 73.

51. See Andrew Gelley, *Narrative Crossings: Theory and Pragmatics of Prose Fiction* (Baltimore, Md.: The Johns Hopkins University Press, 1987), 159–68. "Scene" involves the idea of the Lacanian gaze, in which visibility does not coincide with consciousness and the *cogito*, and the Heideggerian notion of *Schein*, or "showing," which is simultaneously revelatory and illusory. See also Tilottama Rajan, *Dark Interpreter: The Discourse of Romanticism* (Ithaca, N.Y.: Cornell University Press, 1980), 97–142.

52. The fuller passage speaks of the "Idea of all our Passions as of Love [as] all in their sublime, creative of essential Beauty" (*Letters*, 37). While the context suggests the redemptive, transcendental power of Beauty, that "Ideas" and "Love" "create" Beauty rather than express its essential being, suggests itself a subversion of essentialism that will play itself out in Keats's later poetry.

Masks of Anarchy:
Shelley's Political Poetics

Marc Redfield
Claremont Graduate University

TO a markedly greater degree than other period terms, the concept of Romanticism has inspired political passions and assertions. These assertions, however, have ranged across the modern Western political spectrum. Depending on the case, the context, and the interpretive desire, Romanticism's exemplary texts and figures become alternately or simultaneously progressive and nostalgic, atheistic and pious, cosmopolitan and nationalist, revolutionary and reactionary. In Germany, as Maurice Blanchot reminds us, Romanticism knew extreme vicissitudes: "at certain times the most retrogressive regimes laid claim to it (in 1840 Friedrich Wilhelm IV, and then the Nazi literary theorists), at others, it was clarified and taken as a renovating necessity."[1] Even as a term of convenience within our fin-de-siècle American scholarly bureaucracy—for which, to all appearances, the protoprofessional attacks on Romanticism by New Humanists and early New Critics during the first third of the twentieth century simply represent yet more archival material to process—even here, Romanticism retains a whiff of this charged ambivalence.[2] Jerome McGann's *The Romantic Ideology* becomes inconceivable if one imagines it retitled and launched at a different slice of literary history. The handwringing much in evidence in recent books and anthologies written or edited by professional Romanticists has no real equivalent in, say, Victorian studies, where even the most politicized cultural critics seem able to go about their business without worrying that the regal name of their professional field might be a synonym for "ideology." Nor, conversely, do other scholarly fields appear capable of inspiring the kind of passionate advocacy that now and then crops up within academic Romanticism.[3] Romanticism remains a fundamentally ambiguous event in which we seem fated to participate as political and ethical beings.

If Romanticism "is" ideology, as McGann's peculiarly definite article suggests, this is because Romanticism is being understood as another name for aesthetics.[4] Romantic ideology is aesthetic ideology, which is to say ideology in its most exemplary form, as the illicit, and politically consequent, universalization of a particular. In aesthetics, the universal is the human, and the particular is the acculturated subject or the artist or the artwork. By judging subjectively but disinterestedly, the subject obtains a moment of contact with its own essential humanness, while the artist and the artwork speak to all peoples and ages because, transcending their particularity in and through their sensuous immediacy, they represent humanity itself. This idealizing humanism is ideology as aesthetics as Romanticism: the tautologies seem airtight. Yet it seems that Romanticism is inevitably also the *critique* of aesthetic ideology. "Romantic imagination emerges with the birth of an historical sense," McGann observes, to which the historicizing critic is indebted for his existence: "The grand illusion of Romantic *ideology* is that one may escape such a [selfish and unreflecting] world through imagination and poetry. The great truth of Romantic *work* is that there is no escape, that there is only revelation (in a wholly secular sense)."[5] Here, as elsewhere, Romanticism names the source of the values to which the critic appeals, even as he sets out to critique the error from which they spring. There seems no easy exit from Romanticism—particularly, it must be added, if one understands one's project, as McGann does, as that of "return[ing] poetry to a human form": a more Romantic-aesthetic ambition would be hard to conceive.[6] The error generates the critique, but the critique turns out to be hard to tell apart from the error.

Shelley is an interesting figure to examine in this context, not just because his reception has known exemplary extremes—from the varieties of "red Shelley" championed by Spencean socialists, Chartists, and subsequent working-class and socialist movements, to the hyperaestheticized, otherworldly naif of late-nineteenth and early twentieth-century literary scholarship and criticism—but because his work so consistently links aesthetic practice to political struggle and thematizes the complexity as well as the necessity of genuine renovation. His sustained attention to these questions presses us toward the difficulty that composes one of Romanticism's major legacies: how to think the political force of literary texts. The political content of Shelley's writing has proved capable of inspiring wildly different assessments;[7] and this volatility is partly a consequence of the rigor with which his most openly political texts engage the politics of aesthetics as the problem of ideology. Pursuing with unflinching determination the paradox that a critique of aesthetics must risk repeating the error it critiques, Shelley discovers in radical uncertainty the condition of possibility for genuine political engagement. Precisely to the extent that he *fails* to "return poetry to a human form," he opens a space for affirmative action and thought. "[T]he critical redemption value of Shelley's poetry," Forest Pyle proposes, "resides not in its reference to the present or the empirical but in its blank opening onto futurity."[8] That orientation toward futurity represents the temporal dimension of uninsurable risk; and in that risk, Shelley, I suggest, locates poetry's political force and what we may with some caution term aesthetic ideology's political unconsious. My main display texts will be *The Mask of Anarchy* and *The Cenci*; and as is perhaps obvious, I shall be working my way toward a somewhat counterintuitive defense of Shelley's famous, and to some infamous, claim that poets are the world's unacknowledged legislators.

I

"[T]he greatest poem of political protest ever written in English" according to one enthusiastic and knowledgeable reader, *The Mask of Anarchy: Written on the Occasion of the Massacre at Manchester* belongs to a group of poems from the 1819–20 period that Shelley hoped would have immediate political effect, and which at one point he proposed to collect and publish as "a little volume of popular songs *wholly political,* & destined to awaken & direct the imagination of the reformers," as he wrote to Leigh Hunt.[9] Unlike *Prometheus Unbound,* which was intended to "familiarize the highly refined imagination of the more select class of poetical readers with beautiful idealisms of moral excellence," *The Mask* was aimed at a wide readership; furthermore, insofar as it responded to a specific event, the Peterloo atrocity, it assumed some of the excitements and burdens of moving and persuading a specific audience.[10] It did not reach its intended readers. Hunt was unable to publish the poem in 1819 for fear of prosecution; but thirteen years later, when both Peterloo and Shelley had receded into history and the political climate had thawed sufficiently, Hunt published a slightly bowdlerized version, at which point the poem became a Chartist and socialist classic. Shelley thus in fact did reach a wide audience, but not the one implied by the poem's rhetorical occasion. His text knew a certain political impact, though not one he could have predicted.

These facts provide an initial springboard for Susan Wolfson's severe and intelligent scrutiny of *The Mask of Anarchy* in her recent *Formal Charges* (1997): a study that will help speed us on our way toward the problem of aesthetic critique if only because its argument is at times almost diametrically opposable to mine. Wolfson writes as the latest representative of a politically diverse line of Shelley interpreters, from Raymond Williams on the left to Donald Reiman on the right, who are united by degrees of sympathetic skepticism about their poet's political pretensions. Her skepticism goes hand in hand with the traditional contrast she draws between visionary poetry, dreaminess, wishfulness, and aestheticism, on the one hand, and practical politics on the other. Typically in such scenarios, the latter is deemed good, and the former, bad—indeed, because Wolfson understands political poetry as a species of oratory, she finds the text's very boldness a liability: "the bolder aspects of this performance are exactly what rendered it unpublishable—and unable to affect the struggle it addresses."[11] Thus *The Mask* turns out to be "weirdly kin to the elitist visionary poem of the same period with which it is sometimes contrasted, *Prometheus Unbound*" (*FC*, 196). In this account *The Mask of Anarchy* rapidly becomes "an aesthetic processing of politics," an ideological gesture that Wolfson associates with "poetic self-absorption" (*FC*, 195).

These judgments are enriched by Wolfson's sustained attention to formal elements. The poem's unpublishability, she argues, "is troped by the poem itself: the news 'from over the Sea' reaches its poet in a dream state from which he is never seen to awaken" (*FC*, 196). She refers here to the fact that *The Mask* begins with a frame narrative to which it never returns:

> As I lay asleep in Italy
> There came a voice from over the Sea,
> And with great power it forth led me
> To walk in the visions of Poesy.
>
> I met Murder on the way—
> He had a mask like Castlereagh—
>
> (Ll. 1–6)

This narrator flags his own presence in the scene once more, as a reader, when Anarchy appears ("On his brow this mark I saw"); otherwise he is merely an implied spectator, relaying a drama in which he has no real part. That drama—we may take a moment here for plot summary—begins as the grisly antimasque of Murder, Fraud, Hypocrisy (as Castlereagh, Eldon, Sidmouth), and other minions of Anarchy, who pass over "English land" trampling the "adoring multitude" to "a mire of blood" (ll. 39–41). This triumph is crossed by "a manic maid" whose "name was Hope, she said: / But she looked more like Despair" (ll. 86–88). The maid claiming to be Hope lies down before the horses' feet, expecting to be trampled, when "between her and her foes / A mist, a light, an image rose" (ll. 102–3). This phenomenon becomes "a Shape arrayed in mail / Brighter than the Viper's scale" (ll. 110–11), and its motion contrasts with and undoes Anarchy's masque:

> With step as soft as wind it past
> O'er the heads of men—so fast
> That they knew the presence there,
> And looked,—but all was empty air.
>
> (Ll. 118–21)

"Thoughts" spring up "where'er that step did fall," and the oppressor falls—or, more precisely, is discovered to be already fallen:

> And the prostrate multitude
> Looked—and ankle-deep in blood,
> Hope that maiden most serene
> Was walking with a quiet mien:
>
> And Anarchy, the ghastly birth
> Lay dead earth upon the earth
> The Horse of Death tameless as wind
> Fled, and with his hoofs did grind
> To dust, the murderers thronged behind.
>
> A rushing light of clouds and splendour,
> A sense awakening and yet tender
> Was heard and felt—and at its close
> These words of joy and fear arose
>
> As if their Own indignant Earth
> Which gave the sons of England birth
> Had felt their blood upon her brow,
> And shuddering with a mother's throe
>
> Had turned every drop of blood
> By which her face had been bedewed
> To an accent unwithstood,—
> As if her heart had cried aloud:
>
> (Ll. 126–46)

And there follows, encased in quotation marks, an address to "Men of England," spoken by this internal orator. One and a half times longer than the drama that preceded it, this address offers an analysis of political repression and a program of political action that in subsequent months Shelley was to elaborate as *A Philosophical View of Reform*. Like that text, the "Men of England" speech has seemed to many twentieth-century readers a blend of revolutionary, reformist, and even at times agrarian-reactionary advice: the speech's most famous stanza, the twice-repeated refrain "Rise like Lions after slumber . . . / Ye are many, they are few," seems a call to revolutionary action; yet the Men of England are also told to "Let the Laws of your own land, / Good or ill, between ye stand . . . The old laws of England—they / Whose reverend heads with age are grey" (327–28, 331–32), and to avoid retaliatory violence at all costs:

> "And if then the tyrants dare
> Let them ride among you there,
> Slash, and stab, and maim, and hew,—
> What they like, that let them do.
>
> (Ll. 340–43)

The theory being that the tyrants' rage will die away and become shame: "Every woman in the land" will mock them; "the bold true warriors / Who have hugged Danger in wars" will desert them, and the orator's words will then obtain volcanic national force:

> "And that slaughter to the Nation
> Shall steam up like inspiration,
> Eloquent, oracular;
> A volcano heard afar.
>
> "And these words shall then become
> Like oppression's thundered doom
> Ringing through each heart and brain,
> Heard again—again—again—
>
> "Rise like lions after slumber
> In unvanquishable number—
> Shake your chains to earth like dew
> Which in sleep had fallen on you—
> Ye are many—they are few."
>
> (Ll. 360–72)

Thus the poem ends, far distant from the sleeper in Italy; as Wolfson notes, one draft of the poem even lacks closing quotation marks—as though the internal orator's speech had burst its frame to become the poem itself.[12]

The question is what to make of this and other formal complexities or oddities. Wolfson, as we have seen, understands "the suppression of the poem's opening frame" as the mark of a wishful "aesthetic ideology": "If the frame were to return, it would cast the oration as an unreal event—a wish and a dream, a fantasy wrought by visions of Poesy—at the very moment that Shelley wants to insist on its political potency" (*FC*, 204). Aesthetic ideology, here, functions as a synonym for personal and vocational narcissism ("poetic self-absorption"; "aesthetic self-satisfaction" [*FC*, 195, 196]), a narcissism that Wolfson associates with Shelley's substitution of "visionary poetry" for "an analysis of how material change might be realized in the historical moment of 1819" (*FC*, 202). She also suggests that Shelley's program of nonviolent resistance replays the political ambivalence that can be read into his poem's blend of activism and dreaminess, since "passivity . . . can serve the interests of tyranny." The poem's ambiguities thus ultimately compose a nervous reaction to the threat of popular revolution: "What the poem's contradictions contain, in both senses, is a specter of anarchy—not in the Crown, but in the Men of England" (*FC*, 202). When the Chartist and post-Chartist socialists took up this poem, Wolfson implies, they seized on its activist language ("Rise like lions") and filtered out its poetic and political complications. The poem's literary density, according to this account, *is* its ideological vacillation—its bourgeois timidity, its escapism, its Shelleyan dreaminess, narcissism, and impracticality.

Those are not quite Wolfson's terms, but such are the implications of her impressively alert and knowledgeable reading: Shelley, as so often before, is being called to account, this time by a reader ambitious enough to target the politics of literariness itself. And though one would have difficulty quarreling with many of her observations—who can doubt that Shelley indulged himself a little, imagining this address to the Nation?—Wolfson's large claims push one toward large questions: what, for instance, is being taken for granted (politically and otherwise) by a pragmatism that can assimilate a poem's very radicalism (and thus, under the circumstances, its unpublishability) to aestheticism and self-indulgence? Why, for that matter, should self-indulgence weigh so heavily in the ethico-political balance? And why should the political test of Shelley's poem be its viability as a public utterance in 1819, rather than, say, 1832? Wolfson answers that last question more or less directly. Political poetry, in her view, is oratory: it is poetry that does what it intends, realizing within an immediate social field the presence-to-self of an intention. Voice, not writing, composes its essence. Wolfson elabo-

rates this claim by way of a subtle reading of a brace of stanzas from
The Mask's "Men of England" speech:

> "Let a vast assembly be,
> And with great solemnity
> Declare with measured words that ye
> Are, as God has made ye, free—
>
> "Be your strong and simple words
> Keen to wound as sharpened swords,
> And wide as targes let them be
> With their shade to cover ye.
>
> (Ll. 295–302)

"Measured words," as Wolfson comments, suggests not just a speech
act but a poetic act: here "Shelley asserts the authority of poetry in
this fantasy of political performance"; yet she goes on to observe
that his text undermines the fantasy:

> *words* are not just likened to and rhymed with *swords*, but are literally
> infused into them: *swords*. This semantic wit, however, is also the event
> that exposes the poetic self-service of Shelley's fantasy. For both the
> rhyme and the graphemic pun of *words/swords* are forms that register
> only in writing and reading rather than in speech and listening, where
> the rhyme is off at best, or inaudible. The poetic forms that make Shel-
> ley's political point do not translate into oration, and other aspects of
> his verse even contribute to the obstruction: the rhymes that really
> chime are the ones initiated by *assembly be*—the icon of political action
> as static aesthetic spectacle. (*FC*, 200)

Wolfson's dissatisfaction with the text resolves again and again into
the same register: as political poetry *The Mask* is a "posthumous
voice" (*FC*, 195); its poetic politics are "inaudible" effects of "writing and reading" (*FC*, 200). This posthumous, inaudible dimension
of writing is then aligned with self-enclosure: with the "poetic self-
absorption" (*FC*, 195) of a "self-addressed" poem (*FC*, 196) that, as
in the quotation above, exposes "the poetic self-service of Shelley's
fantasy."

Yet surely the posthumous reach of a text and the inaudible effects of writing and reading point less toward self-enclosure or self-
mirroring than toward a certain loss or scattering of the self—what
Wolfson herself calls "the dispersal of authority when writing becomes reading" (*FC*, 194). A narcissistic poetics would need to ward
off such effects of writing and the signifier—and one way of doing
that is by aestheticizing these effects: by seeking, that is, to transform

nonphenomenal differences into sensuous and spectacular tokens of selfhood. My thesis here is that Shelley's texts consistently associate such aestheticization with political violence and that they accept a certain complicity with that violence even as they labor to unmask it. *The Mask of Anarchy* unquestionably stages an aesthetic fantasy: that of the nation as an assembled body, gathered into the presence and presence-to-self of an orator.[13] This fantasy arguably composes the primal scene of aesthetic nationalism, and Wolfson's fine close reading of the *words/swords* stanza suggests not the aestheticism of Shelley's poem but its resistance to aesthetic ideology. Or rather, it suggests—as the history of Shelley's reception amply demonstrates—that a critique of aesthetic ideology will always have to risk a certain "aestheticism." Self-indulgence is no doubt legible at such moments, to the extent that the poet indulges the fantasy he critiques. But it is precisely because the critique outstrips the category of selfhood that it is a *political* critique.

Wolfson has by no means overstated *The Mask of Anarchy*'s formal complexities. Indeed, if anything she has understated them: the text is far more slippery than any reader has yet acknowledged. It complicates its aesthetic-rhetorical occasion beyond all expectation, first and foremost by radically destabilizing the status of the self. Who speaks in this poem? The sleeper in Italy dreams, and never awakes; within the dream a voice emerges to address the nation's citizenry. The more closely one attends to the poem the more difficult it becomes to say who or what this voice is. Critics often name the internal orator Liberty or Britannia—thus, as it were, extending the masque through the entirety of *The Mask*—but all Shelley actually gives us is the twice-repeated qualifier "as if": it is *as if* the indignant Earth had felt the blood of the sons of England on her brow and, in an act of reverse transubstantiation, had turned that blood into language ("an accent unwithstood"); it is *as if* her heart had cried aloud.[14] Wolfson notes the insistence of the "as if" and hears in it an echo of the poem's opening "As I lay asleep"; the effect, she suggests, is to "restrain the political agency of the oratory to a dream" (*FC*, 198). Perhaps; but what then is dreaming and who is doing it? What is the provenance of "these words of joy and fear" that arise from a subject unnameable except through analogy or simile? Why does the poem tease us toward allegory, making it easy for generations of critics to write of "Liberty" 's oration in *The Mask*, and yet refuse, strictly speaking, to allow us to say that a "speaker" speaks, or even that a "voice" gives voice? For though at the beginning of the poem "a voice from over the Sea" calls the sleeping I into Poesy, at the point where the poem turns into internal oration, "words" simply "arise." When we personify these words as an orator we both repeat and efface the poem's "as if": we give voice to a text that, as "these words," is, reflexively and a little blankly, the poem itself. We thereby produce more allegory: allegory that the poem has already provided under the aegis of dream—a dream in which an "I" wanders to the point of losing itself on allegory's road.

Not only does the oration have no certain orator; it also closes with peculiarly excessive self-reflexivity, such that the poem itself threatens to become a machine, even a broken record:

> "And these words shall then become
> Like oppression's thundered doom
> Ringing through each heart and brain,
> Heard again—again—again—
>
> (Ll. 364–67)

The tyrants slash and stab, fall into shame, are mocked on the street and deserted by the militias; the slaughter "steam[s] up like inspiration" to the Nation, "eloquent, oracular" (ll. 361–62)—and the result is not utopia, or even the reforming of Parliament, but rather the production of "these words." Eloquent, oracular words, perhaps, but, as Wolfson would rightly point out, just words and more words, "Heard again—again—again." Precisely where the rhetoric is most stirring, the text hollows itself out most thoroughly, and insists most oddly on its resemblance to what Steven Goldsmith rightly calls the "stifling repetition" of Anarchy's self-promotion ("I AM GOD, AND KING, AND LAW!") in the poem's opening section.[15] Its political theater culminates in a dramatization of the production of the poem—again and again: the refrain "Rise like lions" closes the poem as a figure for the text's endless repetition of itself.

If, therefore, we cast our eyes back over the poem and try to summarize its narrative self-representations, we discover a reiterated, excessive self-reflexivity. On the one hand, the masque—the allegorical triumph and fall of Anarchy of the first thirty-six stanzas—reveals itself to be mere theater; after Anarchy's death we obtain not utopia but an oration. Anarchy's fall is a fiction, a dream, a shadow of futurity: the real political work, as described by the clarion-toned but indeterminate voice that speaks the second part of the poem, lies ahead, beyond and outside the poem, in the extratextual futurity of political struggle. On the other hand, the oration that springs out of the masque and confirms the masque's fictionality is an oration grounded not in voice but in a figure of voice ("as if") that repeatedly effaces its spokenness as the repetition of "these words"

("again—again—again"). The referent of "these words" being un-
decidably and equally the ringing refrain, the stanza that announces
the refrain's repetition, the internal oration, the masque dreamed
by the dreamer, and finally the entire poem, the text returns us to
the mystery of its production as text. If the masque produced nothing but an oration, the oration produces nothing but itself—and the
poem as a whole, which is to say the masque, which is to say the oration. *The Mask* is a dream that generates and destroys its dreamer
both as a character and as a source of authority; it collapses into the
stutter of "these words"—these words on the page that, as professional academics, we read again, again, again.

Though always misreadable as aestheticism, this hyperreflexivity
in fact destroys the self, both as a thematic element within the text
and as a metaphor for the text itself. Offering us nothing more than
the blank fact of its own material occurrence, the text collapses reflexivity into the mechanical iteration of an inscription. At the same
time, it draws attention to the inevitability with which we project
meanings onto inscriptions and give voice to written signs. Voice,
therefore, becomes inseparable from rhetorical personification. *The
Mask* stages a drama of personification: as we have seen, critics inevitably ascribe a voice, and thus an identity and a gender, to "these
words"; and the poem renders that gesture simultaneously necessary and fictional. In this poem, personification is exemplified as allegory. A recent commentator notes that in *The Mask*, "the irony is
that the reality is abstract evil; its appearance merely takes the form
of persons":[16] Murder wears Castlereagh as a mask. Once again,
however, the poem inscribes a difference it encourages us to efface:
Murder's mask is *like* Castlereagh; Fraud has on, *like* Eldon, an er-
mined gown; Hypocrisy is "clothed with the Bible" *like* Sidmouth.[17]
There is never any doubt about the political bite of these "as ifs":
the poem's topical satire is not in the least tempered by them. They
efface themselves before the proper names of the entities they invoke. The masque thus performs felicitously by masking itself: when
we imagine Murder to be incarnate or grounded in Castlereagh, we
make a mask into a person, and fall into the naiveté of taking a mask
for a face, literalizing a prosopopeia: thinking that we have reached
a political or historical referent, we in fact fall into ideology. The
error—the effacement of the "as if"—is necessary and so is the consequent instability of all acts of personification: a lesson Shelley emphasizes by passing from historical masks (Castlereagh) to allegorical
masks (Anarchy, Hope) as the masque develops. The progression
underscores what personification forgets, which is allegory itself: the
figural mode in which sign and meaning remain visibly different.

Like Giotto's Charity in *Du côté de chez Swann,* whose "energetic and vulgar face" shows no trace of the virtue she signifies, and who depends upon the inscription "Caritas" for her legibility, allegorical figures in *The Mask of Anarchy* are arbitrary signs, the meanings of which cannot be intuited; they require supplemental labels.[18] Hope has to gloss her own meaning ("And her name was Hope, *she said*"), because she looks like Despair. The potential for error and deceit in this signifying structure is realized in the figure of Anarchy, the epicenter of the masque:

> He was pale, even to the lips,
> Like Death in the Apocalypse.
>
> And he wore a kingly crown;
> And in his grasp a sceptre shone;
> On his brow this mark I saw—
> "I AM GOD, AND KING, AND LAW!"
>
> (Ll. 32–37)

Anarchy's is a double mask: he mimes allegorical representations of Death (and once again a difference composes this identity: he is pale *like* Death), and he supplements that mask with a "mark" that distills into a list of Shelley's favored targets the lie of ideology itself. To claim to be God, King, and Law is to claim to ground signification in an absolute personification. Anarchy, personified, styles himself the Arche, though only thanks to a label that enacts the difference it denies. Anarchy, in capitals, masks anarchy—masks, that is, the materiality of an uninsurable inscription. Such is the main thrust of Shelley's poem and the reason why it takes the form of a masque in the first place.[19]

The aestheticization of signs thus, within the poem, composes the possibility both of Anarchy's reign and of the poem that dethrones Anarchy. Furthermore, this aestheticization enables the satire—the identification of Murder and Castlereagh, Anarchy and King George—that made the poem unpublishable in 1819 and politically effective in the 1830s. An essential, inescapable ambiguity thus marks the critique. *The Mask* registers this ambiguity in its narrative. Anarchy's horse first tramples the adoring multitude "to a mire of blood" (ll. 40–41) and then, riderless, grinds the murderers to dust (ll. 133–34); the two acts of trampling have wetter or drier results, but are deliberately symmetrical. After Anarchy's overthrow, Hope walks ankle-deep in blood (l. 127)—presumably the blood left over from the first trampling; yet can we be sure that the second didn't spill any? The Shape, it is true, bears only defensive war gear, a helm and coat of mail, yet light rains through the helm's plumes like "crimson dew" (l. 117). Besides being blood-colored, this dew recalls the "dew / Which in sleep had fallen on you" (ll. 53–54) of the reveille—the objective correlative of oppression's sleep, a sleep that in turn recalls the slumber of the poet-narrator in Italy. Political poetry, here, holds out the possibility that it repeats what it condemns: tyrants flee "like a dream's dim imagery" (l. 212) within a dream that to some extent recycles tyrannical imagery. If the poem's endlessly repeated "words" ring "like oppression's thundered doom" (l. 365), the ambiguously objective and subjective genitive (the words ring like the death knell of oppression; the words ring like the sort of doom that oppression is in the habit of thundering) forms no accidental pun: throughout the poem, oppression's overthrow teasingly reiterates oppression's terms and figures. Shelley's attitude toward revolutionary violence can be and often has been read as ambivalent; but his wavering between revolutionary and reform politics, or between an ideal of passive resistance and a pragmatic acceptance of violence, arguably responds to a fundamental ambiguity scripted in the text's figurative language.[20] The poem itself is a mask as well as an unmasking of anarchy. Yet in this ambiguity resides its political force. We may call this ambiguity the text's "political unconscious," so long as we understand that unconscious not as Fredric Jameson's "uninterrupted narrative" or "single great collective story," but rather as something more like interruption itself—an endless interruption, figured in *The Mask of Anarchy* as the mechanical, iterative ringing of the dreamtext's words.[21] Making legible this pulse of death and dispersal within its politico-aesthetic dream, the poem comments on, and offers itself to, the risk that makes politics possible.[22]

II

Shelley's recorded responses to the massacre in Manchester include, besides *The Mask of Anarchy*, two letters to close male friends in which he was inspired to self-quotation. "[T]he torrent of indignation has not yet done boiling in my veins," he wrote to Ollier, shortly after receiving word of Peterloo. "I wait anxiously [to] hear how the Country will express its sense of this bloody murderous oppression of its destroyers. 'Something must be done . . . What yet I know not.' "[23] He was, of course, appropriating the voice of his recently created Beatrice Cenci. Two weeks later, writing to Peacock (who was the friend who had sent him news of the massacre), he allowed Beatrice's *mot* a freer rendering: "What an infernal business this is of Manchester! What is to be done? Something assuredly."[24] The Leninesque echo may be taken, perhaps, as a shadow of futurity caught by the poetic mirror; in a more worldly spirit, thinking along Wolfsonian lines, one might want to pick up on the staginess of these moments—their blend of outrage, self-indulgence and uneasiness, as a poet in exile, highly conscious both of his cultural patrimony and his political impotence, negotiates his relationship to "the Country." But an additional peculiarity bears thinking about here: Shelley's nervous self-reflection occurs as a moment of identification with a traumatized heroine on her way toward the act of vengeance that will destroy her. His ventriloquized Beatrice may be read as a wishful, and to some extent erotically playful, moment of identification with a violated national body; it must also be read as yet another politically ambiguous sign, an appropriate origin for a poem like *The Mask*. Something must be done in advance of, in the absence of, knowledge. The imperative begins in blindness, facing the blankness of futurity. Yet it also quotes; it recalls a scripted, tragic past. What is to be done may turn out, when done, to repeat the violence it sets out to destroy.

I have suggested that *The Mask of Anarchy* forces this ambiguity on us as the condition of all political or historical action. Shelley's quotation compresses the lesson of that text into a fractured, polyvalent phrase. The blindness of the future-oriented imperative is also a blindness to its own past, to its own status as citation: to quote Beatrice, here, is also to forget that one is quoting Beatrice. The imperative's knowledge of its own citationality or iterability haunts it as its condition of possibility, without ever catching up with it. Life itself, Nietzsche tells us, depends upon our ability to forget. Yet in the forgetting, the repressed returns: the poet, identifying with a fictional character of his own creation, repeats that character's blindness. For Beatrice, like Shelley in his letters to Ollier and Peacock, and like many real and fictional characters before and since, is dreaming of an absolute act—a "tremendous deed," as Shelley's preface to *The Cenci* puts it (*SPP*, 238)—that would heal the past by rupturing time and causality with the force of divine redemption, annihilating trauma through a gesture unindebted to and in no way repetitive of that trauma, and thus capable of utterly forgetting it.[25] How else might history be redeemed? Shelley's poems thematize again and again the irreducible double bind of an ethico-political act that must forget the past it must remember and repeat a version of the violence it dreams of effacing.[26] Sometimes his texts mine the self-reflexivity of allegorical personification (as when "Conquest is dragged Captive through the Deep" in Demogorgon's visionary speech at the end of *Prometheus Unbound* [4.556]); occasionally, as at one memorable point in the "Ode to Liberty," he turns to the figure of a violent, ambiguously redemptive inscription:

> O that the free would stamp the impious name
> Of KING into the dust! or write it there,
> So that this blot upon the page of fame
> Were as a serpent's path, which the light air
> Erases, and the flat sands close behind!
>> Ye the oracle have heard:
>> Lift the victory-flashing sword,
> And cut the snaky knots of this foul gordian word.
>
> (Ll. 211–18)

The stanza may be read as a compulsive effort to refigure the initial paradox, according to which the act of stamping repeats what it annihilates: because *stamp* means writing as well as erasing, the ode's narrator first tries to absorb the word's doubleness by reimagining writing as a wind- and sand-obliterated trace, and then constructs a more aggressive scenario in which the reader is interpellated not so much as Hercules as Perseus, cutting the "snaky knots" of a Gorgon-word with a "sword" that, as Wolfson reminds us, contains the word it cuts within it.[27]

These double binds do not add up to nihilism, because the imperative remains absolute ("Something must be done") and the future remains open. But they translate with delusive ease into the terms of despair, the last temptation, as in the Fury's final torment of Prometheus:

> The good want power, but to weep barren tears.
> The powerful goodness want: worse need for them.
> The wise want love, and those who love want wisdom;
> And all best things are thus confused to ill.
> Many are strong and rich,—and would be just,—
> But live among their suffering fellow men
> As if none felt: they know not what they do.
>
> (1.625–31)

Despair, here, may be understood as a name for the illusion that one can *know* the incompatibility between knowledge and performance (from this point of view, cynicism is merely a defensive and inauthentic form of despair). Prometheus feels the force of the temptation, but trumps the Fury: "Thy words are like a cloud of winged snakes / And yet, I pity those they torture not" (1.632–33). In the end, and despite his endless complicity with Jupiter, he is futurity. Shelley keeps faith with the Promethean affirmation; but his mature work understands affirmation as bound up with the strange, inter-twining noncoincidence of performance and knowledge: the incom-patibility of "good and the means of good," as the narrator of *The Triumph of Life* puts it (l. 231).[28] Furthermore, Shelley suggestively complicates the Promethean appeal to affect. Stating that he pities those who fail to feel pity and fear at the spectacle of life's tragedy, Prometheus wards off the Fury by transforming despair into sympa-thy. His pity comprehends the split between knowledge and per-formance by aestheticizing this split as a tragic spectacle; thus his pity repeats the totalizing structure of the despair that pity over-comes. In *The Cenci*, Shelley explores the provenance and structure of tragic affect in ways that allow us to understand Promethean af-firmation in relation to the radical fictionality of the affect it affirms. "In writing the *Cenci*," he told Trelawney, "my object was to see how well I could succeed in describing passions I have never felt, and to tell the most dreadful story in pure and refined language."[29] If Shel-ley's goal in reimagining this Renaissance tragedy is to "clothe it to the apprehensions of my countrymen in such language and action as would bring it home to their hearts" (*SPP*, 239), his retelling in-volves him in acts of fictional identification that receive thematic and figurative elaboration in the text as the pressure, within aesthet-ics, of a certain anaesthesia.

III

We may first rapidly review the well-known spiral of complicity and pain that *The Cenci* sets in motion. Beatrice's tremendous deed—parricide—is, of course, reactive to another deed: the unspeakable crime she has suffered at the hands of her father, the count, who embodies in gothic fashion the full weight of patriarchal oppression. The count appears to have an understanding with God, "whose image upon earth a father is," according to Beatrice (2.1.16–17), and who answers the count's prayers for the death of his sons; the pope's sympathy for the count derives in part from financial self-interest but also from the fact that he stands between God and the count in the patriarchal chain of being: "the paternal power, / Being, as 'twere, a shadow of his own" (2.2.55–56). Earl Wasser-man's influential reading of the play discerns in Cenci a personification of the mystery of evil itself: "Like God, he is the fatherless father, the uncaused cause, the point beyond which evil cannot be traced."[30] It must be added, however, that in *The Cenci* paternal power is also bound up with self-destruction. The count's crimes damage his patrimony, since for each evil deed discovered he pays compensation to the pope; and though from a God's-eye view this self-destructive activity simply feeds resources back up the patriarchal food chain, from the count's perspective it represents a modest step toward the dream of self-annihilation that fuels his villainy: when all is done, he says, he will pile up his remaining riches "And make a bonfire in my joy, and leave / Of my possessions nothing but my name; / Which shall be an inheritance to strip / Its wearer bare as infamy" (4.1.59–62). That autoaesthetic spectacle would for the count be the ultimate act, the most tremendous deed. It would preserve patriarchy as the reflexivity—the fascist dream—of pure autodestruction.

As a surrogate for this absolute deed, the count rapes his daughter Beatrice. It is very much part of the texture of this play, as well as being historically characteristic of this particular sort of violence, that the count's crime is at once unspeakable and overpublicized: we inevitably know the name of this deed, but Beatrice also insists with authority that we do not:

> What are the words which you would have me speak?
> I, who can feign no image in my mind
> Of that which has transformed me: I, whose thought
> Is like a ghost shrouded and folded up
> In its own formless horror. Of all words,
> That minister to mortal intercourse,
> Which wouldst thou hear? For there is none to tell
> My misery; if another ever knew
> Aught like to it, she died as I will die,
> And left it, as I must, without a name.
>
> (3.1.107–16)

Or again: "there are deeds / Which have no form, sufferings which have no tongue" (3.1.141–42). The violence of the count's deed is linguistic in a thoroughly nontrivial sense: it is traumatic; it strips language from its victim, and in doing so it acquires the character of a verbal act even before the literal rape occurs. (To her mother, Lucretia's, anxious question, "What did your father do or say to you?" [2.1.59], Beatrice answers: "It was one word, Mother, one little word" [2.1.63]). The real violence of the count's deed lies in the destruction of the victim's full comprehension of the deed: trauma

destroys the knowledge of its source. "Her spirit," Lucretia concludes, "apprehends the sense of pain, / But not its cause; suffering
has dried away / The source from which it sprung" (3.1.34–36).
With the loss of language or knowledge in trauma comes the victim's
debilitating identification with the torturer. Beatrice answers the
maternal question "What has thy father done?" by asking "What
have I done?" (3.1.69). The count exults precisely in this more than
literal force of rape: "She shall become (for what she most abhors /
Shall have a fascination to entrap / Her loathing will) to her own
conscious self / All she appears to others" (4.1.85–88). He imagines
her having his child, suggesting as the epitome of his "tremendous
deed" the transformation of female generativity into the ghastly
specularity of patriarchal autodestruction: "May [the child] be / A
hideous likeness of herself, that as / From a distorting mirror, she
may see / Her image mixed with what she most abhors, / Smiling
upon her from her nursing breast" (4.1.145–49).

Beatrice's own tremendous deed responds to this unspeakable,
self-destroying injury, and in certain ways repeats its violence, as
nearly every critic of the play has observed.[31] Early on in the text she
calls pain's traumatic effacement of the source of pain "parricide,"
as though the effect were indistinguishable from the cause: responding to Lucretia's comment that "suffering has dried away the source
from which it sprang," she comments: "Like Parricide . . . / Misery
has killed its father" (3.1.37–38). The self-destructive destructive-
ness of patriarchy makes its crime paradoxically congruent with parricide; Cenci, appropriately enough, is the first to utter the word in
the play (in a curious phrase, to which we shall return), and the first
to propose ways of doing it, including the way Beatrice eventually
chooses ("How just it were to hire assassins, or/ . . . smother me
when overcome with wine" [2.1.141, 143]). Thus, in killing her
father, Beatrice slips back into the father's self-immolative logic of
torture. She becomes in her turn a torturer as, at the end of the play,
she wrings a negation of parricide from the hired assassin, Marzio.
After suffering the papal rack, Marzio has confessed all and named
Beatrice as his employer; yet after suffering Beatrice's eloquence, he
retracts his confession: "A keener pain has wrung a higher truth /
From my last breath" (5.2.164–65). The play suggests that Beatrice
has evaded the full trauma of victimage—the ghastly self-alienation
imaged by the mother imaged in the child of incest—only by "becoming the thing she hates" without knowing it. The initial trauma,
which consists in the inability to say what one knows, becomes the
inability to know what one says. The radical, tremendous deed of

parricide in a sense obliterates the self even more thoroughly than the count's original crime was able to do.[32]

It is still not clear, however, why patriarchy's dream of plenitude takes negative—that is, self-immolatively sadistic—form, which suggests that we should look a little more closely at the sadist's account of sadism. "All men delight in sensual luxury," the count generalizes:

> All men enjoy revenge; and most exult
> Over the tortures they can never feel—
> Flattering their secret peace with others' pain.
>
> (1.1.78–80)

This is a significant statement in part because it is a reflection upon tragic affect or catharsis. Pain is the foundation of the sadistic economy, but pain belongs only to the victim, while the sadist experiences a pleasure which has no existence in itself, but resides entirely in the spectacle of the other's pain. Hence the curious insistence, even the bizarre, glancing pathos, of the count's description of men exulting "over the tortures they can never feel." It is as though this inability to feel pain, or at least *those* pains, is a loss, indeed, an absolute loss: the sadist *can never* feel the effect of his own sadistic action. The voluptuous pleasures of sadism cover an underlying numbness or impotence. In a sense this numb foundation creates the voluptuous pleasure which covers it, since the sadist's pleasure (his "secret peace") resides precisely in the irreversibility of the torturer-tortured relation. Yet this irreversibility also shows up as the flickering plangency of a loss.[33]

The sadist's pleasure in pain both politicizes and, willy-nilly, demystifies tragic catharsis. The pleasure we derive from aestheticized suffering is laced with anaesthesia because it is grounded in our inability to identify, except fictionally, with the tragic other of fiction. What we call fiction, in other words, is a name for the absolute otherness of the other. Tragedy, or we may say more generally, poetry, attends to the absolute and infinite loss of the other, even as it betrays this loss by shunting it into the specular illusions of mourning and tragic identification, through powerful and unstable acts of personification. The sadist, trapped in this predicament, seeks to transform loss itself into a ground for self, to exploit the other's otherness; and he succeeds only at the price of destroying others endlessly as part of a self-consuming spiral that can never close. Put another way, God, in this sadistic, patriarchal economy, can do everything except be his own victim. His sacrifice of himself to himself is a lie. He can never know the pain of the other, even the other who is him-

self: such is the infinite pain of his existence, which his sadism fore-
closes and repeats.

The Cenci allows us another way to characterize the sadistic paradox: the sadist seeks to aestheticize his an-aesthesia as the formalism
of a total self. As the play comes to an end, the master trope of patriarchy becomes the machine, the aestheticized figure of form di-
vorced from meaning:

> The Pope is stern; not to be moved or bent.
> He looked as calm and keen as is the engine
> Which tortures and which kills, exempt itself
> From aught that it inflicts: a marble form
> A rite, a law, a custom: not a man.
>
> (5.4.1–5)

To personify a rite or custom—and this personification here defines
patriarchy—is to replay the sadistic economy in which the sadist affirms his inability to feel the victim's pain (the machine being "ex-
empt itself / From aught that it inflicts"), and thereby disavows this
inability. To personify a formal pattern is to deny, by pretending to
celebrate, the word's inability to know its own deed. (Hence Beatrice's apostrophe: "Cruel, cold, formal man; righteous in words, /
In deeds a Cain" [5.4.107–8].) The sadistic economy derives its possibility from a radical incompatibility within itself that it translates
either into the sublime indifference of the machine, or the sublime
spectacle of its own ruin. "Its self-alienation," as Walter Benjamin
wrote of mankind under fascism, "has reached such a degree that it
can experience its own destruction as an aesthetic pleasure of the
first order."[34] Composing yet disarticulating that spectacle is a different, less spectacular parricide, of a sort suggested by the first use of
the word in the play, when Cenci characterizes one of his sons as
having been "taught by rote / Parricide with his alphabet" (2.1.131–
32). The truth of patriarchy's self-immolative aesthetic is allegory,
and "Parricide" appears in *The Cenci* as the exemplary allegorical
figure, destroying its own knowledge of its linguistic provenance
("Like Parricide . . . Misery has killed its father"). It is in making
legible the irreducibility of linguistic play to aestheticization that
poetry's words are swords: politically cutting, if always also double-
edged.

IV

Readers have often observed that Count Cenci is a dark parody of
the artist. He tells stories, manipulates the action, and fathers Be-

atrice's parricidal plot, to the point of appearing "an evil counterpart of the poet who embodies imagination in language," according
to one critic.[35] But "counterpart" suggests a binary opposition more
stable than the play of resemblances one finds again and again in
Shelley's texts. Consider briefly, in conclusion, the famous final sentences of the *Defence of Poetry*, particularly the penultimate sentence,
with its cascade of predicates and uncertain pronouns:

> Poets are the hierophants of an unapprehended inspiration, the mirrors
> of the gigantic shadows which futurity casts upon the present, the words
> which express what they understand not; the trumpets which sing to bat-
> tle and feel not what they inspire: the influence which is moved not, but
> moves. Poets are the unacknowledged legislators of the World. (*SPP*,
> 508)

The cadences are so familiar that we sometimes, I think, have difficulty perceiving how strange Shelley's writing is here. It seems relatively comprehensible that poets should be hierophants or mirrors;
but what is it for them to be "words which express what they understand not"—and who is the "they" here: the poets or the words? But
of course the poets *are* the words: words which enact meanings
blindly. And if at this late hour that trope has a familiar deconstructive ring to it, what do we make of the follow-up clause, that poets are
"the trumpets which sing to battle and feel not what they inspire"?
Is Cenci's anaesthesia lacing this hyperaesthetic performance? In
some sense, yes; for, as legislators, poets seem at once blind and
numb, "unacknowledged" both because the world ignores them
and because they themselves lose their self-awareness—including
their aesthetic sense—as they leave their mark upon the world.

Our reading of *The Cenci* indeed suggests that the closest cousin
to this poetic anaesthesia is a machinal affectlessness that Shelley associates with the worst kinds of political violence. About a year before writing *The Defence of Poetry* he had written about soldiers in *A
Philosophical View of Reform* in terms thematically opposed but rhetor-
ically oddly similar to those he would use to describe poets:

> From the moment that a man is a soldier, he becomes a slave. He is
> taught obedience; his will is no longer, which is the most sacred preroga-
> tive of man, guided by his own judgment. He is taught to despise human
> life and human suffering; this is the universal distinction of slaves. He is
> more degraded than a murderer; he is like the bloody knife which has
> stabbed and feels not; a murderer we may abhor and despise, a soldier
> is by profession beyond abhorrence and below contempt.[36]

The poet is everything the soldier-slave is not—apart from that teasing echo: the former is a trumpet that sings to battle and feels not what it inspires; the latter is a bloody knife that stabs and feels not what *it* inspires. In addition to the rhetorical heightening of a favored Shelleyan inversion ("feels not"), the two figures share an appeal to the particular kind of affectlessness that can be associated with a tool—a technical prosthesis of, in this case, voice (the trumpet) or hand (the knife). That the poetic trumpets "sing to battle" tightens this counterintuitive accord between poet and soldier. Not only are they both tools, blind to the sensation they elicit or the meaning they perform, but they both also seem caught up in political forms of violence. They veer inevitably if sacrilegiously toward each other, such that, at their meeting point, the poet as trumpet unfeelingly inspires the unfeeling soldier to his knife-work.

Perverse though it undoubtedly is to hear such echoes and draw such comparisons, which obviously run counter to Shelley's most prominent themes, in doing so we respond to a vibrant ambiguity in Shelley's work that shows up both on his texts' thematic and figural levels. Poets are not soldiers any more than the Shape is Anarchy or freedom is tyranny or Beatrice (or Shelley) is Count Cenci; yet these all-important differences come into existence only at the price of their potential displacement and repetition. Poetry is risky, given over to the drift of inaudible inscription and posthumous effect. Its tropes are uninsurable, and thus radically ambiguous in their political effects. Tyranny takes its root in the effort to transform this anarchy into the Arche: a gesture that poetry cannot avoid repeating, but one that poetry also endlessly deconstructs, dethroning power by stamping the name of king into the dust, and teaching parricide by rote with its alphabet. By making legible the fact that poetic words do not understand what they express, or feel what they inspire, poetry functions as the political unconscious of aesthetics precisely to the extent that poetry opens aesthetics to the contingency of history and the constitutive uncertainty of futurity. Poetry is the unacknowledged disease of politics, but also its only hope, since poetry insures that the possibility of revolution will always remain absolute. Romanticism remains, for us, another name for this paradox.

Notes

1. Maurice Blanchot, "The Athenaeum," in *The Infinite Conversation*, trans. Susan Hanson (Minneapolis: University of Minnesota Press, 1993), 351, translation slightly modified.

2. German Romanticism inspired sharply political commentary during and

after the Second World War: see especially A. O. Lovejoy, "The Meaning of Romanticism for the Historian of Ideas," *Journal of the History of Ideas* 2 (1941): 257–78 and
Leo Spitzer's reply to Lovejoy, " '*Geistesgeschichte*' vs. History of Ideas as Applied to
Hitlerism," *Journal of the History of Ideas* 5 (1944): 191–203. A fine summary and
analysis of this debate may be found in Orrin N. C. Wang, *Fantastic Modernity: Dialec-
tical Readings in Romanticism and Theory* (Baltimore, Md.: The Johns Hopkins University Press, 1996), 26–36. As late as the 1960s, mainstream Anglo-American scholarship was blaming German Romanticism, or more generally the "German mind,"
for having produced Hitlerism: see, e.g., Ronald Gray, *The German Tradition in Literature, 1871–1945* (Cambridge: Cambridge University Press, 1965).

3. Most recently, as eco- or "green" criticism. The recent tendency to substitute
"early modern" for "Renaissance" has generated discussions similar to but also in-
structively different from those about Romanticism. Though marked by the usual
exchanges between traditionalists and revisionists, the Renaissance/early modern
debate has involved a competition between two terms rather than an obsessive cir-
cling around a single term: "Romanticism" has proved harder to replace than "Renaissance," perhaps in part because the notion of Romanticism, as McGann and
many others recall, names the emergence of a historicism that made possible literary periodization (e.g., terms like "Renaissance") in the first place. Denunciations
of Romanticism as "ideology," have become commonplace among Romanticists
who nonetheless often have no term to offer in its stead, even on the occasions
when they suggest getting rid of it. See, e.g., Anne K. Mellor and Richard E. Matlak,
"General Introduction," *British Literature, 1780–1830* (Fort Worth, Texas: Harcourt
Brace, 1996): "Recognizing that the term 'Romanticism' has become the subject of
interrogation by recent new historical, cultural, and feminist critics, we have set it
aside as a principle of selection" (3). Mellor and Matlak retain the term, however,
to describe "expressive/subjective aesthetics" as opposed to neoclassical aesthetics
or the middle ground called "probabilism" that they ascribe to women writers; ex-
pressive-subjective Romanticism, of course, signifies "an ideological poetics of
whose self-interest or class bias we should be aware" (128). For a helpful summary
of the Renaissance/early modern discussion, see Leah S. Marcus, "Renaissance/
Early Modern Studies," in *Redrawing the Boundaries: The Transformation of English and
American Literary Studies*, ed. Stephen Greenblatt and Giles Gunn (New York: Modern Language Association, 1992), 41–63.

4. McGann's title echoes, of course, the misleading but by now inevitable translation of Marx and Engels's *Die deutsche Ideologie*, but his use of the definite article
is also motivated by his understanding of Romantic ideology as aesthetic ideology
in the sense of elevating art and ideas—"imagination and poetry"—over material
reality: Romanticism is thus ideology itself. See Jerome J. McGann, *The Romantic
Ideology: A Critical Investigation* (Chicago: University of Chicago Press, 1983).

5. McGann, *Romantic Ideology*, 79, 131.

6. Ibid., 160.

7. For two exemplary positions, see Paul Foot, *Red Shelley* (London: Sidgwick &
Jackson, 1980) and Donald H. Reiman, "Shelley as Agrarian Reactionary," in *Romantic Texts and Contexts* (Columbia: University of Missouri Press, 1987), 260–74.

8. Forest Pyle, " 'Frail Spells': Shelley and the Ironies of Exile," in *Irony and
Clerisy*, ed. Deborah White, *Romantic Circles Praxis Series*, http://www.rc.umd.edu/
praxis/irony/pyle/frail. html, 7. Pyle suggestively links this political dimension of
Shelley's writing to Walter Benjamin's notion of a "*weak* Messianic power" capable
of "blast[ing] open the continuum of history." See Walter Benjamin, "Theses on
the Philosophy of History," in *Illuminations*, trans. Harry Zohn (New York:

Schocken Books, 1969), 254, 262. My argument will also have points of affinity with Jerrold Hogle's diagnosis of a "radical transference" at work in Shelley's texts: see Jerrold E. Hogle, *Shelley's Process: Radical Transference and the Development of His Major Works* (New York: Oxford University Press, 1988).

9. *Letters of Percy Bysshe Shelley*, ed. Frederick L. Jones (Oxford: Clarendon Press, 1964), 2:191. The quotation about *The Mask*'s greatness is from Richard Holmes, *Shelley: The Pursuit* (New York: Dutton, 1975), 532, cited in Susan Wolfson, "Social Form: Shelley and the Determination of Reading," in *Formal Charges: The Shaping of Poetry in British Romanticism* (Stanford: Stanford University Press, 1997), 286 n6. Hereafter *FC*, cited in the text. As Wolfson notes, most commentary on *The Mask of Anarchy* has celebrated its power as a political poem.

10. "Preface" to *Prometheus Unbound*, in Donald H. Reiman and Sharon B. Powers, eds., *Shelley's Poetry and Prose* (New York: Norton, 1977), 135. Hereafter *SPP*, cited in the text, for quotations from Shelley's prose taken from Reiman and Powers. All references to Shelley's poetry in what follows are to texts as given in Reiman and Powers, and will be identified simply by book, stanza or line numbers.

11. Wolfson, *Formal Charges*, 195.

12. Ibid., 203; see British Library f. 12V in Donald Reiman, ed., *"The Mask of Anarchy": A Facsimile Edition, with Scholarly Introductions, Bibliographical Descriptions, and Annotations*, vol. 2 of *Percy Bysshe Shelley*, in *The Manuscripts of the Younger Romantics* (New York: Garland Press, 1985), 32.

13. I have examined this fantasy in some detail in "Imagi-Nation: The Imagined Community and the Aesthetics of Mourning," special issue of *Diacritics*, "Grounds of Comparison: Around the Work of Benedict Anderson," ed. Pheng Cheah and Jonathan Culler, 29, no. 4 (1999): 58–83.

14. See, e.g., Carlos Baker, who imagines the address to be spoken by "Liberty" in *Shelley's Major Poetry: The Fabric of a Vision* (Princeton, N.J.: Princeton University Press, 1948), 162; as does Jerrold Hogle forty years later in *Shelley's Process*, 137–38. Tempting though it is to extend the poem's allegorical cast of characters in this way, the text offers us no clear support for doing so. Indeed, since this anonymous orator goes on to apostrophize Freedom and Liberty—"What art thou, Freedom?" (l. 209); "It availed, O, Liberty" (244)—poetic convention suggests that the speaker isn't the entity addressed. We do not even have fully certified warrant for referring to the speaker as "the female orator," as Wolfson does (*Formal Charges*, 203): all we know is that the words arise "as if" a maternal Earth had cried aloud. (Wolfson also characterizes the "Shape" of ll. 110ff. as "a miraculous epiphanic feminine intervention," despite Shelley's use of neuter pronouns in those stanzas.) One of the few critics to emphasize that the Shape "elud[es] any identification" is Steven Goldsmith, in his *Unbuilding Jerusalem: Apocalypse and Romantic Representation* (Ithaca, N.Y.: Cornell University Press, 1993), 245; however, Goldsmith's reading of *The Mask* could hardly be more different from mine: for him the Shape as an embodiment of "decentered" poetic language exists only in order to be negated, "so the rest of the poem can advocate a specific politial program" (ibid). As many critics have shown, *The Mask* draws on contemporary political iconography, and is certainly tempting its readers to personify the speaker as Britannia or a Britannic version of the French Revolution's Liberty, but as so often in this deceptively rough-hewn poem, what it gives with one hand it takes with the other. For a recent study of the poem in relation to the political iconography of the era, see Steven E. Jones, *Shelley's Satire: Violence, Exhortation, and Authority* (De Kalb: Northern Illinois University Press, 1994), 102ff. He personifies the orator as Britannia.

15. For reasons of economy I haven't quoted these stanzas (though a little later

I shall briefly discuss Anarchy's motto); here is Goldsmith's helpful summary in *Unbuilding Jerusalem*: "On his brow Anarchy bears the mark, 'I AM GOD, AND KING, AND LAW'" (l. 37). Every spoken line in the poem's first section merely rearranges this official declaration, as if its terms were the necessary and immutable givens of discourse and social relation. Anarchy's cohorts, for instance, sing, "Thou art God, and Law, and King" (l. 61), and lawyers and priests together whisper, "Thou art Law and God" (l. 69). As if to confirm the tautological unity of the official lexicon, the echoing voices join forces: "Then all cried with one accord, / 'Thou art King, and God, and Lord' (ll. 70–71)" (ibid., 243). I should perhaps note that my reading of *The Mask* is at odds with Goldsmith's claim that it represents a turn on Shelley's part away from the "bankrupt linguistic universals" of *Prometheus Unbound*, and toward a pragmatic idea of "communication" (ibid., 241). Goldsmith's is the sort of privileging of Shelley's "Popular Songs" that Wolfson is setting out to correct— though one should note that Wolfson and Goldsmith share many key assumptions, above all the notion that literary density is the narcissistic opposite of practical politics. Goldsmith's book is in part an extended chastisement of a deconstruction that he imagines to be engaged in "freeing language and its human values from the weight of historical determination" (ibid., 212).

16. Jones, *Shelley's Satire*, 102. Jones notes that Shelley also does this in *The Devil's Walk*.

17. Actually the stanza is even more ambiguous than that. "Clothed with the Bible, as with light, / And the shadows of the night, / Like Sidmouth, next, Hypocrisy / On a crocodile rode by" (ll. 22–25): depending on how one adjudicates the appositions, Hypocrisy is like Sidmouth in being clothed with the Bible, etc., or in riding a crocodile. The historical figure thus blurs into the allegorical figure.

18. Marcel Proust, *Du côté de chez Swann*, in *À la recherche du temps perdu* (Paris: Gallimard, 1954), 1: 81; my translation. Marcel is imagining a resemblance between the Giotto figure and a pregnant kitchen maid who is seemingly "unable to comprehend the meaning" of the "symbol" she bears in her womb.

19. Speculation on Shelley's use of the masque genre has generally not gotten much further than the claim that Shelley is drawing on and debunking an aristocratic genre: see Stuart Curran, *Shelley's Annus Mirabilis: The Maturing of an Epic Vision* (San Marino, Calif.: Huntington Library, 1975), 181–92, for a classic discussion of this point.

20. For a political analysis of *The Mask*, see Michael Scrivener, *Radical Shelley: The Philosophical Anarchism and Utopian Thought of Percy Bysshe Shelley* (Princeton, N.J.: Princeton University Press, 1982): "The idea of massive non-violent response, in the context of a general strike and an egalitarian assembly, is a way for Shelley to express his revolutionary vision while at the same time relieving some of the anxiety this vision produced in him" (210). Wolfson, as we have seen, sharpens that judgment into a perception of "contradictory elements" in Shelley's political stance (*Formal Charges*, 202). It has also proved possible to relate *The Mask*'s "ambivalence . . . toward popular violence" to "a profound ambivalence in the reform movement itself." See Jones, *Shelley's Satire*, 109.

21. Fredric Jameson, *The Political Unconscious: Narrative as a Socially Symbolic Act* (Ithaca, N.Y.: Cornell University Press, 1981), 20, 19: "[T]he all-informing process of *narrative*" Jameson takes to be "(here using the shorthand of philosophical idealism) the central function or *instance* of the human mind" (13).

22. I would thus agree with James Chandler's characterization of *The Mask* as displacing "the everyday time of the periodicals into a quasi-apocalyptic framework,

anticipating the displacement of 'empty homogenous time' by 'messianic time' in Benjamin's twentieth-century analysis." In James K. Chandler, *England in 1819: The Politics of Literary Culture and the Case of Romantic Historicism* (Chicago: University of Chicago Press, 1998), 529.

23. To Ollier, 6 September 1819; *Letters*, ed. Jones, 2:117.

24. To Peacock, 21 September 1819; *Letters*, ed. Jones, 2:120. For Beatrice's line, see *Cenci*, 3.1.86–87.

25. "Aye, something must be done; / What, yet I know not . . . something which shall make / The thing that I have suffered but a shadow/ In the dread lightning which avenges it; / Brief, rapid, irreversible, destroying / The consequence of what it cannot cure." See *Cenci*, 3.1.86–91; ellipses in the text.

26. Sometimes the demonstration undergoes awkward, almost comical, elaboration, as in "The Sensitive Plant," where the Lady goes to great lengths to erase the damage she does in tending her garden: "Her step seemed to pity the grass it prest . . . And wherever her aery footstep trod / Her trailing hair from the grassy sod / Erased its light vestige" (2.21, 25–27). She removes "all killing insects and gnawing worms, / And things of obscene and unlovely forms"; but she removes them gently, exiling them to the "rough woods" in "a basket of grasses and wild flowers full, / The freshest her gentle hands could pull" (2.41–42, 44, 45–46). The irony, of course, is that she still has to pull up grass and flowers and that there has to be a place called the "rough woods" for the killing insects to go on happily killing in. Shelley mercilessly rewrote these images in *The Triumph of Life* (see especially ll. 405–10).

27. The word's persistence within the sword may thus be taken as the mark of language's persistence within and beyond the apocalyptic dream of the "tremendous deed." From this perspective, "Shelley's poetry is the record of a perpetually renewed failure," as J. Hillis Miller writes: "It is the failure ever to get the right formula and so end the separate incomplete self, end lovemaking, end politics, and end poetry, all at once, in a performative apocalypse in which words will become the fire they have ignited and so vanish as words, in a universal light. The words, however, always remain, there on the page, as the unconsumed traces of each unsuccessful attempt to use words to end words." In J. Hillis Miller, "The Critic as Host," in *Deconstruction and Criticism*, ed. Harold Bloom (New York: Continuum, 1979), 237.

28. For a rhetorical study of the complexities of language and speech in *Prometheus Unbound*, see Carol Jacobs, "Unbinding Words: *Prometheus Unbound*," in *Uncontainable Romanticism: Shelley, Brontë, Kleist* (Baltimore, Md.: The Johns Hopkins University Press, 1989).

29. Edward Trelawney, *The Last Days of Shelley and Byron*, ed. J. E. Morpurgo (Garden City, N.Y.: Anchor Books, 1960), 61.

30. Earl R. Wasserman, *Shelley: A Critical Reading* (Baltimore, Md.: The Johns Hopkins University Press, 1971), 87. Wasserman's observation is made in the context of his larger account of free will and causality in Shelley's work generally: "In Shelley's Manichean system, in which evil is an autonomous and pressing potentiality, the count is the original and unmotivated point at which transcendent evil enters human reality and begins its causal sequence, simply because the count *permits* it to enter by assuming man is necessarily evil" (ibid.).

31. Shelley predicted the shape of his play's reception in his "Preface," writing of "the restless and anatomizing casuistry with which men seek the justification of Beatrice, yet feel that she has done what needs justification" (*SPP*, 240). Interpretation of *The Cenci* turns endlessly on whether and to what extent Beatrice is morally

responsible for her crime, and has done so since the earliest reviews, as Stuart Curran shows in *Shelley's Cenci: Scorpions Ringed with Fire* (Princeton, N.J.: Princeton University Press, 1970), 24, passim. For a helpful survey of modern criticism on the issue, see Hogle, *Shelley's Process*, 365n95. Hogle's own analysis of how Beatrice's choice "contorts her into the patterns of patriarchal language" (154) is particularly suggestive.

32. For a rhetorical reading of *The Cenci* that emphasizes the split between action and understanding, see Roger Blood, "Allegory and Dramatic Representation in *The Cenci,*" *Studies in Romanticism* 33 (Fall 1994): 355–89.

33. These observations perhaps gloss Jacques Lacan's suggestive remark that the sadist, projecting outward the death he cannot accept as his own, imagines that he can thereby cast "the pain of existence onto the Other, without realizing that in this manner he also changes into an 'eternal object.' " Jacques Lacan, *Écrits* (Paris: Seuil, 1966), 778; my translation.

34. Walter Benjamin, "The Work of Art in the Age of Mechanical Reproduction," in *Illuminations*, 242.

35. Anne McWhir, "The Light and the Knife: Ab/Using Language in *The Cenci,*" *Keats-Shelley Journal* 37 (1989): 150.

36. As quoted in David Lee Clark, ed., *Shelley's Prose, or, The Trumpet of a Prophecy* (Albuquerque: University of New Mexico Press, 1954), 253.

"Strange Sun": Melancholia in the Writing of Thomas Lovell Beddoes

Frances Wilson

Reading University

I OUGHT to have been among other things a good poet," Thomas Lovell Beddoes wrote in the postscript to the brief and perfunctory note he pinned to his shirt before he swallowed a lethal dose of poison. He was forty-five and had published nothing, save the odd poem, for a quarter of a century, although it had been very much on his mind to do so. A melancholic, exile, eccentric, atheist, and political malcontent, Beddoes was, like the Ancient Mariner or Wandering Jew, the archetypal Romantic outsider. Proclaimed heir at the age of nineteen to the recently deceased Keats and Shelley, Beddoes has been mostly ignored by the nineteenth and twentieth centuries. He is best known now as a poet of ruins and broken parts: taut, muscular fragments and scattered scraps of words, lines without beginning or end which he considered worthless and discarded like so much rubbish. Pathologically unable to finish his writing, in form his poems are as broken, raw, and unresolved as was Beddoes himself. But to be known as a poet at all today would have surprised him: Beddoes wrote poems so as to break them open and watch them die.

At the same time as ruthlessly dissecting himself—during an earlier suicide attempt he stabbed a leg which then had to be removed—Beddoes dismembered his work. Exchanging a promising poetic career to train as a physician in Germany, Beddoes's accounts of writing are frequently described in anatomical terms. "Dismemberment and reassembly become . . . the central articles of a powerful analogy between the corpus and the corpse,"[1] as Michael Bradshaw puts it; physiognomy and poetry were both concerned with fragmentation, dissection, and death. But Beddoes was the first to allude to the relation for him between the physical and the figurative: "Apollo has been barbarously separated by the moderns: I will endeavour to reunite him,"[2] he wrote, elsewhere arguing that "the studies . . . of the dramatist and physician are closely, almost inseparably allied." He had no intention, however, of uniting these two parts. The gesture that shapes Beddoes's career is not one of joining but one of turning away. He "swerved," as Beddoes put it, from "the path to reputation" when he turned his back on England and poetry, and his life can be seen as an assortment of swerves and turns. He swerved into anatomy to avoid writing and once writing, he swerved from completion. This image of "swerving" recalls Freud's description of the work of mourning as a defensive "turning away from reality,"[3] and it is the relation of Beddoes's troubled writing to the broken language of melancholy which interests me here.

The idea of wholeness or unity as something to be achieved through the pen is resisted by Beddoes at every level, but most particularly in his fear of endings ("for ever to be continued," he wrote with weary irony on a tale he then, predictably, discarded). He went to great lengths in order not to write, but once he had begun, there was no end to the lengths he then wanted to go in his work. In his hands poetry overcame blocks and crossed through boundaries, and Beddoes's aim was to push language and the self as far as they could go—beyond signification, representation, and identity.

The suggestion in his suicide note that Beddoes had failed as a poet disguises the contending feelings he had toward his work, the battle being waged between the part of him that wrote and the part which rejected writing. The scene of his writing was fraught with psychic conflict. He wrote lyric poetry "almost against his will," H. W. Donner recognized, and he saw his shockingly original work not as an expression of the self but rather as a foreign body. The disease of self-consciousness is an idea central to Romanticism, but Beddoes oscillated between seeing the self as the affliction to be got rid of and writing as the impurity. Writing for Beddoes was a self-destructive and high-risk activity, staging a fight to the death between artist and art. This is why he chose to exile himself as soon as he had achieved poetic success—he turned to medicine to cure him of words and as protection from their powers. His years as a poet were spent trying to expel poetry from his system and to stem the flow of his verse in the outside world.

Beddoes saw in writing the possibility of self-dissolution. As such it both thrilled and thwarted him; here he was brought to the heart of the division between conscious and unconscious life, to the very edge of his identity and of what it was possible to say. Devoured by unspeakable sadness, Beddoes lived in the realm of the inexpressible. His poetry encrypted his peculiar melancholy and became for him an object he loathed but refused to let go. It provided a stage on which he could dramatize the symbolic collapse which defines what Julia Kristeva calls the "dead language" of depression, in which words become wasteful and lose their meaning.[4]

I

This essay explores Beddoes's violent ambivalence toward a poetic voice, "the greatness of whose work," Donner argues, "ranks in the kind where there is no comparison" (*W*, 389). In Beddoes we have the perverse case of a poet who mastered language but did not believe in it, whose poems represent an attempt to proclaim, not his enduring reputation or his poetic strength, but his poetic mortality; who sought *noncanonicity* in his writing; who tried everything to rid himself of the impulse to write whilst never being able to rid himself of the writing. His greatest ambition was not to be recognized but to become invisible, to achieve what Thoreau called "the absence of the speaker from his speech." In a few spare lines written "On Himself," Beddoes mocked the

> Poor bird, that cannot ever
> Dwell high in tower of song:
> Whose heart-breaking endeavour
> But palls the lazy throng.

But he sought this dejected position as well. He shifted between denouncing his poetry as worthless and denouncing the poet. "I prefer being anonymous," he confided, elsewhere writing that he was "contented with oblivion." He repeatedly claimed that he was not "genuine" and that, "my nature is not that of one, who is destined to achieve anything very important in this department of literature." While feeling he was "essentially unpoetical in character, habits, and ways of thinking; and nothing but the desperate hanker for distinction . . . ever set [him] upon rhyming," he resisted that temptation with a will of iron. [5]

This central ambivalence as to the object of his aggression and melancholy dominates Beddoes's attitude to writing and recalls Freud's description of melancholy:

In melancholia the relation to the object is no simple one; it is complicated by the conflict due to ambivalence . . . In melancholia . . . countless

separate struggles are carried on over the object, in which hate and love
contend with each other; the one seeks to detach the libido from the
object, the other to maintain this position of the libido against the as-
sault.[6]

As part of this struggle, much of Beddoes's work he destroyed or
lost, but what survives has the appearance of a series of occassionally
brilliant interrupted ideas. This is either due to the striking similes
which sometimes blaze out from the whole—"cool as an ice-drop in
a dead-man's eye"—or to the incomplete nature of the work to
begin with. ("Let us keep in mind," Kristeva writes, "the speech of
the depressed—repetitive and monotonous . . . they utter sentences
that are interrupted, exhausted, come to a standstill," *BS*, 33.) The
reason Beddoes's poems and plays survive at all is because of the
efforts of admirers who collected, copied, and cared for his unloved
manuscripts following his death in 1849. This was no easy task: considering his writing a waste, he ensured that it was debris to begin
with, and he wrote on "the backs of letters or any scrap of vilest
paper,"[7] squeezing his poems into minute corners, into margins of
receipts, and around the borders of those margins. His altered drafts
were veritable palimpsests and barely legible. Having produced this
refuse Beddoes then added it, for the most part, to his "never-ending" and increasingly unwieldy sprawl, *Death's Jest-Book*, which drama
became his life's work, occupying him for twenty-four years and remaining unfinished when he died. The songs and bits and pieces
he composed over the years were "stuck" into his play—his term
appropriately suggests not only insertion but blockage—like "scattered limbs." His description of writing depicts a scene of carnage
similar to the one he was writing about.

No critical attempt at writing Beddoes off has been so successful
as his own endeavors to write himself out. From the start he abjected
his writing, although his earliest work was cast aside after publication
rather than during composition. His first success came in 1821
when, as an undergraduate, he published a play, *The Bride's Tragedy*,
which was praised by the *Edinburgh Review* as displaying "more
promise (we ought to say, perhaps, more power) than that of almost
any young poet, whose works have come before us for the first
time." He described his drama however as being "a very sad boyish
affair" which he "would not now be condemned to read through
for any consideration."[8] The previous year, Beddoes brought out his
first collection of poems, *The Improvisatore* (the only volume of
poetry he ever saw published), and he experienced such distress at
their perceived worthlessness that, once complete, he destroyed

every copy he could find. Readers discovered that following a visit by the poet their edition had been disembowelled; Beddoes had cut out the pages before replacing the book on the shelves. This gesture typically perverts what Geoffrey Hartman describes as the Romantic desire to overcome self-consciousness and return to what Yeats called "Unity of Being."[9] When he separated the inside pages of *The Improvisatore* from the outside cover, Beddoes performed the fear of wholeness that would dog his writing to the last. His act of mutilation reveals the urgency of his need to cut himself off from his work: cutting open his leg or cutting out his poems, what is crudely apparent in Beddoes is his profound resistance to the idea of unity. He resisted completion because he resisted wholeness: he ruined his poetry because he wrote ruins; the ruin was his poetic form. But Beddoes's dissection of *The Improvisatore* suggests that he also feared being separated from it and felt a horror of letting his work go into circulation. In future, as if it were a vital limb his body could not do without, Beddoes ensured that his poetry would never leave him. He developed an anxiety about ever stopping his writing, ever reaching the point where he should let it go.

An empty book disguising itself as complete—the mockery of Beddoes's act has about it all the trademark signs of his black humor and provides an ironic comment on what Harold Bloom recognizes as Beddoes's fatal flaw, his "want of a subject."[10] *The Improvisatore* was now hollow at the core, but hollowness *was* Beddoes's subject; the dismembered pages of *The Improvisatore* figure the imaginative space left between his desire to write and the nothing he wrote about. His poems resound with images of emptiness, his "dead language" breaks down into asymbolia. "If my friend Death lives long enough to finish his jest-book," Beddoes wrote, suggesting not only that his writer is dead but that completing his work finishes it off too, "it will come with its strangenesses—it contains nothing else."[11] Beddoes's subjects, his "strangenesses," are not only the wastes the *Jest-Book* contained—waste being what his writing represented to him—but also emptiness, silence, and nothingness. It was not that he had nothing to write about—Beddoes wanted to write about nothing:

> I begin to hear
> Strange but sweet sounds and the loud rocky dashing
> Of waves, where time into Eternity
> Falls over ruined worlds.

Blocks, blanks, blindspots, and "boundless emptiness" are what dominate Beddoes's work. They are not obstacles to his poetic expression: they are what he came to express.

II

Beddoes saw the failure of language as the aim of poetry. He kept coming up against barriers in expression which made him stop dead in his tracks, and his fascination with death was just another expression of this block. Death in Beddoes is not explored, embraced, or exceeded but endured, succumbed to, suffered. Bloom sees this as the "baffling theme"—because Beddoes too was baffled by it—on which he chose to "waste his genius," but perhaps this was Beddoes's aim. Profoundly atheistic, Beddoes "found it difficult to scrape together hints for a doctrine of immortality" and he was "haunted for ever" by the question of an afterlife.[12] He returns to the idea of death not as a close or the start of something better but as a nightmarish endless continuation of living, "an area which stops just short of annihilation," Judith Higgens suggests, "a suspended area of confusion, dissolution without re-creation, where this world and the next interpenetrate."[13] "But dead and living, which are which? A question / Not easy to be solved," Beddoes wrote in the *Jest-Book*, and he cannot go beyond posing the question. He could find no conclusion to either his poems or to his vision of life; death is not the end for him. When the dead return in his imagination, as they recurrently do, it is as no more than the living dead, corpses which carry on wandering regardless of point or reason:

> I'll dethrone
> The empty skeleton, and be thy death,
> A death of grinning madness.—Fear me now:
> I am a devil, not a human soul—

Beddoes's writing describes an impossible mourning; his world is littered with lost objects from which he cannot part. His dead take on the ambivalent position that melancholy ascribes to loss: both desired and despised, these things become like waste in Beddoes's psychic economy.

In *Black Sun*, Kristeva describes the mourning of the depressed narcissist, "struggling with signs, going beyond, threatening, or modifying them" (*BS*, 24). Instead of containing aggressiveness toward the lost object as in Freudian accounts of mourning, the narcissist feels instead a sadness "which would point to a primitive self—wounded, incomplete, empty . . . [This sadness is] the archaic expression of an unsymbolizable, unnameable narcissistic wound, so precocious that no outside agent . . . can be used as a referent" (*BS*, 12). Mourning such as this is not for "the object but the Thing . . .

the real that does not lend itself to signification, the centre of repulsion and attraction" (*BS*, 13; my emphasis). Kristeva describes this lost "Thing" as buried alive in the language of depression; it is "an insistence without presence, a light without representation." It cannot be symbolized or translated; it is beyond the signified. "It is a waste" Kristeva continues, "with which, in my sadness, I merge" (*BS*, 15). Melancholy dispenses with the boundaries by which we separate ourselves from the unclean or abject; the melancholic collapses into his own refuse.

The poet Nerval, whom Kristeva quotes, called the silence or Thing which is walled up in the place where signification should be, "the black sun of melancholia": "It is a well known fact that one never sees the sun in a dream, although one is often aware of some far brighter light" (*BS*, 13). In Beddoes the asymbolic Thing which his writing encrypts stalks through his writing as the living dead, but it also appears as the "strange sun," both absent and present, appearing and disappearing, whose light remains after it has set:

> My waking is a Titan's dream,
> Where a strange sun, long set, doth beam
> Through Montezma's cypress bough . . .

This "strange sun" is Beddoes's sublime moment, in which signification fades in nothingness. His writing swerves away from the path to reputation and toward the annihilating pull to this unrepresentable light; to reach the strange sun is his aim as a poet because here is an end to language.

But swerving can also be a self-preservative mechanism: swerving and turning are movements away from the linear progression Beddoes resisted in his writing. Swerving from his drive to write and from finishing what he wrote suggest that writing poetry and confronting himself as a poet contained a threat from which Beddoes needed to be shielded. "I fear there is some maddening secret / Hid in your words," is how he puts it in a fragment.[14] But he was not interested in preservation and he fought against his ego's attempt to defend and assert itself in his work. His instinct was to fear words, and Beddoes's work is remarkable for its lack of self-protection and for the violent encounters with blocks he did not swerve to avoid.

The term *anaclisis* describes an unconscious leaning or propping gesture in which the self-preservative instinct "rests" against or props itself up against a sexual instinct;[15] the anaclitic object is one, like the breast, in which need reappears as desire. Beddoes profoundly lacked any instinct of this sort; there are no safe props in his imagination, and his writing mercilessly deprived him of comfort. But leaning exerts a motionless pressure which prevents further progress and as such it is a gesture which does interest Beddoes. In his hands, however, it becomes not a protective action but one exposing the subject to danger. In a fragment called "Life in a Glass Window," he wrote

> Let him lean
> Against his life, that glassy interval
> 'Twixt us and nothing

and the isolated subject leaning on his reflected image from which he is divided by a break is Beddoes's signature. Instead of recognition, the glass offers a vision of "nothing"; in the place where the self looks for confirmation of himself he finds only emptiness. For Beddoes there could be no union between broken parts, and these lines reveal his sense of irreconcilability between the self who wrote and the self who was revealed in the writing.

Nor is there any relation between the subject and its perceptions in his poetry; Beddoes's writing attempts to have done with egotistic self-reflection. The eye, traditionally perceived as window to the soul and representative of the "I," is Beddoes's most potent image of emptiness and separation. Neither blind, seeing, nor reflecting what is seen, the "cold gazing eyes" that stare blankly from his verse are looked at rather than looking out:

> Just now a beam of joy hung on his eye-lash;
> But as I looked, it sunk into his eye
> Like a bruised worm writhing its form of rings
> Into a darkening hole.
>
> ("Concealed Joy")

> Did you not see a white convulsion
> Run through his cheek and fling his eyelids up?
>
> Alive but in his eyes, and they were fixed
> On a smeared, earthy, bleeding corpse . . .
>
> (Fragment of "The Last Man")

> There's a fellow
> With twisted root-like hair up to his eyes,
> And they are streaked with red and starting out
> Under their bristling brows . . .
>
> ("A Ruffian")

Beddoes's poetry is full of images of visionless seeing. The very possibility of the self collapsing into its object and thus sealing the divide between them is blocked off by his separation of subject from vision.

> How my eyes ache
> With gazing on this mighty vacancy
> (Fragment of "The Last Man")

Continually caught in a confrontation between opposing drives, even the desire for separation, so potently expressed in his writing, is fraught with ambivalence in his imagery.

III

"And so I weave my Penelopean web and rip it up again: and so I roll my impudent Sisyphean stone," Beddoes said of the endless, joyless strain of writing *Death's Jest-Book*. Like the web which Penelope spun by day and unraveled by night and the stone which Sisyphus perpetually rolled to the top of the hill only to let go again, the *Jest-Book* was restarted, expanded, and completed to be then restarted once more. Beddoes's play absorbed—like a "bottomless well" (*W*, 326)—any fragments he cared to throw into it and it spread out until it was longer than *Hamlet*.[16] Had it been published as Beddoes wished in 1829, four years after its inception—"because it is written and can't be helped," he characteristically reasoned—this maverick poetic drama, while perhaps not reviving (or killing) British theater like an "electric shock"[17] as he at one time hoped, might have made Beddoes the strongest voice of his generation. But as it was, the near fatal criticism of friends who found it a blend of "obscurity, conceits and mysticism" resulted first in Beddoes's decision that he "had no real poetical call"[18] and a subsequent attempt at suicide, and then in the play's endless revision. "What good was got by suppressing the poem?" Robert Browning mourned forty years later. "Suppose it had been laughed at . . . Beddoes would not have much cared, but probably made a clean breast, and begun on something else."[19] While he continued to write—and his best poetry was written, but not published, a year later, in 1830 —Beddoes was never able to "free his mind from [this] poetic foetus"[20] which he also called a "still birth."

A year after it was begun he spoke of *Death's Jest-Book* as "never-ending" and the following year he wrote that it had "grown deuced grey." Writing became interminable. He variously described the *Jest-*

Book as a slowly growing "Yew tree," a "tortoise—slow and sure," and a "snowball—I give it a kick every now and then out of mere scorn and ill humour."[21] While the first two images are of certain and solid progress, the last describes an accumulation of bulk which can melt away without trace: precisely the fate he both feared and desired both for his play and for himself as an author and precisely what he suspected occurred in death.

To delay reaching the end, Beddoes began *Death's Jest-Book* again and again, creating greater and more assertive openings. His revised title pages, bearing his pseudonym, suggest a concern about origins and about himself as origin of his work, but also a desire to enclose, or rather to entomb, the play, like Kristeva's Thing, within more writing. Before *Death's Jest-Book* has even begun it is presented as without beginning or end. It is represented, like the missing pages of *The Improvisatore*, or like the ever-expanding center of the play itself, or even like one of his numerous poetic fragments, as a "floating middle."[22]

CHARONIC STEPS
A Dramatic Pocket-book for 1833
Containing
DEATH'S JEST BOOK
A Dithyrambic in the florid Gothic Style
by
Theobald Vesselldoom

THE IVORY GATE
DIDAKILIA-ELEUTHERIA-ANTHESTERIA
THANATOS OR THE PRIVATE THEATRE
A story including
DEATH'S JEST-BOOK
OR
THE FOOL'S TRAGEDY
IN FIVE ACTS
BY THEOBALD VESSELLDOOM
A dramatic keepsake with engravings for 1838

When Beddoes did hand a finished product over to the public he anticipated, with enjoyment, how it would then be torn to shreds. He "murdered to dissect," as Wordsworth put it, when he destroyed copies of *The Improvisatore:* "How I envy you the pleasure of dissecting and laughing at such a grotesque fish as 'The Improvisatore,' " he wrote to Kelsall, whose edition of his poems was still in one piece.[23] Yoking together dissection with laughter, Beddoes beckons the ghost of his father, inventor of laughing gas, dissector of the dead. A Renaissance man, Dr. Beddoes also wrote poetry, social history, radical politics: in his final letter to the scientist Humphry Davy he described himself as "one who has scattered abroad the Anena Fatua [wild oats] of knowledge, from which neither branch nor blossom nor fruit has resulted,"[24] and this fruitlessness is echoed in his son's accounts of his own life's work. "My unhappy devil of a tragedy . . . is done and done for" Thomas Lovell wrote of *Death's Jest-Book,* "its limbs [were] as scattered and unconnected as those of the old gentleman whom Medea minced and boiled young."[25] Both "done and done for," Beddoes developed a Blakeian language of contraries to describe his poetic progress. As Bradshaw observes, "the growth of the *Jest-Book* is simultaneously its ruin and death" ("SL," 14–15). Elsewhere Beddoes calls the drama "dead-game"; the work which at various points is described as "repeatedly touched up," "a strange conglomerate," "written over," "stitched," "cemented" and "stuck" together, is dead on arrival, and the poet lived with this albatross for the rest of his life. Just as the father's dissemination of knowledge bore no fruit, so the son's scattering of what he called "man's puny words" created a stillbirth.

In *Death's Jest-Book* Beddoes stuck together from bits of broken body a Frankenstein's monster who pursued him to the end. The drama was finally patched up and completed by his devoted champion, Thomas Forbes Kelsall, who determined to see it posthumously published. The version which at last appeared in 1850 is Kelsall's own—"excluding everything that might shock a delicate taste by eccentricity, ruthless disregard of convention, or a grotesque and coarse sense of humour"[26]—rather than one of the three versions left behind by Beddoes. Kelsall's editorship turned "an inchoate tangle of alterations, corrections, forethoughts and afterthoughts, into a finished work" (*W,* xxiii).

My Dear Kelsall
Up at 5, Anatomical reading till 6—translation from English into German till 7—Prepare for Blumenbach's lecture on comp. Anatomy and breakfast till 8—Blumenbach's lecture till 9—Stromeyer's lecture on chemistry till 18. 10 to half past 12, Practical Zootomy—half p. 12 to 1 English into German or German literary reading with a pipe—1 to 2 Anatomical lecture. 2 to 3 anatomical reading. 3 to 4 Osteology. 4 to 5 Lecture in German language. 5 to 6 dinner and *light* reading in Zootomy, Chem. or Anatomy. 6 to 7, this hour is very often wasted in a visit, sometimes Anatomical reading till 8. Then coffee and read Greek till 10. 10

to 11, write a little Death's Jest book which is a horrible waste of time, but one must now and then throw away the dregs of the day.[27]

A year into its inception, *Death's Jest-Book* is already a waste of time. After *The Bride's Tragedy* was published, Beddoes saw this drama as "little better than waste paper" too.[28] Writing produces waste and causes time to decay; waste and dregs, like the corpses who stalk through his poems, are the left-overs we expel in order to live. For Beddoes, poetry was something to be recycled or thrown away, something which, as Kristeva says of the abject, "disturbs identity, system, order . . . does not respect borders, positions, rules,"[29] but it is also something to which he returns, again and again. "I have tried 20 times at least to copy it fair," Beddoes wrote to Kelsall of the *Jest-Book*, "but have given up with disgust."[30]

What is it in the idea of waste that haunts Beddoes? What does it mean that he wasted twenty years of his life on a poem he refused to publish? What does it mean that he turned *The Improvisatore* into waste paper after publication or that he saw *The Bride's Tragedy* as "waste paper" once it appeared, that he scrawled his poems on the margins of waste paper, that he "wasted his talent," as Bloom puts it, on the continual pursuit of a theme which thwarted his imagination, or that he "wasted on wild and impracticable subjects a genius only second to the highest in tragic poetry," as the Victorian critic John Forster claimed?[31] Beddoes had a compulsion to make waste and his critics have a compulsion to treat him as such: each poem or play, fragmented or otherwise, was written as waste or written off as waste and all this accumulated waste becomes excessive. Death itself creates excess: in Beddoes's imagination, death simply results in left-over bodies which won't go away and spill over into the living world:

> If I can raise one ghost, why I will raise
> And call up doomsday from behind the east.
> Awake then, ghostly doomsday!
> Throw up your monuments, ye buried men
> That lie in ruined cities of the wastes!

For Beddoes, waste is not only what is considered worthless but what is considered excessive, that which—like the writing of the *Jest-Book* or the publication of *The Improvisatore* and *The Bride's Tragedy*— becomes overwhelming and subsequently overloads him. Beddoes was continually expelling the excess—be it of ideas, of words, of time, of books—by which he was burdened, and this became his preoccupation. His letter above is an example of the cumulative build-up which resulted in throwing away the dregs. When he treats poetry as waste, Beddoes can be seen hovering at the borders of his sublime "strange sun": excess and emptiness confront the ego with a threatening vastness and a war of contraries which stubbornly resist integration. Beddoes's vision of death as an infinite endlessness that his imagination could not match, and his sense of the inadequacy of writing—however endless that too became—to deal with the vision, pushed him to the limit. If the dilemma of the sublime is whether it enlarges or diminishes us, in Beddoes's aesthetic it did the latter. He lived and wrote at the threshold of sublimity, and it is at that threshold that we find Beddoes's melancholy Thing. "The Thing is a waste with which, in my sadness I merge," Kristeva writes, and this collapse with the melancholy object occurs at Beddoes's sublime moment.

Beddoes reaches a blockage in his letter to Kelsall when, at the end of his list of hours in the day and the activities he has to squash into his limited space, he confronts the "horrible waste of time" he identifies with *Death's Jest-Book* and can go no further. He has arrived at a moment in which excess, waste, and inexpressibility combine to prevent further progress in what he finds it possible to think or to say. "For Burke and Kant," Adam Phillips writes, "the sublime was a way of thinking about excess as the key to a deeper kind of subjectivity,"[32] and the "horror" of waste which Beddoes feels before writing is itself a kind of sublime blockage, a violent reaction to confronting this deeper self. Beddoes experienced writer's block as the sublime, and he used the language of waste—both in his words and in his actions—to symbolize the excess of "self" which must be got rid of. Neil Hertz at the beginning his remarkable essay on "The Notion of Blockage in the Literature of the Sublime" writes:

> There is, according to Kant, a sense of the sublime—he calls it the mathematical sublime—arising out of sheer cognitive exhaustion, the mind blocked not by the threat of an over-whelming force, but by the fear of losing count or of being reduced to nothing but counting—this and this and this—with no hope of bringing a long series or a vast scattering under some sort of conceptual unity.[33]

The sublime blockage appears as a "drama of collapse and compensation" and its compensation is to consolidate a self who is "single, whole, and distinct from its representations."[34] Kant's account of the blockage describes a self-preservative mechanism, the mind's turning back on itself as a way of preventing further progress in the face of an overwhelming threat. Saved from an experience which exposes the self as nothing, the blockage achieves the fantasy of "Unity of Being": "For there is here a feeling of the inadequacy of [the] imagination for presenting the ideas of a whole, wherein the imagination reaches its maximum, and, in trying to surpass it, sinks back into itself, by which, however, a kind of emotional satisfaction is produced."[35] The result of the blockage is the consolidation of the ego: "the mind's exultation in its own rational faculties, its ability to think a totality that cannot be taken in through the senses."[36]

And yet Beddoes's subject was "strangenessess . . . and nothing else," wastelands, empty visions, splintered selves in "glassy intervals." The reassurance offered by becoming blocked and turning back into an integrated self were counterproductive to him. When he experienced completion, as in the case of the published *Improvisatore*, he destroyed it. Beddoes operated in the language of melancholy and the realms of division, fragments, broken bodies: "Art not sewn up with veins and pegged together / With bony sticks and hinges." His aim was to move beyond—"Getting at length beyond our tedious selves"—beyond the "borders, positions, rules" which waste rejects, beyond death, language, and blockage, and in this he felt he had failed as a poet. His poetic ambition was to extinguish his voice, to write himself out by taking language as far as it would go. Poetry, like disease, was no respecter of boundaries; for Beddoes writing should not end, should not have limits or be hindered by blocks. He wanted to merge with his Thing, to write himself into oblivion, and not being able to do so made his work a waste of time.

If the mark of a strong text is the critic's repetition of that text's unconscious gestures, so that he "*does* the same thing,"[37] then Beddoes's afterlife becomes, like his life's work, "strangenesses . . . and nothing else." "By a fatality which seemed to pursue the author of 'Death's Jest-Book,' " as Edmund Gosse puts it,[38] his writing has continued to exert blocks, excite fears, and waste away in the hands of those readers who have tried to resurrect him. Judith Higgens, whose edited selection of Beddoes partially revived him in 1976, writes that she was "seized . . . with writer's block" during her compilation of the edition, after which her editor at Carcanet found during the typesetting that "Beddoes gave him dreadful nightmares."[39] A hundred years earlier, Beddoes's entire oeuvre had ended up in the care of Robert Browning, who was bequeathed the papers by Kelsall when Browning expressed his admiration for the poet. Initially enthusiastic about the project of publishing Beddoes, Browning became increasingly resistant to even reading the manuscripts and held off opening the box: "I have not opened it—and may delay a little in what I feel to be a serious business," he wrote to Mrs. Kelsall a day after its arrival.[40] His delay lasted for the next eleven years. "Nothing," Gosse recalled, "would induce him" to open what had become "that dismal box." Browning seemed to have " an unaccountable horror of what would be discovered,"[41] and eventually he asked Gosse to unlock it and examine the contents. The "Browning Box," as it is known, has now disappeared. It seems as if Beddoes's will to obscurity was stronger than even he could have predicted: who could have foreseen that, like the snowball he described his *Jest-Book* as resembling, "the adverse fate that pursued Beddoes in life should continue its work of destruction until nearly every trace of his existence was obliterated from this earth?"[42]

Notes

1. Michael Bradshaw, "Scattered Limbs: The Making and Unmaking of *Death's Jest-Book*" (Derbyshire: Thomas Lovell Beddoes Society, 1996), 25. Hereafter "SL," cited in the text.

2. *The Works of Thomas Lovell Beddoes,* ed. H. W. Donner (London: Oxford University Press, 1935), 611. Hereafter *W,* cited in the text.

3. See Freud, "Mourning and Melancholia," Pelican Freud Library (Harmondsworth: Penguin Books, 1984), 11: 253.

4. Julia Kristeva, *Black Sun: Depression and Melancholia,* trans. Leon S. Roudiez (New York: Columbia University Press, 1989), 53. Hereafter *BS,* cited in the text.

5. *Works,* letter to Kelsall, October 1827, 636.

6. Freud, "Mourning," 266.

7. See *The Browning Box, or, The Life and Works and Thomas Lovell Beddoes as Reflected in Letters by His Friends and Admirers,* ed. H. W. Donner (London: Oxford University Press, 1935); letter from Kelsall to Browning, 13 November 1867, 97.

8. *Works,* letter to Kelsall, October 1827, 637.

9. Geoffrey Hartman, "Romanticism and Anti-Self Consciousness," reprinted in Cynthia Chase, ed., *Romanticism* (London: Longman, 1993), 47.

10. Harold Bloom, *Visionary Company* (London: Faber & Faber, 1969), 428.

11. *Works,* letter to Kelsall, 1 April 1826, 616–17.

12. Letter to Kelsall, April 1827: "I am now already so thoroughly penetrated with the conviction of the absurdity and unsatisfactory nature of human life, that I search with avidity for every shadow of a proof or probability of an after-existence, both in the material and immaterial nature of man. Those people . . . are greatly to be envied, who believe, honestly and from conviction, in the christian doctrines: but really in the New Testament it is difficult to scrape together hints for a doctrine of immortality" (*Works,* 630).

13. Judith Higgens and Michael Bradshaw, eds., *Thomas Lovell Beddoes: Selected Poems* (Manchester: Carcanet, 1999), xv.

14. Beddoes, "Anticipation of Evil Tidings."

15. See Freud, "Three Essays on the Theory of Sexuality," Pelican Freud Library (1977), 7: 71.

16. Absorption is the recurring metaphor chosen by all Beddoes's critics to describe the composition of *Death's Jest-Book:* the poems, verses, and prose speeches of which the play was composed resembled, James Thompson writes, "the liver of his

imagination—absorbing and retaining the embittered products of his eccentric sensibility." In *Thomas Leve Beddoes* (Boston: Twayne, 1985), 51. For Donner: "There was no end to *Death's Jest-Book*. It absorbed all the treasures thrown into it, and it gradually came to absorb many more of Beddoes's most beautiful poems."

17. *Works,* letter to Kelsall, 1 April 1826, 617.

18. *Works,* letter to Proctor, 19 April 1829, 642.

19. *Browning Box,* letter from Browning to Kelsall, 22 May 1868, 104.

20. *Browning Box,* letter from Kelsall to Browning, 16 June 1868, 109.

21. *Works,* letter to Kelsall, 1 April 1826: "The never-ending Jest-book . . . lies like a snow ball and I give it a kick every now and then out of mere scorn and ill humour," 616.

22. Bradshaw, "Scattered Limbs," 4.

23. *Works,* letter to Kelsall, 3 April 1826, 618.

24. Quoted in Roy Porter, *Doctor of Society* (London: Routledge, 1992), 187.

25. *Works,* letter to Kelsall, 5 October 1826, 620.

26. *Browning Box,* introduction, lxxiii.

27. *Works,* letter to Kelsall, 5 December 1825, 608–9.

28. *Works,* letter to Kelsall, undated, 611.

29. Julia Kristeva, *Powers of Horror: An Essay on Abjection* (New York: Columbia University Press, 1982), 4.

30. *Works,* letter to Kelsall, 5 October 1826, 620.

31. In his Forster's life of *Walter Savage Landor,* quoted in a letter from Browning to Kelsall in *Browning Box,* 123.

32. Edmund Burke, *A Philosophical Enquiry into the Sublime and the Beautiful,* ed. Adam Phillips (Oxford: Oxford University Press, 1990), lx.

33. Neil Hertz, "The Notion of Blockage in the Literature of the Sublime," in Geoffrey H. Hartman, ed., *Psychoanalysis and the Question of the Text* (Baltimore, Md.: The Johns Hopkins University Press, 1978), 62.

34. See Chase, *Romanticism,* 78.

35. Kant, quoted in Hertz, "Notion of Blockage," 72.

36. Hertz, ibid., 62.

37. See Chase: "In Hertz's reading, a critical or theoretical text illuminates a poetic text not chiefly through what it says about it but in so far as it *does* the same things" (*Romanticism,* 78).

38. Sir Edmund Gosse, *The Complete Works of Thomas Lovell Beddoes, with a Memoir* (London: Fanfrolico Press, 1895), x.

39. Judith Higgins, *The Thomas Lovell Beddoes Society Newsletter,* vol. 1, no. 2.

40. *Browning Box,* 138.

41. Gosse, *Complete Works,* 11.

42. *Browning Box,* 1. xxv.

A Woman's Desire to Be Known: Expressivity and Silence in *Corinne*

Toril Moi

Duke University

L'humanité est mâle et l'homme définit la femme non en soi mais relativement à lui; elle n'est pas considérée comme un être autonome.

[Humanity is male and man defines woman not in herself but as relative to him; she is not regarded as an autonomous being.]
—Simone de Beauvoir, *The Second Sex*

J'aurais pu, ce me semble, envoyer à ma place une poupée légèrement perfectionnée par la mécanique; elle aurait très bien rempli mon emploi dans la société.

[It seems to me that I could have sent a delicately improved mechanical doll in my place. It would have fulfilled my function in society very well.]
—Madame de Staël, *Corinne, or Italy*

Efterhaanden blev da Hørelsen mig den kjæreste Sands; thi ligesom Stemmen er Aabenbarelsen af den for det Ydre incommensurable Inderlighed, saaledes er Øret det Redskab, ved hvilket denne Inderlighed opfattes, Hørelsen den Sands, ved hvilken den tilegnes.

[Little by little, hearing became my favourite sense; for just as it is the voice that reveals the inwardness which is incommensurable with the outer, so the ear is the instrument whereby that inwardness is grasped, hearing the sense by which it is appropriated.]
—Søren Kierkegaard, *Either/Or*

143

Introduction

W E no longer die for love. When relationships break up, we
soldier on, seeking solace in work, family, friends, or casual
sex. Sooner or later we start looking for new relationships. Not so
with Corinne, Madame de Staël's pathbreaking woman of genius.
When her lover marries another, Corinne loses all her formidable
talents, her interest in art, books, other people, her voice, and, finally, her life. Why? What does the brilliant Corinne's lingering
death mean?

I want to show that Corinne's death is not simply the result of
Staël's failure of feminist nerve. In spite of Corinne's sad demise,
the novel offers a radical analysis of women's situation in 1807. (*Corinne* was written in 1806–07, and published in April 1807.) And although there is much melodrama in *Corinne*, to think that one can
dismiss Corinne's death by calling it "melodramatic," is to blind
oneself to the philosophical and psychological meanings of the
melodramatic mode. Peter Brooks speaks of melodrama's aesthetics
of *excess*, and shows that it is immensely influential on nineteenth-
century literature and theater.[1] In particular, the influence of pictorial melodrama is ubiquitous in *Corinne*.[2] All the crucial scenes in
the novel are staged as if they were paintings, or in theatrical terms:
tableaux. In the world of *Corinne*, as in the world of melodrama, aesthetics and ethics are deeply intertwined. In this novel pictures are
expected to convince by their contents, not just by their color or
technique. Corinne and Oswald both expect paintings to have
strong ethical implications.[3] Corinne's death scene exemplifies this
aesthetic program: it is at once a tableau and the outcome of Staël's
meditations on the relationship between love and expressivity, and
between love and our capacity to understand others.

A major concern in *Corinne* is the problem of knowing others and
of being known by them. Philosophers usually refer to these questions as "skepticism concerning other minds," and the problem
arises when someone comes to experience his or her existential sep-
arateness from others. But Staël does not ponder such questions in
the abstract, as so many philosophers have done. Pitting England
against Italy, and male against female, *Corinne* asks us to think about
what it takes to understand human beings separated from us by national or sexual differences. These are uncannily modern problems,
as relevant today as two hundred years ago.

Corinne explores these questions through an almost obsessive concern with Corinne's expressivity, represented both in terms of her
capacity to show others who she is, and in terms of her capacity to

understand others. Yet, in spite of the insistence on expressivity, Corinne's sudden silence in book 17 is the turning point of the plot.
The novel's explicit preoccupation with the aesthetics of theatricality and absorption, to draw on Michael Fried's useful terms, is closely
connected with its understanding of expressivity and silence, love
and knowledge. Thus Corinne's ceaseless attempts to show herself
to others is contrasted with her rival and half-sister Lucile's constant
efforts to hide herself from others. Against Corinne's direct gaze,
the novel sets Lucile's lowered eyelids; against Corinne's rhapsodiz-
ing voice it sets Lucile's constrained silence. Moreover, it would
seem that Oswald falls in love with Lucile precisely because her silence prevents him from getting to know her: "[I]l aimait Lucile
presque sans la connaître, car il ne lui avait pas entendu prononcer
vingt paroles," the narrator comments (F17.8.494)[4] [He loved Lucile almost without knowing her, for he had not yet heard her utter
twenty words] (E17.8.337). In fact, the contrast between Lucile and
Corinne is used to illustrate all the important themes in this novel:
while it is crucial to its aesthetic considerations, it is also central to
its ruminations on women's position in society, and on love and
knowledge. The novel's treatment of love and knowledge, moreover,
returns us to the question of melodrama: *Corinne* now seems to me
to be the prototype, or the literary precursor, of the film genre Stanley Cavell has called the "melodrama of the unknown woman."

One final question needs to be addressed: why write on *Corinne* at
all? I think I owe my enduring fascination with *Corinne* to Ellen
Moers's chapter on the "Myth of Corinne" in her pioneering book
Literary Women, first published in 1976. Moers's vivid account of the
importance of *Corinne* for nineteenth-century readers enthralled
me. "[*Corinne*] is an immortal book, and deserves to be read three
score and ten times—that is once every year in the age of man," Elizabeth Barrett wrote at the age of twenty-six.[5] Jane Austen, Mary God-
win Shelley, George Sand, George Eliot, Charlotte Brontë, Harriet
Beecher Stowe, Margaret Fuller ("The Yankee Corinna"), Kate
Chopin—all of them read *Corinne*, passionately. Daisy Miller's visit
to the Coliseum in moonlight is taken straight out of *Corinne*. Even
Ibsen's Nora dances the tarantella in secret homage to Corinne, who
danced it first. *Corinne* was published in more than forty editions (in
French alone) between 1807 and 1872.[6] The success and influence
of this novel was quite simply immense.[7]

But does *Corinne* matter today? Of course, a book that mattered
so intensely to a whole century is of enormous historical interest.
For Staël's contemporary admirers, male and female, *Corinne* was a
"remarkably courageous celebration of the rights of spiritual genius

and intellectual freedom, in defiance of the spreading imperial rule of a military genius named Napoleon."[8] For its post-Waterloo readers, however, the novel's appeal lies in what Moers calls the "ultimate fantasy of the performing heroine."[9] "What Oswald is made to love in Corinne," Moers writes, "is not the woman in the genius but, if the expression is pardonable, the whole package: the woman of genius at the moment and in the place of her greatest public triumph."[10] As long as passionate love affairs keep going badly wrong, as long as some people believe in the myth of the unbearable ugliness of the intellectual woman, as long as some girls feel that they have to "dumb down" in order to be loved, there is good reason to reread *Corinne*.[11]

Absorption and Theatricality

Corinne is a highly theatrical novel, in the sense that it constantly invites its readers to approach it as if it were the text of a play, the kind of play that relies on tableaux for its greatest effects.[12] Thus we are supposed to *see* Corinne at the Capitol, Corinne at Cape Miseno, Corinne in her dying moment pointing toward the cloud over the moon, and so on. Tableau in French means painting or picture, and paintings play an important part in the novel. Oswald and Corinne visit picture galleries together, and Corinne's own collection of paintings is detailed at length. Lucile identifies with Coreggio's *La Madonna della Scala*, Corinne with Domenichino's *The Sibyl*.[13] Modern editors always stress the importance of these paintings. Thus my French editions of *Corinne* and *De la littérature* both reproduce a detail of François Gérard's *Corinne at Cape Miseno* on the cover, whereas the Oxford edition of *Corinne* opts for Domenichino's Sibyl.

Nothing provides a better grasp of the contrast between Corinne and Lucile than the novel's first representation of the two women. Corinne is, famously, introduced in book 2, where Oswald witnesses her crowning at the Capitol in Rome. Lucile, on the other hand, is not seen until book 16, when Oswald catches a glimpse of her in the park of Lady Edgermond's Northumberland estate. I shall start with Oswald's first impression of Lucile, which also is the novel's first description of her:

> [Oswald] se promena dans le parc et aperçut de loin, à travers les feuilles, une jeune personne de la taille la plus élégante, avec des cheveux blonds d'une admirable beauté, qui étaient à peine retenus par son cha-

peau. Elle lisait avec beaucoup de recueillement. Oswald la reconnut pour Lucile, bien qu'il ne l'eût pas vue depuis trois ans . . .

C'était Lucile, qui entrait à peine dans sa seizième année. Ses traits étaient d'une délicatesse remarquable: sa taille était presque trop élancée, car un peu de faiblesse se faisait remarquer dans sa démarche; son teint était d'une admirable beauté, et la pâleur et la rougeur s'y succédaient en un instant. Ses yeux bleus étaient si souvent baissés que sa physionomie consistait surtout dans cette délicatesse de teint qui trahissait à son insçu les émotions que sa profonde réserve cachait de toute autre manière. . . [Oswald] rêvait à la pureté céleste d'une jeune fille qui ne s'est jamais éloignée de sa mère, et ne connaît de la vie que la tendresse filiale. (F16.5.450)

[(Oswald) went for a stroll in the grounds. Through the foliage he saw, in the distance, a girl with the most elegant figure and with wonderfully beautiful fair hair barely contained under her hat. She was reading very attentively. Oswald recognized her as Lucile, despite not having seen her for three years . . .

It was Lucile, who was just sixteen.[14] Her features were remarkably delicate, her figure almost too slender, for a little weakness could be seen in her walk. Her complexion was wonderfully beautiful and paleness gave way to blushes in a moment. Her blue eyes were lowered so often that her expression lay mainly in that delicate complexion which, unknown to her, betrayed emotions which her deep reserve concealed in every other way . . . (Oswald) meditat(ed) on the heavenly purity of a young girl who has never left her mother's side and whose only knowledge of life is filial affection.] (E16.5.306)

Readers of *The Mill on the Floss* will remember that this is the exact point where Maggie Tulliver gives up on *Corinne:* "I didn't finish the book," said Maggie. "As soon as I came to the blond-haired young lady reading in the park, I shut it up, and determined to read no further. I foresaw that that light-complexioned girl would win away all the love from Corinne and make her miserable."[15]

Lucile is reading attentively. Her eyes are not lifted. She does not look at Oswald or anyone else. She doesn't know that she is being watched. Even if she had known, she would never knowingly have revealed her feelings. The young, blond girl reading in the park is the very definition of *absorption,* as defined by Michael Fried in *Absorption and Theatricality,* his epochal study of Diderot's aesthetics and eighteenth-century French painting.

Briefly put, Fried understands absorptive art as art that seeks to absorb the beholder, to fix her in front of the canvas. Fundamentally, the point of absorptive art is to allow the beholder to forget that she *is* a beholder, to "establish the fiction that no one is standing before the canvas."[16] There is a paradox here: the fiction that there is no beholder serves to stop and hold the beholder precisely there, in front of the canvas (AT, 108). In its effort to eradicate self-consciousness in the beholder, absorptive art is the antithesis of modernism. In the eighteenth-century people visiting an art exhibition would remain transfixed in front of a canvas, often for hours on end. Today, such behavior would probably strike us as a highly theatrical, self-dramatizing gesture on the part of the beholder. We'd think that the person doing this was making an exhibition of herself. In the eighteenth-century, however, such experiences were sought after, and taken as evidence of the greatness of the art that induced them. Absorption, then, is a state of intense reverie, in which the beholder is able totally to forget herself, to let herself dream (free-associate) without self-restraint.

In early to mid-eighteenth-century French painting, painters sought to inspire the desired state of absorption in beholders by representing characters who were themselves absorbed. In the first half of the century, this could be done through the representation of everyday activities (think of Chardin's paintings of young people blowing soap bubbles or building card castles). By the 1760s, Fried writes, absorption could only be induced by more extraordinary means. Greuze still represents absorbed young girls, but now seemingly everyday activities—a girl crying over a broken mirror or a dead bird—are suffused with a dramatic and emotional intensity absent in Chardin.[17] Corinne's representation of Lucile instantly brought Greuze's Une jeune fille qui pleure son oiseau mort (A young girl crying over her dead bird, 1765) to my mind.[18]

Lucile's (self-)absorbed inexpressiveness becomes the source of erotic fantasies for Oswald:

> [S]a complète réserve lui laissait toujours du doute et de l'incertitude sur la nature de ses sentiments. Le plus haut point de la passion, et l'éloquence qu'elle inspire, ne suffisent pas encore à l'imagination; on désire toujours quelque chose de plus; et ne pouvant l'obtenir, l'on se refroidit et on se lasse, tandis que la faible lueur qu'on aperçoit à travers les nuages tient long-temps la curiosité en suspens, et semble promettre dans l'avenir de nouveaux sentiments et des découvertes nouvelles. Cette attente cependant n'est point satisfaite; et quand on sait à la fin ce que cache tout ce charme du silence et de l'inconnu, le mystère aussi se flétrit, et l'on en revient à regretter l'abandon et le mouvement d'un caractère animé. (F17.5.485–86)

> [(H)er complete reserve always left him in doubt and uncertainty about the nature of her feelings. The highest point of passionate love and the

eloquence it inspires still do not satisfy the imagination. You[19] always want something more, and if you cannot get it you become cold and weary. But the faint glimmer you can see through the clouds holds curiosity in suspense for a long time and seems to promise new feelings and new discoveries in the future. This expectation, however, is not satisfied. In the end, when you know what is hidden by all the charm of silence and the unknown, the mystery, too, fades, and you come back to regretting the lack of restraint and the animation of a lively personality.] (E17.5.331–32)

Oswald's attraction to Lucile is the attraction of a lover to a blank screen. This is transference love: Oswald admiring his own projection.

It is tempting to assume that if Lucile is presented as the quintessential absorptive painting, then Corinne must be theatricality incarnate. This conclusion seems all the more compelling to anyone reading *Corinne* after the advent of modernism. To us, it is almost impossible to understand Corinne as anything else than a misguided painting by, say, Bouguereau or Alma-Tadema, a kind of camp incarnation of theatricality and bad taste. But these are anachronistic associations. The character of Corinne embodies the aesthetic ideals of *Corinne*, and these have to be understood on their own terms before we choose to embrace or reject them. The "modernist" response to *Corinne* has another flaw: it can't account for the emotions, feelings, identifications that the novel still stirs up in many readers. Such readers (I am one of them) are not necessarily aesthetic morons: there are reasons why the hopeless love affair and death of the supertalented Corinne still have the power to move. I shall return to this.

In order to avoid the "modernist" response to *Corinne*, we need to understand what theatricality meant in late eighteenth and early nineteenth-century France. Again I'll rely on Fried's study of the term. It is crucial to note that theatricality and absorption are not in fact binary opposites. Theatricality is a feature of a work of art or of a particular artistic performance, whereas absorption is a mental and emotional state experienced by the beholder. Theatricality destroys this state because it brings about a jarring awareness in the beholder of her own act of beholding, one might say. Already in the 1760s it had become evident that the mere representation of absorptive states was no longer enough to secure absorption in the beholder. Fried shows that a new, dramatic conception of art was being established at this time:

The dramatic conception calls for establishing the fiction of the beholder's nonexistence in and through the persuasive representation of figures wholly absorbed in their actions, passions, activities, feelings, states of mind. (As we have seen, increasingly strong measures came to be required in order to persuade contemporary audiences that a figure or group of figures *was* so absorbed.) (*AT*, 131–32)

For Diderot, anything that reminds the beholder that he *is* a beholder, was theatrical. He used the term *le théâtral* [the theatrical] to mean "consciousness of being beheld," and took it to be synonymous with falseness (*AT*, 100). Diderot also distinguished between *attitudes* and *actions*: "Autre chose est une attitude, autre chose une action. Toute attitude est fausse et petite; toute action est belle et vraie" [An attitude is one thing, an action is another. Attitudes are false and petty, actions are all beautiful and true.][20] Fried comments:

> Diderot's distinction between actions and attitudes asserted a difference not of degree, but of kind, i.e. between natural, spontaneous, largely automatic realizations of an intention or expressions of a passion on the one hand and conventional, mannered, and (in the pejorative sense of the term . . .) theatrical simulacra of those on the other. (*AT*, 101)

A Diderotian critic, then, would want to know whether the performing Corinne strikes attitudes, or expresses deeply passionate actions. The answer to this question would decide whether she should be rejected as theatrical or applauded for being simple and natural.

Let us turn to the novel's first description of Corinne, as seen through Oswald's eyes. He catches his first glimpse of her as her triumphal chariot is moving through admiring crowds:

> Elle était vêtue comme la Sybille du Dominiquin, un schall des Indes tourné autour de sa tête, et ses cheveux du plus beau noir entremêlés avec ce schall; sa robe était blanche; une draperie bleue se rattachait au-dessous de son sein, et son costume était très pittoresque, sans s'écarter cependant assez des usages reçus, pour que l'on pût y trouver de l'affectation. Son attitude sur le char était noble et modeste: on apercevait bien qu'elle était contente d'être admirée; mais un sentiment de timidité se mêlait à sa joie, et semblait demander grace pour son triomphe; l'expression de sa physionomie, de ses yeux, de son sourire, intéressait pour elle, et le premier regard fit de lord Nelvil son ami, avant même qu'une impression plus vive le subjuguât. Ses bras étaient d'une éclatante beauté; sa taille grande, mais un peu forte, à la manière des statues grecques, caractérisait énergiquement la jeunesse et le bonheur; son regard avait quelque chose d'inspiré. L'on voyait dans sa manière de saluer et de remercier, pour les applaudissements qu'elle recevait, une sorte de naturel qui relevait l'éclat de la situation extraordinaire dans laquelle elle se trouvait; elle donnait à la fois l'idée d'une prêtresse d'Apollon,

qui s'avançait vers le temple du Soleil, et d'une femme parfaitement simple dans les rapports habituels de la vie; enfin tous ses mouvements
avaient un charme qui excitait l'intérêt et la curiosité, l'étonnement et
l'affection. (F2.1.52)

[She was dressed like Domenichino's Sibyl. An Indian turban was wound
round her head, and intertwined with her beautiful black hair. Her dress
was white with a blue stole fastened beneath her breast, but her attire,
though very striking, did not differ so much from accepted styles as to
be deemed affected. Her demeanour on the chariot was noble and modest; it was obvious that she was pleased to be admired, but a feeling of
shyness was mingled with her happiness and seemed to ask pardon for
her triumph. The expression on her countenance, in her eyes, and in
her smile aroused interest in her, and the first sight of her inclined Lord
Nelvil in her favour even before he was conquered by any stronger feeling. Her arms were dazzlingly beautiful; her tall, slightly plump figure,
in the style of a Greek statue, gave a keen impression of youth and happiness; her eyes had something of an inspired look. In her way of greeting
people and thanking them for the applause she was receiving, there was
a kind of naturalness which enhanced the effect of (*qui relevait l'éclat de*)
her extraordinary situation. At one and the same time she gave the impression of a priestess of Apollo who approaches the sun-god's temple,
and of a woman who is completely natural (*simple*) in the ordinary relationships of life. In short, all her movements had a charm which aroused
interest and curiosity, wonder and affection.] (E2.1.23)

This is in many ways an extraordinarily melodramatic scene. A man
struck by love at the sight of a woman's public triumph: nothing
could be more pictorial, more unlikely, more excessive, than the
novel's enthusiastic description of Corinne's crowning at the Capitol. But although *Corinne* may strike modern readers as theatrical
("mannered," Diderot would say), it doesn't follow that its contemporary readers saw the novel in that way.

Oswald's vision of Corinne has been preceded by aural impres-
sions. As she approaches, the ecstatic crowd talks about her accom-
plishments and the mystery surrounding her name and birth, concluding that "Quoi qu'il en soit . . . c'est une divinité entourée de
nuages" (F2.1.51) [Whatever the truth may be . . . she is a goddess
surrounded by clouds"] (E2.1.22). This phrase contains the same
apparent ambiguity as the longer description of Corinne. She is at
once extraordinarily elevated (a priestess of Apollo, the god of art)
and completely ordinary (she is straightforward or unaffected [*simple*] in ordinary relationships). Corinne is "noble" and "modest,"
"pleased to be admired," and yet marked by "shyness" and a sense
that she needs to be "pardoned" for her success. While transgres-

sing all rules for female behavior, Corinne exudes a charming (in Oswald's eyes) awareness that such transgressions are not to be condoned. Identifying with the Sibyl, she dresses in blue and white, the traditional colors of the Madonna.[21] The myth of the Cumaean Sibyl contains a similar blend of paganism and Christianity, since this pagan prophetess was venerated by Christians because she was said to have foretold the coming of Christ. Corinne, then, unites in her person all kinds of traditional oppositions. She shines like the sun (Apollo was the sun god, too), yet she is veiled behind a cloud. She is at once pagan and Christian, transgressive and submissive, extraordinary and ordinary, goddess and mortal woman. It seems obvious that Staël is trying to represent the half English and half Italian Corinne as the triumphant synthesis of traditional opposites. No wonder that many modern readers have found her ludicrously idealized.

Idealized or not, Corinne is explicitly described as "simple" and "natural." Absorption is still the novel's aesthetic ideal: "[L]e calcul du succès est presque toujours destructeur de l'enthousiasme" (F8.3.223) [(T)o work for success is nearly always to destroy strong feeling] (E8.3.144), Corinne says to Oswald in one of their discussions of paintings. Corinne moves her interlocutors, but not by calculating her effects. Her art moves because it is all genuine *expression* of passionate inner feelings. It is no coincidence that Corinne's most admired art is that of public improvisation on a given theme.

Staël repeatedly demonstrates Corinne's overwhelmingly absorptive effect on Oswald. The description of her arrival at the Capitol, which I just quoted, continues in the following way:

> L'admiration du peuple pour elle allait toujours en croissant, plus elle approchait du Capitole, de ce lieu si fécond en souvenirs. Ce beau ciel, ces Romains si enthousiastes, et par-dessus tout Corinne, électrisaient l'imagination d'Oswald. . . .
> Oswald était tellement absorbé dans ses réflexions, des idées si nouvelles l'occupaient tant, qu'il ne remarqua point les lieux antiques et célèbres à travers lesquels passait le char de Corinne. (F2.1.52–53)

> [The nearer she came to the Capitol, that place so rich in memories, the more the crowd admired her. The beautiful sky, the wildly enthusiastic Romans, and above all Corinne, fired[22] Oswald's imagination. . . .
> Oswald was so lost in his thoughts, so absorbed by new ideas, that he did not notice the famous, ancient places through which Corinne's chariot passed.] (E2.1.23–24)

That Corinne is supposed to have supremely "absorptive" effects is borne out by the paroxysmatic chapter in which her performance as Juliet leaves Oswald in a state where he is unable to distinguish between reality and fiction. At one point Corinne, on stage as Juliet, stretches out her arms, and Oswald "crut voir qu'elle étendait les bras vers lui comme pour l'appeler à son aide, et il se leva dans un transport insensé, puis se rassit, ramené à lui-même par les regards supris de ceux qui l'environnaient, mais son émotion devenait si forte qu'elle ne pouvait plus se cacher" (F7.3.199) [thought she was stretching out her arms to him to summon him to her aid, and, in a crazy outburst of passionate love, he got up. Then he sat down again, brought to his senses by the surprised looks of the people around him, but his emotion became so strong that he could hide it no longer] (E7.3.127). When the performance is over, Oswald is so moved that he still can't tell the difference between reality and fiction: "Dans l'excès de son trouble, il ne savait pas distinguer si c'était la vérité ou la fiction" (F7.3.200) [In his great disarray, he could not distinguish between truth and fiction] (E7.3.127). Throwing himself at Corinne's feet, Oswald starts speaking Romeo's lines to her.

Oswald, in fact, behaves exactly like Diderot reading Richardson:

Ô Richardson! On prend, malgré qu'on en ait, un rôle dans tes ouvrages, on se mêle à la conversation, on approuve, on blâme, on admire, on si'irrite, on si'indgine. Combien de fois ne me suis-je pas surpris, comme il est arrivé à des enfants qu'on avait menés au spectacle pour la première fois, criant: "Ne le croyez pas, il vous trompe . . . Si vous allez là, vous êtes perdu."[23]

[O Richardson! whether we wish to or not, we play a part in your works, we intervene in the conversation, we give approval and blame, we feel admiration, irritation and indignation. How many times have I caught myself, as happens with children being taken to the theatre for the first time, shouting out: *Don't believe him, he's deceiving you . . . If you go there it will be the end of you.*][24]

For Diderot, nothing is better evidence of the absence of theatricality in art than this. For Diderot and Oswald are here "forgetting the fiction"—forgetting that what they are experiencing is a work of art. They are so absorbed, in other words, that they experience art as reality. Elsewhere, Diderot speaks of a supremely antitheatrical quality which he calls *le naïf* [the naive]. The naive, understood as something simple, innocent, original and true, is found in all beautiful art: "C'est la chose, mais la chose pure, sans la moindre altération. L'art n'y est plus" [It is the thing, but the thing in itself, without the slightest alteration. Art is no longer there].[25] When spectators take

art for reality, when they want to storm up on stage in order to rescue Ophelia from her doom, they testify to the supreme greatness
of the art that provoked the response.[26]

I have compared Lucile reading in the park to a painting by
Greuze. By the time of the French Revolution, however, Greuze had
lost his fortune, his popularity, and his power to move the beholder.
In 1807 Greuze was dead, and David reigned supreme over French
painting. Corinne at the Capitol is not in the least Greuzelike. The
intensely expressive drama of the crowning of Corinne recalls,
rather, the 1780s masterpieces of David, which are usually said to
inaugurate modern painting.[27] The contrast between Greuze and
David is repeated in the contrast between Lucile and Corinne. Corinne embodies an aesthetics of dramatic expressivity which was radically modern in 1807, and which also turned out to point to the
future of Western painting. Set against such a radically modern aesthetic ideal, the inexpressive, absorbed Lucile must have seemed
pale and old-fashioned. I shall now show that the aesthetic contrast
between Corinne and Lucile, between radical modernity and prerev-
olutionary past, is repeated on the political level.

Expressivity, Silence, Individuality:
Corinne as a Modern Woman

Because Corinne is a woman, her extraordinary expressivity—the
very feature that secures her antitheatricality according to Diderot's
dramatic conception of art—makes her exceptionally vulnerable
precisely to accusations of theatricality. The scenes emphasizing the
clash between Corinne's personality and the norms of womanhood
in England bring this out. Explaining her hostility to Corinne, Lady
Edgermond says to Oswald: "Il lui faut un théâtre où elle puisse
montrer tout ces talents que vous prisez tant, et qui rendent la vie si
difficile" (F16.6.461) [She needs a theatre where she can display all
those gifts you prize so highly and which make life so difficult]
(E16.6.313). More alarming to Oswald is the fact that his own re-
vered father turns out to have said the same thing, in the fatal letter
explaining why he doesn't want Corinne to marry Oswald:

> elle a besoin de plaire, de captiver, de faire effet. Elle a plus de talents
> encore que d'amour-propre; mais des talents si rares doivent nécessaire-
> ment exciter le désir de les développer; et je ne sais pas quel théâtre peut
> suffire à cette activité d'esprit, à cette impétuosité d'imagination, à ce
> caractère ardent enfin qui se fait sentir dans toutes ses paroles: elle en-

traînerait nécessairement mon fils hors de l'Angleterre; car une telle femme ne peut y être heureuse; et l'Italie seule lui convient. (F16.8.466–67)

[she needs to please, to charm, to attract attention. She has far more gifts than vanity, but such exceptional talents are bound to arouse the desire to develop them, and I do not know what audience (*théâtre*) can satisfy the intellectual activity, the eager imagination, the ardent nature, which can be felt in all she says. She is bound to lead my son to leave England, for such a woman cannot be happy here, and Italy alone will suit her.] (E16.8.318)

To align oneself with this kind of antitheatricality is to align oneself with the defenders of silence and anonymity for women. This is why *Corinne* works so hard to establish its heroine as an intensely dramatic woman who nevertheless avoids theatricality. Corinne's performances are high-wire balancing acts, one wrong step and she will be perceived as theatrical. To agree with the novel's antitheatrical forces is also, of course, to cast Italy, Corinne's double (the novel is after all called *Corinne, or Italy*), as a place of dubious reputation, the site of excess and social transgression. Somewhat paradoxically, then, the common "modernist" reaction to *Corinne*—the one that finds it excessive, melodramatic, lacking in artistic restraint and self-awareness—ends up in the same camp as Lady Edgermond and the elder Lord Nelvil. In order to avoid the condescending (and uninteresting) conclusion that Corinne's expressivity is simply excessive, that she is a ludicrous figment of Staël's narcissistic imagination, we need to read it against what the novel posits as the norm for women, namely silence. For Staël a silent woman is one who is not recognized as an individual. In *Corinne* silence *is* anonymity.

When Lucile and Oswald, now long married, finally travel to Italy, Lucile does not express a single wish: "Lord Nelvil craignait les souvenirs que lui retraçait la France; il la traversa donc rapidement: car Lucile ne témoignant, dans ce voyage, ni désir ni volonté sur rien, c'était lui seul qui décidait de tout" (F19.5.548) [Lord Nelvil was afraid of the memories which France recalled to him. So he crossed it quickly for, on the journey, Lucile showed no wish or desire for anything; he alone decided everything] (E19.5.376). To express wishes and desires is to assert one's subjectivity; Lucile's idea of perfect womanhood is to eradicate herself as a subject. According to Staël this is the English idea of ideal womanhood. It also happens to be Hegel's.

It is a delicious irony that both *Corinne* and *The Phenomenology of Spirit* were published in 1807. For the character of Corinne magnifi-

cently challenges Hegel's analysis of women's place in society. All
commentators agree that Staël's first trip to Germany in 1803–04
had decisive impact on *Corinne*. Madelyn Gutwirth reminds us that
the philosopher August Wilhelm von Schlegel was tutor to Staël's
children and one of her closest friends. He was instrumental in in-
troducing Staël to the German intellectual elite and also accompanied her on the voyage to Italy in 1805.[28] In Germany, Staël discovered dialectics. Whether or not she saw excerpts from Hegel's
Phenomenology of Perception, the future author of *De l'Allemagne* (On
Germany) would have been exposed to conversations about Hegel's
work. Insofar as women were concerned, Hegel was in any case only
systematizing the dominant antifeminist views at the time, which
Staël could hardly have failed to discover.

It would carry too far to discuss Hegel's view of women in detail.[29]
Suffice it to say that according to *The Phenomenology of Spirit* men, but
not women, can achieve self-consciousness, that is to say, become
fully individualized human beings. Men achieve this by engaging in
conflict and collaboration (work) with other men in the public
sphere. Men thus become citizens endowed with the capacity and
right to participate in public life; women, on the other hand, belong
only to the family. Because they do not oppose themselves to others
in the arena of the universal (society or the state), women do not
achieve self-conscious subjectivity. They therefore have no understanding of the universal, which here means the common good, that
which serves the state or community as a whole. Women are incapable of transcending themselves toward the universal, that is, they will
never sacrifice their own petty self-interest for the well-being of all.
To Hegel, women remain generic creatures. When they do behave
altruistically (Antigone comes to mind), they do so in virtue of their
function as mother, sister, wife. Modern feminism can be defined as
the attempt to prove Hegel wrong, to produce a society which recognizes women as individuals, as citizens, as human beings. (No literary text expresses the conflict between the Hegelian and the feminist view on women better than *A Doll's House*.)

By making her a woman who does not hesitate to speak on matters
of public interest, Staël represents Corinne as the perfect antidote
to Hegel's unindividualized, generic family woman. Corinne wishes
to be recognized as a human being in her own right in a society
which does not consider this to be an option for women. Asking for
recognition as a subject, Corinne is asking to be recognized as a fully
individualized ("self-conscious," in Hegelian terms) human being,
and as an Other in relation to men (so that she can become their
opponent, collaborator, enemy or friend). Corinne thus refuses to

become the "relative being" sexist ideology expects her to be. "L'humanité est mâle et l'homme définit la femme non en soi mais relativement à lui; elle n'est pas considérée comme un être autonome"[30] [Humanity is male and man defines woman not in herself but as relative to him; she is not regarded as an autonomous being],[31] Simone de Beauvoir writes, in what amounts to a pointed rebuttal of Hegel.

The contrast between Lucile and Corinne on all these points is striking. Whereas the character of Corinne points to the future, to a time of bourgeois democracy in which a woman—an ex-show girl at that—can become the respected speaker of the British Parliament,[32] Lucile points to the past, to a time when women were the undifferentiated property of feudal clans or dynasties. Politically, Corinne may be the first modern woman in Western literature, in that she is trying to find a way out of a dilemma typical of modernity, namely one in which women are invited to consider themselves either as women or as human beings, but not as both at once. In 1807, Corinne's very modern efforts to avoid this impossible "choice" doomed her.

The aesthetic and political difficulties Staël was up against are now clear: in a culture that denied women the right to participate in the struggle to define political, ethical, and aesthetic values, a culture that thought of women as somehow less individual and more generic than men, she had to show that Corinne was worthy of participation in the sphere of the universal. Ipso facto Corinne had to be represented as extraordinary, and in particular as capable of extraordinary public and private expressivity. This is why Staël can't just make Corinne less expressive, why she had to expose her heroine to the risk of theatricality. If Corinne is endowed with extraordinary talents, learning, and expressiveness, it is in an attempt to make men accept her as an individual, that is to say as a human being *like themselves.*

But the phrase "like themselves" points to the obvious difficulty of the project. For Corinne does not want to be taken for a man. This is difficult to avoid, however, in a culture that thinks of the individual and of "mankind" as male. Just think of Staël's ex-lover Talleyrand's quip: "I have heard that in her novel, Madame de Staël depicted us both disguised as women."[33] No wonder, then, that Staël overemphasizes Corinne's female and heterosexual charms, just as she overemphasizes her expressive individuality. In the crucial scene of Corinne's crowning at the Capitol, to give an obvious example, Oswald is deeply moved by Corinne's public triumph, but also by what he takes to be evidence of her womanliness, defined by him as her need for protection by a male friend.[34] But Staël can't win this game: the very excess of Corinne's female charm and individual expressiveness is precisely what will give rise to accusations of "disguise," or in other words, of theatricality.[35]

The same dilemma does not apply to men. In a sexist society a man can assert himself as a political and intellectual subject without risking that his sex (or sexuality) is going to be brought into question. Nor does a man's capacity for public self-expression cast doubt on his ability to love. Insofar as Corinne's dilemma has come to seem less pressing to women in the year 2001, it is because we have succeeded in loosening the grip of sexist ideology. *Corinne* issues a challenge to its readers, asking us whether we are capable of acknowledging a woman as a human being without converting her into an abstraction (into an ungendered "human being," for example), and without stripping her of her femaleness.[36]

Now we are in a position to realize the importance of Oswald to Corinne. During Corinne's triumphal ascent to the Capitol, Oswald is immediately struck by her individuality. When Roman poets praise Corinne, Oswald suffers:

> Déjà lord Nelvil souffrait de cette manière de louer Corinne; il lui semblait déjà qu'en la regardant il aurait fait à l'instant même un portrait d'elle plus vrai, plus juste, plus détailleé, un portrait enfin qui ne pût convenir qu'à Corinne. (F2.1.54)

> [Lord Nelvil was already suffering from this way of praising Corinne. He felt already that, just by looking at her, he would have produced right away a more true, accurate, and detailed portrait, a portrait which would have fitted no one but Corinne.] (E2.1.24)

The "portrait which would have fitted no one but Corinne" is a testimony to Corinne's uniqueness, to her individuality. Whereas the pretty first picture of Lucile could only have a generic Greuzelike title, such as "Young girl reading in a garden," the first glimpse of Corinne produces a David-inspired individualized portrait of a brilliant, triumphant woman, entitled "Corinne at the Capitol." Oswald's instant recognition of Corinne's individuality is in part based on Corinne's intensely expressive body, face, and clothes. Her astonishingly expressive face is noted by everyone, even the dour old Mr. Dickson who meets her in Scotland when she is sick with the loss of Oswald, and no longer capable of much speech: "—Et sa figure?—Oh! la plus expressive que j'aie vue, quoiqu'elle fût pâle et maigre à faire de la peine" (F19.2.534) [—And her face?—Oh, the most expressive I have ever seen, although she was painfully thin and pale] (E19.2.367).

Because she says nothing, reveals nothing, Lucile is not truly Other to Oswald. Oswald does not discover that Lucile is another human being; to him she is just a pretty picture, of the kind that made Diderot dream of erotic experiences. Ultimately, Staël points out, such narcissism will come to grief. Genuine love requires recognition and acknowledgment of the Other's otherness. Meeting Corinne, Oswald meets another human being, with all the potential for conflict, pain, and disappointment that that entails; meeting Lucile he meets his own fantasies. Oswald's tragedy is that he simply can't sustain his initial recognition of Corinne. Retreating from Corinne to Lucile, he retreats from genuine reciprocity to silent adoration of his own fantasies.

Readers have always recognized that the scene of Corinne's crowning at the Capitol is deeply fantasmatic. It is a scene in which Oswald recognizes all at once Corinne's individuality, her femaleness, and her humanity. He is, as it were, granted an immediate understanding of Corinne's way of being in the world. The fantasy here is of a relationship between a man and a woman, in which the woman does not have to struggle to "say all" in order to be understood. *This* is the fantasy that fires Staël's erotic imagination, the fantasy that so many women responded to throughout the nineteenth century. It is still the source of the novel's power. The question then becomes: Why does Corinne's fantasy have to be crushed? Why does Staël doom Corinne to isolation, silence, and death? The answers to these questions will start to emerge if we take an even closer look at Corinne's relationship to expressiveness and silence.

The "Perfected Doll": Fearing and Desiring Inexpressiveness

In a striking passage, Corinne complains of the silence imposed on women in Northumberland, and compares her silent self to "a doll slightly perfected by mechanics":

> J'aurais pu, ce me semble, envoyer à ma place une poupée légèrement perfectionnée par la mécanique; elle aurait très bien rempli mon emploi dans la société . . . L'existence des femmes, dans le coin isolé de la terre que j'habitais, était bien insipide. (F14.1.369–70)

> [(I)t seems to me that I could have sent a delicately improved mechanical doll in my place. It would have fulfilled my function in society very

well . . . (W)omen's lives, in the isolated corner of the earth where I was living, were very dull]. (E14.1.249)

The figure of the mechanical doll, the automaton or the robot is a *locus classicus* in skepticist philosophy. In his *Meditations* Descartes looks out of his window on the street below, and notes that all he really sees from his window are "hats and cloaks that might cover artificial machines, whose motions might be determined by springs."[37] In *The Claim of Reason* Stanley Cavell shows (among other things) that there are no criteria for existence, by exploring the example of a craftsman perfecting an automaton to the point where it becomes indistinguishable from a human being.[38] Corinne's fear of being interchangeable with a "doll perfected by mechanics" is a fear of loss of humanity, a fear of not being recognized as human, a fear of not being known. The "body snatcher" theme, so prominent in science fiction and horror stories, trades on the same fear, the sense of horror that arises when we start doubting that another person is human, or worse: when we start to feel that others doubt our own humanity. (Relevant examples here are the *Alien* movies, particularly the Sigourney Weaver character, but also the more simplistic *Species* movies.)

Corinne's casual reference to the "mechanical doll" is also picked up by another Romantic writer, E. T. A. Hoffmann, who explores it in "The Sandman," a story given everlasting fame by Freud's reading of it in "The Uncanny."[39] Hoffmann too connects the silence of women to the idea that women might just as well be dolls. There's a feminist twist here: any man who falls for a doll-woman (Lucile, Olympia), deserves what he gets: misery, madness, death.

Corinne makes it clear that sexism encourages women to identify themselves with mechanical dolls. This is what happens to Lucile. In her marriage to Oswald, Lucile behaves like a mechanical doll: she fails to assert herself, remains silent, leaves him to guess what her feelings might be. As we have seen, the blankness of the woman-doll is at first a source of pleasure and delight for the man. Lucile's behavior aids and abets Oswald's failure to recognize her as a human being. But Lucile's eradication of her own subjectivity also prevents her from understanding Oswald. Their marriage—succinctly represented in book 19 as undone by the silence and reticence of both partners—is a breeding ground for projections, conjecture, and mistrust. Lucile suspects Oswald of not loving her; Oswald first manages to persuade himself that Lucile genuinely has no wishes and desires and then gets furious when he discovers that she hides her desires and fears from him (this is shown in the description of Lucile's un-expressed fear at crossing the Alps in winter).

The text's comparison between the silent woman and a "per-fected mechanical doll" tells us that a woman's voice and speech are the very emblems of her humanity. Yet Staël's novel also contains a very different attitude to voice, words, and expression. *Corinne* is a text haunted by the theme of exile (Staël herself was half way through her own ten years of exile when she wrote the novel). In book 14, devoted to Corinne's exile in Northumberland, the hero-ine appears to take refuge in a fantasy of the mother tongue as home, as a guarantee of understanding and communion:

> [M]ille intérêts qui vous sont communs avec vos compatriotes ne sont plus entendus par les étrangers; il faut tout expliquer, tout commenter, tout dire, au lieu de cette communication facile, de cette effusion de pensées qui commence à l'instant où l'on retrouve ses concitoyens. Je ne pouvais me rappeler, sans émotion, les expressions bienveillantes de mon pays. *Cara, Carissima,* disais-je quelquefois en me promenant toute seule, pour m'imiter à moi-même l'acceuil si amical des Italiens et des Italiennes; je comparais cet acceuil à celui que je recevais. (F14.3.378)

> [A thousand interests you share with your compatriots are incomprehen-sible to foreigners. You have to explain everything, comment on every-thing, say everything, instead of the instant communication, the out-pouring of thoughts, which begins the moment you are reunited with compatriots. I could not recall without emotion my country's kindly words. Sometimes, as I took a solitary walk, I would say *Cara, Carissima,* to imitate to myself the friendly welcome of Italian men and women, and I compared this welcome to the one I was receiving.] (E14.3.255; transla-tion amended)

Corinne is describing her life with her stepmother, the hostile Lady Edgermond, the incarnation of the severe English view of women. In England, any expression of Corinne's is, per definition, a faux pas. In this situation, it is understandable that Corinne repeats words of affection to herself: *Cara, Carissima.* Thinking of Italy, Co-rinne thinks of a world in which her experiences of life and of cul-ture are shared with others. Corinne's longing for her homeland is a longing for community, for immediate understanding. A world of exile is a world of silence, alienation, and hostility. Exile means isola-tion, separation, the absence of understanding, a life in which she is denied recognition as a subject.

So far, the passage would seem to elaborate the same fear of inex-pressivity as the figure of the mechanical doll. But this is not all. For this passage also thinks of Italy as a place where Corinne will finally be relieved of the burden of having to "explain everything." How does this fit with our image of Corinne, a renowned poet, actress, musician, singer, and dancer, the woman who is crowned at the Capitol for her expressive improvisations? The passage draws, I think, an implicit distinction between *having* to "say everything" and *choosing* to do so. For Corinne, exile would seem to mean enforced expressivity. Having to express herself, having endlessly to explain her (Italian) ways to these English strangers, is quite different from choosing to express the feelings of her soul to an enraptured audience, whether at the Roman Capitol or the romantic Cape Miseno. Thus the text intimates that there may be friendly forms of silence. The mechanical doll may have her counterpart in a restfully silent woman, in the woman who feels understood without having to use words (we remember here the novel's fantasmatic representation of Oswald's immediate understanding of Corinne at the Capitol). But how can this attitude coexist with the novel's intense promotion of expressivity? What exactly is *Corinne* telling us about women, humanity, expressivity, and silence?

In order to reach a coherent answer to this question, I want to examine a final set of passages. They come from the pivotal book 17, entitled "Corinne in Scotland." This is the book in which Corinne, having followed Oswald to England and Scotland, renounces Oswald, without ever meeting with him, and without letting him know why she suddenly sets him free from his many oaths of eternal fidelity. In fact, even for an enthusiastic admirer of *Corinne*, it's not at all obvious why the heroine suddenly chooses such a self-defeating course of action. In my view we will not understand Corinne's erotic defeat and death unless we understand the meaning of Corinne's silence in book 17.

In chapter 4 of book 17, the disguised Corinne goes to the theater in London to see the famous Mrs. Siddons in *Isabella, or the Fatal Marriage*. Inevitably, she happens to be in the audience the same night as Oswald and Lucile. (Book 17 insists on the reversal of Corinne's fortunes: three times Corinne, the star performer, is placed in the position of being the unknown and unnoticed spectator in relation to Lucile and Oswald.)[40] We are quickly informed that the fictional Isabella commits suicide by stabbing herself with a dagger. In a text awash with presentiments and warnings it is difficult to escape the thought that this suicide is intended to prefigure Corinne's own end. But if this is right, then Corinne's death is not simply the result of Oswald's betrayal, of his metaphorical murder of her spirit. Rather, we are encouraged to believe that Corinne also *chooses* silence and death. What fate seems worse than death to Corinne? Here's the scene in the theater, where Corinne sees Lucile:

> Lucile s'était plus parée qu'à l'ordinaire en venant au spectacle; et depuis long-temps, même en Angleterre où les femmes sont si belles, il n'avait paru une personne aussi remarquable. Corinne fut douloureusement surprise en la voyant: il lui parut impossible qu'Oswald pût résister à la séduction d'une telle figure. Elle se compara dans sa pensée avec elle, et se trouva tellement inférieure, elle s'exagéra tellement, s'il était possible de se l'exagérer, le charme de cette jeunesse, de cette blancheur, de ces cheveux blonds, de cette innocente image du printemps de la vie, qu'elle se sentit presque humiliée de lutter par le talent, par l'esprit, par les dons acquis enfin, ou du moins perfectionnés, avec ces graces prodiguées par la nature elle-même. (F17.4.481)

> [Lucile had dressed more elegantly than usual to come to the theater, and even in England, where the women are so beautiful, no one had seen such a remarkably beautiful girl. Corinne was painfully surprised when she saw her. It seemed impossible to her that Oswald could resist the attraction of such a face. Mentally she compared herself to Lucile, and she thought herself so inferior, she exaggerated to herself, if that were possible, the charm of youth, of that fair complexion, of that blond hair, of that innocent picture of the springtime of life; and so she felt almost humiliated to struggle by means of talent and wit, in short, by acquired or at least perfected gifts, against these charms lavished by nature itself.] (E17.4.328)

The importance of the passage is shown by the fact that Staël chooses to reinforce the same points just a few pages later:

> L'imagination de Corinne était tellement frappée des avantages de sa sœur, qu'elle avait presque honte de lutter avec de tels charmes. Il lui semblait que le talent même était une ruse, l'esprit une tyrannie, la passion une violence à côté de cette innocence désarmée; et bien que Corinne n'eût pas encore vingt-huit ans, elle pressentait déjà cette époque de la vie où les femmes se défient avec tant de douleur de leurs moyens de plaire. Enfin la jalousie et une timidité fière se combattaient dans son ame; elle renvoyait de jour en jour le moment tant craint, et tant désiré, où elle devait revoir Oswald. (F17.6.487–88)

> [Corinne's imagination was so impressed by her sister's advantages that she was almost ashamed to fight against such charms. It seemed to her that even talent was a ruse, wit a tyranny, and passionate love (*la passion*) a violence beside this unarmed innocence, and although Corinne was not yet twenty-eight, she already foresaw that period of life when, with so much pain, women mistrust their ability to be attractive. In short, jeal-

ousy and shy pride fought against each other in her soul. From day to day she put off the dreaded, longed-for moment when she was to see Oswald again.] (E17.6.333)

Together these two passages tell us why Corinne chooses not to see Oswald again. In the first passage, Lucile is described as astonishingly beautiful. Her blond innocence is contrasted with Corinne's talents and wit [*esprit*]. Described entirely in terms of her looks, Lucile could be a painting. Her appeal is to the eye. Described entirely in terms of her inner capacities, Corinne's appeal is to the ear. Kierkegaard's preface to *Either/Or* brings out the value of this contrast. Kierkegaard begins by exploring his sense of mistrust of a person's outside, his sense that the outside does not necessarily reveal the inside. The eye deceives us, he writes, which is why he has come to cherish the sense of hearing:

Efterhaanden blev da Hørelsen mig den kjæreste Sands; thi ligesom Stemmen er Aabenbarelsen af den for det Ydre incommensurable Inderlighed, saaledes er Øret det Redskab, ved hvilket denne Inderlighed opfattes, Hørelsen den Sands, ved hvilken den tilegnes.[41]

[Little by little, hearing became my favourite sense; for just as it is the voice that reveals the inwardness which is incommensurable with the outer, so the ear is the instrument whereby that inwardness is grasped, hearing the sense by which it is appropriated.][42]

For Corinne to feel "almost humiliated" to use her wit and talents—her words—to win Oswald from Lucile, is to say that she now thinks that Oswald no longer knows how to hear her words. She is saying, in fact, that it would be humiliating for her to try to express herself, to struggle to exteriorize her inner feelings for someone who has shown himself to be deaf, someone who has capitulated to the treacherous pleasures of the gaze.

We note, too, that all of Corinne's qualities are now understood as "acquired or at least perfected gifts," as opposed to Lucile's charms, which are said to be "lavished by nature itself." Gone are Corinne's many references to her God-given talents. It is as if Corinne now is renouncing her education, since education—the acquiring of "culture"—is a way to "perfect" nature. Losing her faith in Oswald's capacity to hear her, Corinne also loses her pride in the very culture and learning that enabled her to improvise so gloriously at the Capitol. It would seem that nothing short of an astonishing transformation of Corinne's identity is now under way.

Contrasting Corinne's "acquired or at least perfected gifts" with

Lucile's "natural charms," the text echoes the opposition already established between the "perfected mechanical doll" and a woman, between that which is dead and that which is alive, between the inhuman and the human. But now the relationship between Lucile and Corinne is reversed. Lucile is the real woman, Corinne the one who has come to doubt her own humanity, her own "perfectedness." What the novel so far has seen as the emblem of Corinne's humanity—her expressive language—has now, in a strange reversal, come to be the humiliating sign of her artificiality and inhumanity. It is difficult to avoid the conclusion that Corinne *desires* inexpressiveness.

The second passage amplifies this impression. Corinne is "most ashamed to fight against [Lucile's] charms." A series of stunning comparisons follows: "It seemed to her that even talent was a ruse, wit [*esprit*] a tyranny, and passion a violence beside this unarmed innocence." Ruse, tyranny, violence: these are fighting words. A ruse is a stratagem, a form of trickery. If talent is a ruse, it means that Corinne's talents doom her to inauthenticity and theatricality, to a kind of violent, tyrannical self-expression which can only turn her into a termagant, an older woman (there is the reference to her advancing age—she's all of twenty-seven) whose very expressions do violence to young innocence. No longer identified with the Sibyl, Corinne casts herself as Medea to Lucile's Creusa. Again the underlying fantasy would seem to be a dream of not having to exteriorize her feelings.

From now on Corinne is a silent woman. She never speaks to Oswald again. Before she leaves Scotland, she catches several glimpses of him, always disguising herself, always hiding herself among the crowd or among the trees, always keeping secret those feelings she used so candidly to reveal. There is no denying, then, that Corinne quite deliberately chooses silence, isolation, and death rather than speech, expression, and marriage to Oswald. (As if to reinforce the point, book 17 keeps repeating that if only Corinne had revealed herself to Oswald, then their destinies would have been different.)[43] There is no denying, either, that Corinne has come to think of her words as histrionic, artificial, and violent. Having dedicated her life to expression, expression now disappoints her. Why is this? The answer, I think, can be found if we manage to understand Corinne's seemingly contradictory attitude to expression and silence. As I shall now go on to show, *Corinne* is quite possibly the very prototype of the genre Stanley Cavell has called the "melodrama of the unknown woman."[44] By "prototype" I mean that Corinne is something like the literary foremother of the Hollywood heroines discussed by Cavell.

Suffocation and Exposure: *Corinne* as Melodrama
of the Unknown Woman

The "melodrama of the unknown woman" is a term coined by Cavell to describe the connection between four Hollywood films: *Letter from an Unknown Woman, Now, Voyager, Gaslight,* and *Stella Dallas.* There are differences between these films, and in my view, *Corinne* is more like *Letter from an Unknown Woman* and *Now, Voyager* and less like *Gaslight* and *Stella Dallas.* The principal features of the genre are as follows:

—the woman's father is not on the side of her desire, but on the side of
    law
—the woman is shown in relation to a child (as a mother)
—the woman searches for a mother, or the loss of her mother is always
    present
—there is a negation of communication between the principal couple
—the genre's answer to the question: "What does a woman want?" is "A
    woman wants to be known"
—the woman's superior knowledge becomes the object of the man's fan-
    tasy
—the ineffectuality and irrelevance of the man is underscored
—the man's struggle is against recognition
—the woman's struggle is to understand why recognition by the man has
    not happened or has been denied or has become irrelevant
—the woman undergoes a radical change of identity
—there is a final negation of marriage itself
—the woman chooses solitude (figured as a refusal of marriage)
—the woman's choice of solitude is a judgment of the world[45]

Corinne contains *every one* of these features. We have already considered a number of them. I will not tire readers by going through all the others. Anyone who reads the book can see how apposite they are. In this last section, I shall concentrate on the woman's sense that she is not known, and never will be, and particularly not by the man she has chosen as her erotic partner.

We have seen that Corinne fears inexpressiveness (the mechanical doll). She also fears enforced expression (*having* to say all in exile). At the same time, book 17 shows her longing for a state of inexpressiveness. In his masterly exploration of skepticism, *The Claim of Reason*, Stanley Cavell writes:

> So the fantasy of a private language, underlying the wish to deny the publicness of language, turns out, so far, to be a fantasy, or fear, either of inexpressiveness, one in which I am not merely unknown, but in which I am powerless to make myself known; or one in which what I express is beyond my control.[46]

Cavell, then, considers that the fear of inexpressiveness and the fear of involuntary expressiveness are reactions to the *same* metaphysical and existential predicament. Both fantasies, after all, share a picture of a person who is powerless in relation to her own expressions. Both fantasies have their roots in a fundamental disappointment with expression; they reveal a loss of faith in words, a conviction that our words necessarily betray us. Cavell connects such anxieties to a deep-rooted anxiety about meaning: "Why do we attach significance to *any* words and deeds, of others or of ourselves?" is a question that this mood gives rise to, just as it produces an "anxiety that our expression might at any time signify nothing. Or too much," or "an anxiety over there being nothing whatever to say."[47]

This fear, Cavell writes, is at once a fear and a wish. But how can anyone come to *wish* for inexpressiveness? If we could answer this question, we would know why it is that Corinne chooses silence. Cavell writes:

> A fantasy of necessary inexpressiveness would solve a simultaneous set of metaphysical problems: it would relieve me of the responsibility for making myself known to others—as though if I were expressive that would mean continuously betraying my experiences, incessantly giving myself away; it would suggest that my responsibility for self-knowledge takes care of itself—as though the fact that others cannot know my (inner) life means that I cannot fail to. It would reassure my fears of being known . . . it would reassure my fears of not being known . . .—The wish underlying this fantasy covers a wish that underlies skepticism, a wish for the connection between my claims of knowledge and the objects upon which the claims are to fall to occur without my intervention, apart from my agreements. As the wish stands, it is unappeasable. In the case of my knowing myself, such self-defeat would be doubly exquisite: I must disappear in order that the search for myself be successful.[48]

I shall try to gloss this difficult, but immensely suggestive, passage. The wish underlying the fantasy of inexpressiveness is a wish for a state in which words would have absolutely objective meanings. This

is a yearning for a language which would not depend on the intervention of human subjectivity for its meanings. There is a dream
here of a world in which all objects and human beings somehow nat-
urally come equipped with big labels naming their essence. The "labels" would have to be of a magical kind so that everyone who
looked at them would instantly grasp that the label and the thing
were, as it were, one and the same thing. In such a world there
would be no language differences, no translation from "horse" to
"cheval," simply because there would be no language in any mean-
ingful sense of the word. Skepticism is born of the realization that
the world is not like this. (Skepticism, one might say, is fixated on
the idea that there *must* be an unbridgeable gap between words and
things.)

Cavell (and Wittgenstein) reaches a different conclusion. We may
be made of language, but language is also made of us: there can
be no meanings without speakers of the language. Each one of us
participates in the production of the meaning of our words. The
fundamental question, then, is not about reference or the floating
of signifiers, but about my responsibility for my words. For if I am in
part responsible for the meaning of language, then I am also responsible for making myself known to others. I can't just sit back and wait
for others to decipher me, as if I were the Rosetta stone of humanity.
Nor am I justified in assuming that my illegibility to others somehow
guarantees my legibility to myself. To believe something like this
would be to take refuge in a fantasy of an inner, private subjectivity
unreadable and unreachable by all others. The idea of unplumbable
inner depths is the flip side of the dream of objective decipherment.
Both fantasies share a deeply skeptical picture of a human being as
a swamp-infested treasure island, an isolated, inaccessible, treacherous surface hiding rich inner depths. (This is pretty much the
thought that bothers Kierkegaard in the introduction to *Either/Or*.
As we have seen, *Corinne* is filled with the very same concerns.)

We can now see what the dream of inexpressivity has to do with
Wittgenstein's critique of the idea of a private language, namely that
it is underpinned by a metaphysical picture of utterly private inner
depths. Such a vision completely fails to understand the relationship
between language and subjectivity. There can be no concepts, no
language, without shared criteria. We all participate in shaping the
meaning of language; nobody can be the sole dictator of meaning.
Not even my knowledge of myself (if "knowledge" is the right word
here) can exist apart from the dense weave of shared human meanings we all belong to.

Corinne, however, is a skeptic at heart. Throughout the novel, she has struggled to "say all." In book 17 she gives up on that struggle. She moves, in other words, from a fantasy of perfect communion with the beloved Other, to an outright denial of that fantasy, from excessive expressivity to total silence. This is the terrain of melodrama. In *Contesting Tears*, Cavell picks up precisely the passage from *The Claim of Reason* that I have just quoted, and adds a few comments to it:

> I am led to stress the condition that I find to precede, to ground the possibility and the necessity of, "the desire to express all," namely the terror of absolute inexpressiveness, suffocation, which at the same time reveals itself as a terror of absolute expressiveness, unconditioned exposure; they are the extreme states of voicelessness. (I claim that these are the polar states expressed in the woman's voice in opera.)[49]

Corinne is an opera, I am tempted to say. The dying Corinne, struggling for breath, is not at all unrelated to the dying Violetta in *La Traviata*.[50] She is also—and this may be more surprising—the predecessor of Ibsen's heroines, who constantly find themselves caught between suffocation and exposure (none more so than Irene in *When We Dead Awaken*, yet Nora, Mrs. Alving, and Hedda Gabler all struggle with the same dilemma).

Giving up on Oswald, giving up on language, Corinne chooses death. In her dying moment she directs her last words to the faithful Prince Castel-Forte:

> —Mon ami, lui dit-elle, en lui tendant la main, il n'y a que vous près de moi dans ce moment. J'ai vécu pour aimer, et sans vous je mourrais seule. —Et ses larmes coulèrent à ce mot; puis elle dit encore: Au reste ce moment se passe de secours; nos amis ne peuvent nous suivre que jusqu'au seuil de la vie. Là commencent des pensées dont le trouble et la profondeur ne sauraient se confier. (F20.5.586)

> ["My friend," she said, holding out her hand to him. "Only you are with me at this moment. I have lived for love, and but for you I would die alone." At these words, her tears flowed. Then she spoke again. "Besides, no help is possible at this moment. Our friends can follow us only to the threshold of life. The thoughts beginning there are so confused and deep, they cannot be confided."] (E20.5.404)

Corinne's last words speak of human separation and of thoughts "so confused and deep, they cannot be confided." The ultimate realization of human finitude is doubled by a zealous protection of her own, separate and secret interiority. Corinne's dying words affirm her intense conviction that she has remained *unknown*.

Corinne dies seated in an armchair by a window from which she can see the sky. As she is about to breathe her last, the "malheureux Oswald" rushes into the room and falls on his knees in front of Corinne:

> Elle voulut lui parler, et n'en eut pas la force. Elle leva ses regards vers le ciel, et vit la lune qui se couvrait du même nuage qu'elle avait fait remarquer à lord Nelvil quand il s'arrêtèrent sur le bord de la mer en allant à Naples. Alors elle le lui montra de sa main mourante, et son dernier soupir fit retomber cette main. (F20.5.586)

> [She wanted to speak to him, but was not strong enough. She raised her eyes to heaven and saw the moon covered with the same cloud as the one she had pointed out to Lord Nelvil when, on the way to Naples, they had stopped by the seashore. Then, with her dying hand, she pointed it out to him, and with her last breath that hand dropped down.] (E20.5.404)

The reference is to an evening the two spent in Terracina, a little village fragrant with the smell of orange and lemon trees, an earthly paradise where children spontaneously throw flowers into the carriages of strangers. That moonlit evening by the sea inspires the greatest transports of love in the whole book. As the evening ends, Corinne suddenly becomes sad. A cloud covers the moon, and she takes it as an omen: "[J]e vous le dis, Oswald, ce soir [le ciel] condamnait notre amour" (F11.1.289) [I tell you, Oswald, this evening (heaven) condemned our love] (E11.1.191). Oswald protests and Corinne replies that perhaps the sky threatened only her. Two months later, they return to Terracina, on their way north. This time the mood is one of pain and bitterness. The truth about the past has been told, and Oswald has decided to return to England. Again they spend the night in Terracina, again they sit on the same cliff by the sea, again the moon is covered by a cloud. This time Corinne takes it as a warning of death: "N'oubliez pas, Oswald, de remarquer si ce même nuage ne passera pas sur la lune quand je mourrai" (F15.2.400) ["Do not forget, Oswald, to notice if this same cloud passes across the moon when I die"] (E15.2.270).

Pointing to the moon in her dying moment Corinne, like so many of Cavell's "unknown women," is affirming her connection to the transcendent at the end of her story. But she is also delivering a stinging rebuke to Oswald. Given her previous warnings, the obvious meaning of the gesture is "I told you so." In a brisk final paragraph Oswald is dispatched. He follows Corinne's funeral procession to Rome, and nearly goes mad before finally returning to his wife and daughter. The text stresses Oswald's reintegration into society, as if to make Corinne's exile all the more bitter. After his crisis, we are told, Oswald returns to "le monde qui l'approuva" (F20.5.587) ["society's approval"] (E20.5.404).

The "moon behind the cloud" motif is only the last reinforcement of a well-established theme: Oswald's failure to acknowledge Corinne. The end of the novel loses no opportunity to remind us of Oswald's betrayal, for example by pointedly comparing the dying Corinne to the wronged Dido.[51] Throughout the novel, Madame de Staël has never tired of demonstrating Corinne's emotional and spiritual superiority over Oswald. The melancholic Oswald we first meet in chapter 1 was always too ambivalent, too guilt-ridden, to commit himself wholly to a woman, we now realize.[52] Corinne's rejection of Oswald leads to death because she is not just rejecting a man, she is rejecting the world that approves of him. No man can provide Corinne with the "apt and cheerful conversation" Milton thought was the very meaning of marriage.[53] Rejecting marriage, rejecting Oswald, Corinne looks at the world and judges it worthless to her. It is difficult to say that she was altogether wrong.

Notes

I would like to thank Ghislaine McDayter for being an immensely understanding editor, David L. Paletz, Roberta Pearson, and Karin Sanders for giving feed-back on some very early (and very incoherent) drafts, Yunyi Wang at Duke's Lilly Library and Helene Baumann at Duke's Perkins Library for expert help at the last minute.

1. The phrase "melodramatic mode" is taken from Peter Brook's foundational study *The Melodramatic Imagination: Balzac, Henry James, Melodrama, and the Mode of Excess* (1976; reprint, with a new preface, New York: Columbia University Press, 1985), 4.

2. The phrase "pictorial melodrama" is inspired by *Realizations: Narrative, Pictorial, and Theatrical Arts in Nineteenth-Century England* (Princeton, N.J.: Princeton University Press, 1983), Martin Meisel's thought-provoking study of nineteenth-century British art, narrative, and theater. Meisel writes: "In the new dramaturgy, the unit is intransitive; it is in fact an achieved moment of stasis, a picture . . . What is striking and characteristic in the nineteenth-century theater is that its dramaturgy was pictorial, not just its mise-en-scène . . . Its pictorialism could flourish, if necessary, in the absence of much that is normally associated with theatrical spectacle . . . the most powerful expression of its pictorial dramaturgy was . . . melodrama" (38–39).

3. There are differences of opinion between Oswald and Corinne. Oswald prefers history paintings, or paintings based on famous tragedies or histories, whereas Corinne prefers religious paintings. But they both agree that paintings have to be immediately understandable, which is why any scene represented must be well known. For their discussions of painting and for a description of Corinne's own picture gallery, see book 8, chapters 3 and 4. Margaret Cohen's discussion of painting and sculpture in *Corinne* considers the question of realism. See Margaret

Cohen, "Melancholia, Mania, and the Reproduction of the Dead Father," in *The Novel's Seductions: Staël's "Corinne" in Critical Inquiry*, ed. Karyna Szmurlo (Lewisburg, Penna.: Bucknell University Press, 1999), 95–113.

4. All references to *Corinne* will be given in the text. The French text used is Germaine de Staël, *Corinne ou l'Italie* (1807), ed. Simone Balayé (Paris: Gallimard, 1985). References to the French text are preceded by "F." The English text used is the widely available *Corinne, or Italy*, ed. and trans. Sylvia Rafael (Oxford: Oxford University Press, 1998). References to the English text are preceded by "E." References are given to book and chapter as well as page. F17.8.494 thus means book 17, chapter 8, page 494 in the French edition.

5. Moers's chapter 9 is devoted to *Corinne*. See Ellen Moers, *Literary Women* (London: Women's Press, 1977), 173–210. The quote from Elizabeth Barrett Browning can be found on page 172.

6. See Madelyn Gutwirth, "Seeing *Corinne* Afresh: *Corinne*'s Second Coming," in *The Novel's Seductions*, ed. Szmurlo, 27.

7. On this topic, see also Ellen Peeland and Nanora Sweet, "Corinne and the Woman as Poet in England: Hemans, Jewsbury, and Barrett Browning," in *The Novel's Seductions*, ed. Szmurlo, 204–20; Katharine Rodier, "Nathaniel Hawthorne and *The Marble Faun*: Textual and Contextual Reflections of *Corinne, or Italy*," in *The Novel's Seductions*, ed. Szmurlo, 221–42.

8. Moers, *Literary Women*, 182.

9. Ibid., 179.

10. Ibid., 181.

11. I briefly discuss the relationship between seduction and brainpower in the "Afterword," to Toril Moi, *Simone de Beauvoir: The Making of an Intellectual Woman* (Oxford: Blackwell, 1994), 253–57.

12. In an early study of Staël, Carl Benzoni documents her constant and life-long passion for and involvement with theater. See *Staël og Theatret* (Copenhagen: Wienes, 1906).

13. There are black and white reproductions of these paintings in Madelyn Gutwirth, *Staël, Novelist: The Emergence of the Artist as a Woman* (Urbana: University of Illinois Press, 1978), 238–39.

14. This must be a translator's error. Lucile "entrait à peine dans sa seizième année," Staël writes, which means that she had just turned fifteen.

15. George Eliot, *The Mill on the Floss* (1860) (London: Everyman, 1991), 312.

16. Michael Fried, *Absorption and Theatricality: Painting and Beholder in the Age of Diderot* (Chicago: University of Chicago Press, 1980), 108. Hereafter *AT*, cited in the text. Fried also refers to this idea as the "supreme fiction of the beholders non-existence" (149).

17. "Chardin and Greuze represent different *worlds*," Fried writes (*Absorption*, 61). For more examples and some black and white reproductions of Chardin and Greuze, see ibid., 50–60.

18. This, of course, is also the painting which inspired Diderot to indulge in a long, explicitly sexual fantasy. "Diderot finds in Greuze's canvas a scarcely veiled allegory of the young girl's loss of virginity," Fried writes, after giving a delicious quote from Diderot's 1765 *Salon* (*Absorption*, 59).

19. I think I would have translated Staël's "on" by "we" rather than "you" in this passage.

20. Denis Diderot, "Essais sur la peinture" (1765), in *Oeuvres*, vol. 4: *Ésthéthique—Théâtre*, ed. Laurent Versini (Paris: Laffont, 1996), 471; my translation.

21. Although Domenichino's Sibyl does have white sleeves and a small blue rib-

bon or shawl under the chest, the dominant colors in his Sibyl are gold, ochre, and red (the turban, the shawl, the outer dress).

22. It is a pity that the English translation here chooses to forego the verb *électriser*. In 1807, the verb *électriser* was a very modern one. The Robert *Dictionnaire historique de la langue française* defines it as "to transmit electrical qualities to a body," and claims that the figurative usage about people ("to produce an exciting impression on someone") dates from 1772.

23. Denis Diderot, "Éloge de Richardson" (1761), in *Oeuvres*, 4: 155–56.

24. Denis Diderot, "In Praise of Richardson," in *Selected Writings on Art and Literature*, trans. Geoffrey Bremner (London: Penguin Books, 1994), 82.

25. Denis Diderot, "Pensées détachées sur la peinture" (1781), in *Oeuvres*, 4: 1051; my translation. Fried also quotes this passage (in *Absorption*, 100).

26. There is a connection to be made here between Diderot's aesthetics and Stanley Cavell's analysis of the reality of theater, where the figure of the child screaming at Red Riding Hood is crucial to the argument. See Cavell, "The Avoidance of Love: A Reading of *King Lear*," in *Must We Mean What We Say?* (Cambridge: Cambridge University Press, 1969), particularly 326–31.

27. Fried writes: "[T]he history of modern painting is traditionally—in my view, rightly—seen as having begun with David's masterpieces of the 1780s, most importantly the *Serment des Horaces* (1784, exhibited 1785), which at once established itself as paradigmatic for ambitious painting: as exemplifying, down to the smallest details of its execution, what painting had to do and be if it were to realize the highest aims open to it" (*Absorption*, 72). One of David's 1780s masterpieces was *Bélisaire, reconnu par un soldat qui avait servi sous lui au moment qu'une femme lui fait l'aumône* (Belisarius, recognized by a soldier who had served under him at the moment when a woman gives him alms, 1781). Corinne actually has a painting of Belisarius receiving alms in her own picture gallery.

28. Madelyn Gutwirth discusses the origins of *Corinne* in chapter 5 of her important study of Staël. According to Gutwirth, three factors were particularly important in the gestation of the book: Staël's first voyage to Germany in 1803–04, when she stayed in Weimar; the death of Necker (Staël's father) on 10 April 1804, while she was away in Germany; and her voyage to Italy in 1805. See Gutwirth, *Staël*, 154–82.

29. This dangerously brief account gestures toward a more serious account of Hegel's analysis of *Antigone*, which leads him to conclude that woman is the "eternal irony of the community." See G. W. F. Hegel, *Phenomenology of Spirit* (1807), trans. A. V. Miller (Oxford: Oxford University Press, 1977), particularly §§473–75. I discuss Hegel's analysis of women at greater length in my introduction to the new Norwegian translation of Beauvoir's *The Second Sex*. See Toril Moi, "Innledende essay," in *Det annet kjønn* by Simone de Beauvoir, trans. Bente Christensen (Oslo: Pax, 2000), particularly xix–xxv.

30. Simone de Beauvoir, *Le deuxième sexe*, vol. 1 (1949) (Paris: Gallimard, 1986), 15.

31. Simone de Beauvoir, *The Second Sex*, trans. H. M. Parshley (New York: Vintage Books, 1989), xxii.

32. I am referring, of course, to Betty Boothroyd, who announced her retirement as speaker of the British House of Commons in the summer of 2000.

33. Quoted in Marie-Claire Vallois, "Voice as Fossil; Germaine de Staël's *Corinne, or Italy*: An Archeology of Feminine Discourse," in *The Novel's Seductions*, ed. Szmurlo, 127. Talleyrand actually said this about *Delphine*, not *Corinne*, but the remark remains an excellent illustration of how little it took for a writing woman to be accused of being a man in disguise, i.e., of not being "feminine."

34. [M]ais au milieu de tout cet éclat, de tous ces succès, il lui semblait que Corinne avait imploré, par ses regards, la protection d'un ami, protection dont jamais une femme, quelque supérieure qu'elle soit, ne peut se passer; et il pensait en lui-même qu'il serait doux d'être l'appui de celle à qui sa sensibilité seule rendrait cet appui nécessaire (F2.1.54) [(I)n the midst of all this splendour and success it seemed to him that Corinne's eyes had sought the protection of a man friend, a protection no woman, however superior she may be, can ever dispense with. And he thought it would be pleasing to be the support of a woman who would feel the need for such support only because of her sensitivity] (E2.1.24).

35. This is an extremely condensed analysis of the dilemma sexism poses for women: they are enjoined, either to consider themselves women, or to consider themselves "just a human being." This is a choice, Beauvoir would say, between being imprisoned in one's subjectivity, and being asked to eliminate it altogether. *The Second Sex* is a passionate denunciation of this dilemma. I analyze the philosophical and existential implications of such sexism in *What Is a Woman? And Other Essays* (Oxford: Oxford University Press, 1999), particularly in chapter 2, 200–207 and 212–19.

36. In August 2000 the British press gave much play to a Tory attack on Cherie Blair. The British Prime Minister's wife had committed the unpardonable sin of co-authoring a defense of the European Human Rights legislation for a British news-paper. This legislation was about to be incorporated into British law, and Cherie Blair (Booth, by her professional name), is a QC specializing in human rights law. The Tory MP accused her of being a combination of Hilary Clinton and Lady Macbeth, simply because she had the temerity to express her own views in public. As the Prime Minister's wife, he felt, her proper role was to say nothing about anything at all in public, whatever her own professional expertise and commitments might be. Otherwise there would be a dangerous "conflict of interests," the Tories claimed. There are remnants here of the ideology which is under attack in *Corinne*.

37. René Descartes, *Discourse on Method and the Meditations*, trans. John Veitch (Buffalo, N.Y.: Prometheus Books, 1989), 84. Veitch correctly translates the 1647 French text. But this is itself a translation of Descartes's 1641 Latin original, albeit a translation corrected and reviewed by Descartes himself. The phrase "artificial machines, whose motions might be determined by springs" translates a single Latin word, namely *automata*. For the French 1647 text and the 1641 Latin original, see René Descartes, *Méditations métaphysiques*, ed. and trans. Florence Khodoss (Paris: Quadrige/PUF, 1956), 49.

38. See Stanley Cavell, *The Claim of Reason: Wittgenstein, Skepticism, Morality, and Tragedy* (1979; reprint, with a new preface, New York: Oxford University Press, 1999), 403–11.

39. See E. T. A. Hoffmann, "The Sandman," in *Selected Writings of E. T. A. Hoffmann*, ed. and trans. Leonard J. Kent and Elizabeth C. Knight (Chicago: Chicago University Press, 1969), 93–125, and Sigmund Freud, "The 'Uncanny' " (1919), *The Standard Edition of the Complete Psychological Works*, ed. and trans. James Strachey (London: Hogarth Press, 1955), 17:217–52.

40. Nancy K. Miller has explored the meaning of the gaze and its reversals in *Corinne* from a feminist and psychoanalytic point of view in "Performances of the Gaze: Staël's *Corinne, or Italy*,"in *The Novel's Seductions*, ed. Szmurlo, 84–94.

41. Søren Kierkegaard, *Enten—Eller*, vol. 1 (1843) (Copenhagen: Gyldendal, 1988), 9.

42. Søren Kierkegaard, *Either/Or: A Fragment of Life*, abridged and trans. Alastair Hannay (London: Penguin Books, 1992), 27.

43. See for example F17.8.494 (E17.8.337–38); F17.9.501 (E17.9.342); F17.9.502 (E17.9.343).

44. I am referring to Stanley Cavell, *Contesting Tears: The Hollywood Melodrama of the Unknown Woman* (Chicago: University of Chicago Press, 1996).

45. This list simplifies, and in some cases flattens out, some of the nuances in Cavell's extraordinarily suggestive text. The list is extracted from Cavell's introduction to *Contesting Tears*, 3–45.

46. Cavell, *Claim of Reason*, 351.

47. Ibid. for all the quotations in this paragraph.

48. Ibid., 351–52.

49. Cavell, *Contesting Tears*, 43. This passage is, at least in part, a response to Peter Brooks's discussion of the desire to "say all" in melodrama.

50. See here Cavell's interesting comments on Garbo in *Camille*, in *Contesting Tears*, 17–20.

51. When the dying Corinne sees Oswald in the audience at her last improvisation, she turns away her face, "comme Didon lorsque'elle rencontre Énée dans un monde où les passions humaines ne doivent plus pénétrer" (F20.5.581) [like Dido when she met Aeneas in another world, impervious to human passions] (E20.5.400). The pointed reference is to a painting in Corinne's own picture gallery, described in book 8, which functions as a clear warning of the fate awaiting Corinne: "Le premier représente Énée dans les Champs-Élysées, lorsqu'il veut s'approcher de Didon. L'ombre indignée s'éloigne et s'applaudit de ne plus porter dans son sein le cœur qui battrait encore d'amour à l'aspect du coupable. La couleur vapoureuse des ombres, et la pâle nature qui les environne, font contraste avec l'air de vie d'Énée et de la Sibylle qui le conduit" (F8.4.234) [The first shows Aeneas in the Elysian Fields when he wants to approach Dido. The indignant ghost moves away and congratulates herself on not bearing any longer in her breast the heart that would still throb with love at the sight of the guilty man. The misty colour of the ghosts and the pale countryside which surrounds them afford a contrast with the appearance of life in Aeneas and the Sibyl who is his guide] (E8.4.152). Corinne's fate is here outlined: she is to be transformed from colorful, live Sibyl to shadowy, dead Dido. And it's all going to be Oswald's fault.

52. Oswald is so clearly Hamlet's descendant, and equally clearly Adolphe's twin brother. Although it wasn't published until 1816, Benjamin Constant, Staël's long-time lover, wrote *Adolphe* in 1806, at the same time and at times in the same house where Staël was writing *Corinne*.

53. John Milton, "The Doctrine and Discipline of Divorce Restored to the Good of Both Sexes" (1643), in *John Milton*, ed. Stephen Orgel and Jonathan Goldberg (Oxford: Oxford University Press, 1991), 183.